Literature of the 1920s

The Edinburgh History of Twentieth-Century Literature in Britain
General Editor: Randall Stevenson

Published:
Vol. 3 *Literature of the 1920s: Writers among the Ruins*
    Chris Baldick
Vol. 6 *Literature of the 1950s: Good, Brave Causes*
    Alice Ferrebe
Vol. 9 *Literature of the 1980s: After the Watershed*
    Joseph Brooker

Forthcoming:
Vol. 1 *Literature of the 1900s: The Great Edwardian Emporium*
    Jonathan Wild
Vol. 4 *Literature of the 1930s: Border Country*
    Rod Mengham
Vol. 5 *Literature of the 1940s: War, Postwar and 'Peace'*
    Gill Plain
Vol. 8 *Literature of the 1970s: Things Fall Apart, Again*
    Simon Malpas

Literature of the 1920s

Writers among the Ruins

Chris Baldick

EDINBURGH
University Press

For Dorothy

© Chris Baldick, 2012

Edinburgh University Press Ltd
22 George Square, Edinburgh

www.euppublishing.com

Typeset in 10.5/13 Adobe Sabon
by Servis Filmsetting Ltd, Stockport, Cheshire, and
printed and bound in Great Britain by
CPI Group (UK) Ltd, Croydon, CR0 4YY

A CIP record for this book is available from the British Library

ISBN 978 0 7486 2730 1 (hardback)
ISBN 978 0 7486 3143 8 (webready PDF)
ISBN 978 0 7486 7457 2 (epub)
ISBN 978 0 7486 7458 9 (Amazon ebook)

The right of Chris Baldick
to be identified as author of this work
has been asserted in accordance with
the Copyright, Designs and Patents Act 1988.

Contents

Preface		vi
General Editor's Preface		vii
	Introduction: In Search of the Twentyish	1
1	A Literature of Ideas	36
2	Mixing Memory and Desire: Modernism and Anachronism	71
3	Never Such Innocence: Versions of Experience and Disillusionment	100
4	Impunities: Crime, Comedy and Camp	137
5	But It Still Goes On: The Passing of the Twenties	170
Works Cited		182
Index		186

Preface

In preparing this work I have benefited from discussions on specialised aspects of 1920s literature with my colleagues Len Platt and Frank Krause. Pippa Roscoe also kindly gave up some of her time to go sleuthing for me among the minutiae of detective plots. My children too deserve thanks for their forbearance during the more absorbing stages of composition. My principal debt, though, is to the series editor, Randall Stevenson, whose sustained encouragement, pertinent suggestions and timely corrections have made this a better book than it could have been without his guidance; needless to say, he is not to be held responsible for its specific arguments or emphases.

General Editor's Preface

One decade is covered by each of the ten volumes in *The Edinburgh History of Twentieth-Century Literature in Britain* series. Individual volumes may argue that theirs is *the* decade of the century. The series as a whole considers the twentieth century as *the* century of decades. All eras are changeful, but the pace of change has itself steadily accelerated throughout modern history, and never more swiftly than under the pressures of political crises and of new technologies and media in the twentieth century. Ideas, styles and outlooks came into dominance, and were then displaced, in more and more rapid succession, characterising ever-briefer periods, sharply separated from predecessors and successors.

Time-spans appropriate to literary or cultural history shortened correspondingly, and on account not only of change itself, but its effect on perception. How distant, for example, that tranquil, sunlit, Edwardian decade already seemed, even ten years later, after the First World War, at the start of the twenties. And how essential, too, to the self-definition of that restless decade, and later ones, that the years from 1900 to 1910 *should* seem tranquil and sunlit – as a convenient contrast, not necessarily based altogether firmly on ways the Edwardians may have thought of themselves. A need to secure the past in this way – for clarity and definition, in changeful times – encourages views of earlier decades almost as a hand of familiar, well-differentiated cards, dealt out, one by one, by prior times to the present one. These no longer offer pictures of kings and queens: King Edward VII, at the start of the century, or, briefly, George V, were the last monarchs to give their names to an age. Instead, the cards are marked all the more clearly by image and number, as 'the Twenties', 'the Thirties', 'the Forties' and so on. History itself often seems to join in the game, with so many epochal dates – 1918, 1929, 1939, 1968, 1979, 1989, 2001 – approximating to the end of decades.

By the end of the century, decade divisions had at any rate become a firmly-established habit, even a necessity, for cultural understanding and analysis. They offer much virtue and opportunity to the present series. Concentration within firm temporal boundaries gives each volume further scope to range geographically – to explore the literary production and shifting mutual influences of nations, regions and minorities within a less and less surely 'United' Kingdom. Attention to film and broadcasting allows individual volumes to reflect another key aspect of literature's rapidly changing role throughout the century. In its early years, writing and publishing remained almost the only media for imagination, but by the end of the century, they were hugely challenged by competition from new technologies. Changes of this kind were accompanied by wide divergences in ways that the literary was conceived and studied. The shifting emphases of literary criticism, at various stages of the century, are also considered throughout the series.

Above all, though, the series' decade-divisions promote productive, sharply-focused literary-historical analysis. Ezra Pound's celebrated definition of literature, as 'news that stays news', helps emphasise the advantages. It is easy enough to work with the second part of Pound's equation: to explain the continuing appeal of literature from the past. It is harder to recover what made a literary work news in the first place, or, crucially for literary history, to establish just how it related *to* the news of its day – how it digested, evaded or sublimated pressures bearing on its author's imagination at the time. Concentration on individual decades facilitates attention to this 'news'. It helps recover the brisk, chill feel of the day, as authors stepped out to buy their morning newspapers – the immediate, actual climate of their time, as well as the tranquillity, sunshine or cloud ascribed to it in later commentary. Close concentration on individual periods can also renew attention to writing that did *not* stay news – to works that, significantly, pleased contemporary readers and reviewers, and might repay careful rereading by later critics.

In its later years, critics of twentieth-century writing sometimes concentrated more on characterising than periodising the literature they surveyed, usually under the rubrics of modernism or postmodernism. No decade is an island, entire of itself, and volumes in the series consider, where appropriate, broader movements and influences of this kind, stretching beyond their allotted periods. Each volume also offers, of course, a fuller picture of the writing of its times than necessarily-selective studies of modernism and postmodernism can provide. Modernism and postmodernism, moreover, are thoroughly specific in their historical origins and development, and the nature of each can be usefully illumined by the close, detailed analyses the series provides. Changeful, tumultuous and challenging, history in the twentieth century perhaps pressed harder and more variously on literary imagination than ever before, requiring a literary history correspondingly meticulous, flexible and multifocal. This is what *The Edinburgh History of Twentieth-Century Literature in Britain* provides.

The idea for the series originated with Jackie Jones in Edinburgh University Press, and all involved are grateful for her vision and guidance, and for support from the Press, at every stage throughout.

Randall Stevenson
University of Edinburgh

Introduction: In Search of the Twentyish

A Decade Overlooked

This is the first book to attempt a general – although of course far from comprehensive – account of literature in Britain during the 1920s. To some readers, this will seem surprising. The Twenties have become an almost invisible decade in British literary history, certainly by comparison with the Thirties. There are numerous books about Thirties poetry, Thirties fiction and Thirties literature as a whole, but they have very few counterparts in studies of the Twenties.[1] W. H. Auden famously characterised the Thirties as a 'low, dishonest decade', and although there is room for debate about quite how low and dishonest those years were, at least there is little dispute that they constitute a decade. About the 1920s we appear to be much less certain.

One reason why we have come to regard 1930–9 as a proper decade with its own distinct cultural and literary agenda while we hesitate to grant the preceding decade such recognition is that the ascendancy of Modernism in academic literary studies since the 1970s has brought about a habitual substitution of a movement – and for all its undoubted importance, a minority movement – for a chronological period in the terminology of early twentieth-century literary history. The phase of 'High' Modernism that runs approximately from 1910 to 1930 not only overshadows the rich and varied non-Modernist writing of the time but resists that segmentation into decades to which lesser cultural developments are still subject. By calling the literary 1920s almost invisible, I do not at all suggest that its major writings go unread. Quite to the contrary, some of them are accorded critical respect verging on adulation, so there will be no rhetorical snivelling about 'neglect' in these pages. I refer rather to the occlusion of the period than of its literary fruits, and to the impression that the calendar of modern letters has been curiously suspended so as not to impede the procession of Modernism, with the result that to speak now of any decades intervening between the Edwardian period (1901–10) and the Thirties may seem like an irrelevance or even an impertinence. This book attempts to correct those distortions of literary history, taking as its object not Modernism alone (although that certainly has the attention it merits, especially in Chapter 2), but the much broader 'modern movement' that I have mapped out in an earlier study (Baldick 2004).

The academic construction of Modernism is one important factor, then, in the failure of the 1920s to emerge as a recognised literary period in Britain, but it is not the only one. There have been local historical factors at work also, that may best be highlighted by bringing in the American case for comparison. In the United States, where Modernism comes even closer to monopolising academic discussion of early twentieth-century literature, there is nonetheless in the national memory a sharper recollection of the Twenties as a period to itself, opened by the enforcement of Prohibition from January 1920, and punctually closed by the Wall Street Crash of October 1929. American culture has also taken greater care to immortalise its 1920s on film, not only in the superior gangster movie *The Roaring Twenties* (1939), starring James Cagney, but also in one of the world's favourite film comedies, Billy Wilder's *Some Like it Hot* (1959). British history lacks such conveniently placed turning-points as decade-markers, and British culture is bereft of memorable cinematic reconstructions of the 1920s. Political, social and economic historians of Britain, who in any case usually prefer to work across periods longer than a single decade, have for good reasons most often segmented the early twentieth century according to its wars, giving us numerous studies of Britain either in the age of world wars, thus 1914–45, or in the interval between wars, thus 1918–39.[2]

Further impediments to the visibility of the 1920s arise from the configuration of the decade's literary scene itself, which in some respects does not offer a picture of coherence. Several incoherences, imbalances and internal divisions of Twenties literary life will be considered under various heads in this Introduction. For the time being, it will suffice to point out that this decade, unlike the Thirties, failed to throw up a cohort of new young poets who could be identified as a collective voice of changed times. There was little doubt at the time that T. S. Eliot was the most formidable new presence in poetry, but with the departure of his mentor Ezra Pound from the British scene in 1920, Eliot was neither able nor visibly willing to surround himself, as W. H. Auden was to do in the 1930s, with like-minded peers and collaborators. Eliot had his imitators (Richard Aldington, Herbert Read and the far inferior Osbert Sitwell among them), but no solid-looking phalanx of poets emerged that could be identified under the heading 'Twenties Poets'. Indeed, such a phrase looks almost meaningless compared with the assumption of a common project that is evoked by the term 'Thirties Poets'.[3]

Distinctive new voices did emerge in the 1920s, some of them quickly associated with the new moods of the times. The arrivals of Noël Coward in the theatre, of Aldous Huxley in prose fiction, and of Edith Sitwell and Hugh MacDiarmid in poetry were all noticed as portents of the new, while detective fiction was being refashioned by the arrival of Agatha Christie and Dorothy L. Sayers. At the same time a number of writers who had already launched themselves in the previous decade, including Eliot, Virginia Woolf and D. H. Lawrence, commanded growing critical attention as they adopted new tones and styles: Eliot modulated from fastidious wit to morose lamentation, Woolf switched from orthodox narrative construction to experimental design and Lawrence moved on from provincial growing-pains to exotic misanthropy. Novelty and originality were plentifully evident, but they did not seem to be arriving under any common banner, nor to conform to any single 'new wave' or identifiable trend. Even if we adopt such a capacious term as Modernism to cover the teeming variety of literary innovations found in the 1920s, we would struggle to accommodate Coward, Lawrence and Huxley under that label, let alone Christie or such late-Twenties debutants as Evelyn Waugh. We need, to consider, then, a range of other perspectives that might allow us to bring the literary Twenties into focus. We are engaged here upon a search for that which is 'Twentyish' – meaning characteristic of the 1920s.[4]

Ruinations

Our first resort is to find some common basis of belief from which most 1920s writers proceed, and which most 1920s readers would accept from them. As for positive beliefs, any hope of finding common ground there is simply doomed: as we shall see in Chapter 1, a disputatious contrariness is the norm for the period. On the other hand, the negative terrain of unbelief or disbelief turns out to be far more promising. Virginia Woolf's attempt to make critical sense of recent literary developments in her essay 'How it Strikes a Contemporary' (1923; revd 1925) makes this point, dwelling upon the unspoken but secure conviction that Walter Scott and Jane Austen had shared with their readers, that the human world was 'of a certain quality' (Woolf 1994: 239). Woolf is careful not to tie this conviction to any specific religious, philosophical or political creed: at issue is the capacity to believe in anything, rather than in something. Her backward glance at Scott and Austen provides the ground of a telling contrast with the modern writer of Woolf's own day. 'So then our contemporaries afflict us,' she writes, 'because they have ceased to believe' (Woolf 1994: 240). Unable to summon up a whole world of commonly held assumptions, the modern writer can give us only transitory personal impressions, fragments of what had once been a secure whole. 'It is an age of fragments,' Woolf declares in the same essay (Woolf 1994: 236), drawing upon an image already resonantly employed near the end of the decade's most famous poem, T. S. Eliot's 'The Waste Land' (1922): 'These fragments I have shored against my ruins' (Eliot 2001: 20). If there was one thing upon which writers of the Twenties could agree, it was that their very disagreements arose from the collapse of some formerly coherent order of civilisation that had recently been left in ruins by the Great War of 1914–18.

This book takes its title from a forthright version of the same claim about the post-War condition, in the opening sentences of D. H. Lawrence's novel *Lady Chatterley's Lover* (1928):

> Ours is essentially a tragic age, so we refuse to take it tragically. The cataclysm has happened, we are among the ruins, we start to build up new little habitats, to have new little hopes. It is rather hard work: there is now no smooth road into the future: but we go round, or scramble over the obstacles.[5] (Lawrence 1990: 5)

The ruins to which Lawrence refers were of course metaphorical. There had indeed been some aerial bombardment of London and other eastern parts of England during the War, and there was economic ruin in the form of severe deflation and unemployment, especially in the steep recession of 1920–1, which was in fact worse than anything seen later in the Thirties. The damage that truly concerned 1920s writers, however, had been done less to the physical fabric of British civilisation or to its productive capacity than to its collective morale, its self-belief and cultural self-confidence. The name most commonly given to that general spiritual depression, both at the time and since, is 'disillusionment'. If we think we know anything about the prevailing mood of the 1920s, it is that it was disillusioned. One writer, indeed, the journalist C. E. Montague, devoted an entire book, entitled *Disenchantment* (1922), to analysing that 'general post-war condition of mind with its symptoms of apathy, callousness, and lassitude' (Montague 1928: 66), and to retracing its origins to the wartime experience of what were now returned ex-servicemen. Recalling the moment of victory in November 1918 that had ushered in the post-War age, Montague writes,

> And now the marred triumph would leave us jaded and disillusioned, divided, half-bankrupt; sneerers at lofty endeavour, and yet not the men for the plodding of busy and orderly peace; bilious with faiths and enthusiasms gone sour in the stomach. (Montague 1928: 176)

The significantly 'disillusioned' strain of literature in the 1920s, especially in relation to recollected wartime experiences, will be considered at length in Chapter 3, in which I propose that we would benefit from shedding some of our illusions about disillusionment. At this stage, though, our focus remains upon perceived discontinuity, with the aid of Lawrence's picture of tragic ruination.

The 'smooth road' that had once seemed to connect the past with the present and the future according to most pre-War assumptions about the progressive march of civilisation had, in the eyes of many observers, now vanished, leaving a moral landscape without directions or customary signposts; or, to pursue the architectural metaphor, without reliable foundations upon which to build anew. The impact of the cataclysm upon British culture in the 1920s was widely felt to have taken the form of a sudden historic disconnection, a disturbing discontinuity between past and present, such that the pre-War world now seemed to many observers to resemble a strangely remote, even prehistoric era. Only fifteen years after the War's outbreak, the narrator of Richard Aldington's novel *Death of a Hero* (1929) could put the matter like this:

> Pre-war seems like pre-history. What did we do, how did we feel, what were we living for in those incredibly distant years? One feels as if the period 1900–14 has to be treated archaeologically, painfully recreated by experts from slight vestiges. (Aldington 1984: 199)

Aldington's conversion of a period within living memory into a long-vanished era may well have been prompted by similar observations in the preface to Osbert Sitwell's earlier novel *Before the Bombardment* (1926), which, as its title suggests, is set in the pre-War world, specifically in 1907–8. Sitwell advises his readers to regard the story as a historical romance set in a now-forgotten age more remote to them than Greek antiquity, further inviting them to compare the figures in a fashion-magazine of 1906 with those of an ancient Cretan wall-painting. 'The distant, mysterious inhabitants of that lost world are infinitely nearer to us in their clothes, and probably in their outlook, than our own parents' (Sitwell 1985: 9). Sitwell, who detested his own parents, adds here to his version of the problem an element of generational antagonism that is also found in Aldington's repeated disparagement of his elders as 'Victorian' fossils and as Old Fools. We shall come to consider the generational divisions and conflicts of the 1920s below, but for the time being our attention is devoted to the larger sense of discontinuity of which the discredited parent-figure is only one symptom.

Virginia Woolf addresses the same question in the essay from which I have already quoted, 'How it Strikes a Contemporary':

> We are sharply cut off from our predecessors. A shift in the scale – the sudden slip of masses held in position for ages – has shaken the fabric from top to bottom, alienated us from the past and made us perhaps too vividly conscious of the present. Every day we find ourselves doing, saying, or thinking things that would have been impossible to our fathers [...] No age can have been more rich than ours in writers determined to give expression to the differences which separate them from the past and not to the resemblances which connect them with it. (Woolf 1994: 238)

It is clear from these remarks that Woolf detects in contemporary writing an unbalanced attitude to the past, a determined effort to suppress continuities in favour of disruptions, and to cancel one's debts to prior tradition in an excessive focus upon the unprecedented features of the present day. She seems to be aware that the striking originality of her contemporaries in literature is of a curiously rootless kind that, already culturally orphaned by the loss of that 'belief' enjoyed by Austen and Scott, risks weakening itself further by deliberate repudiation. It is significant that Woolf refrains here from widening an already uneasy gulf between past and present by mythicising the pre-War years as 'archaeologically' remote, as Sitwell and Aldington were to do.

The sense of radical disconnection from the past to which Woolf and others bear witness is one aspect of a more general temporal disorientation that afflicts Twenties literature, often in curious and contradictory forms. The present book takes the time-sense of the 1920s as a major clue to the decade's distinctive preoccupations, devoting Chapter 2 to the examination of time-shifting and anachronism in the literature of the period, and Chapter 3 to its strong sense of distance from the pre-War world. At this point, we shall note more briefly the problem of contemporaneity in 1920s writing.

Times of the Twenties

On the second page of her novel *Mrs Dalloway* (1925), Virginia Woolf establishes the setting of the fiction, first mentioning that we are in Westminster, and then, in free-indirect rendition of the thoughts of Clarissa Dalloway, letting us know the time:

> For it was the middle of June. The War was over, except for some one like Mrs Foxcroft at the embassy last night eating her heart out because that nice boy was killed and now the old Manor House must go to a cousin; or Lady Bexborough who opened a bazaar, they said, with the telegram in her hand, John, her favourite, killed; but it was over; thank Heaven – over. (Woolf 1992b: 4–5)

Here we have encapsulated the central paradox of historical self-awareness in the 1920s, of which the literature of the time is the principal record: that the War is now over, except that it is not over. Woolf builds into the novel an important secondary character, Septimus Warren Smith, a traumatised war-veteran whose harrowing hallucinations of dead comrades remind us that the War is not over for him or for many others – and they would include a good share of the novel's first readers – in similarly war-haunted states of mind. Twenties literature is overshadowed, possessed and 'haunted' by the Great War, even when that War is not directly mentioned, as Samuel Hynes's major study, *A War Imagined* (1990), has argued persuasively. To make that uncontroversial claim would seem, however, to be in contradiction to Woolf's contemporary assertion, quoted above, that the writer of her time is sharply cut off from her or his predecessors. We find ourselves here in a related paradox: 1920s literature feels itself to be disconnected from the past, even from the relatively recent past, but at the same time is obsessed with the past, especially the relatively recent past.

It is at this point that we come upon a further, and perhaps surprising, factor in the relative invisibility and indefiniteness of the 1920s in British cultural memory. This is that so little of its significant literature actually takes the measure of contemporary life. We have seen that Virginia Woolf thought her generation was 'perhaps too vividly conscious of the present', and yet if she had in mind literature rather than contemporary thought and conversation at large, she need not have worried greatly. Her own *Mrs Dalloway*, of which the action is set in June 1923, is of course a novel of contemporary life, but it is one of very few major novels of the 1920s that come under that description. Modernist fiction on an international scale is indeed in great part a literature of retrospect and historical reconstruction, of which the principal monuments are Marcel Proust's novel sequence *A la recherche du temps perdu* (1913–27), set mostly around the turn of the century, and James Joyce's *Ulysses* (1922), set in 1904. Its British wing is best represented by Dorothy Richardson, whose novel-sequence *Pilgrimage* (1915–38) covers events of the 1890s and shortly after; by Ford Madox Ford, whose masterpiece *Parade's End* (1924–8) treats the period 1912–18 except in its final Twenties-set volume; and by Woolf herself, who devotes most of *Jacob's Room* (1922), *To the Lighthouse* (1927) and *Orlando* (1928) to the pre-War world. We could add that all the short stories of Wyndham Lewis's *The Wild Body* (1927) are set some time before the War, as is D. H. Lawrence's major work, *Women in Love* (1921). Katherine Mansfield did not live long enough to capture much of 1920s life in her stories, of which some of the best are set in the period of her 1890s childhood in New Zealand. Fantastical fictions also tend to delve back into the Victorian age, as is the case with Walter de la Mare's *Memoirs of a Midget* (1921), David Garnett's *Lady into Fox* (1922) and Rose Macaulay's *Orphan Island* (1924). If we go looking for portrayals of British society in the 1920s, we find them in only a handful of truly notable novels, all from the decade's second half: *Mrs Dalloway*, *Lady Chatterley's Lover*, Henry Green's *Living* (1929), Aldous Huxley's *Point Counter Point* (1928) and, through the distorting lens of grotesque farce, Evelyn Waugh's *Decline and Fall* (1928); although there are also lesser novels – again, mostly of the decade's later years – that set out to picture the contemporary scene: John Galsworthy's second Forsyte trilogy *A Modern Comedy* (1928) and J. B. Priestley's romance of travelling players, *The Good Companions* (1929), are among them.

Most kinds of poetry being unsuited to capturing impressions of contemporary social life, it is in broadly satirical verse that we find them, most memorably in passages of Eliot's 'The Waste Land', less memorably in the 1920s verse of Siegfried Sassoon and Richard Aldington. The drama is another matter: here the presentation of contemporary life was the norm, although it is worth noting that the Twenties stage witnessed a vogue for historical and biographical plays including John Drinkwater's *Robert E. Lee* (1923), Clemence Dane's *Will Shakespeare* (1921) and Bernard Shaw's *Saint Joan* (1924). Otherwise the dominance of the comedy of manners almost guaranteed audiences a conventionally restricted glimpse of contemporary life, in the form of a drawing-room set populated by smartly-dressed modern socialites wielding cigarette-holders. The reigning master of this form in the early part of the decade was W. Somerset Maugham, notably in *The Circle* (1921) and *Our Betters* (1923), although he came to be eclipsed by the arrival of newer comic playwrights – Frederick Lonsdale, the farceur Ben Travers and most importantly Noël Coward – in whose works the drawling accents of fashionable Twenties conversation are heard in a new style of slang-enlivened informality.

Returning to the realm of the novel, we find a significant new configuration in lighter 'genre' fiction of the decade. Put simply, historical fiction – in the strong sense, set in times beyond living memory – shrinks in importance, while detective stories and comical fiction come to the fore. There is little historical fiction of any note in the 1920s apart from the romantic bestseller *Precious Bane* (1924) by Mary Webb, John Buchan's *Witch Wood* (1927) and Naomi Mitchison's feminist reinterpretations of antiquity in *The Conquered* (1923) and *Cloud Cuckoo Land* (1925). Meanwhile the new generation of detective writers led by Agatha Christie established the murder-puzzle story as a kind of national craze; and P. G. Wodehouse's tales of spineless aristocratic buffoons commanded the sphere of lighter literary amusements. Detective fiction in particular emerged as the only literary genre that consistently, although within a narrow social range, addressed the forms and idioms of contemporary life, and indeed it pursued them in its relentless fashion down to the very minutiae. This is why it still shapes the impressions we now retain of life and manners in 1920s Britain, which are more likely to derive from Christie – and in other genres from Wodehouse and Coward – than from the higher levels of its mainstream fiction.

To summarise this brief review of contemporaneity and its diminished role in 1920s writing, we might say that the most talented writers of that decade largely failed to immortalise their own times. Putting the matter more fairly, they did not, aside from exceptions already noted, even attempt to. The following decade offers a striking contrast here: it seems that the documentary impulse to seek out and record the unique sights and sounds of the present day was as underdeveloped in the Twenties as it was overdeveloped in the Thirties. If we ask why this should have been so, then the answer seems to be indicated in part by the pre-1920 and mostly pre-War settings of so many novels mentioned above, while the decline of remotely-set historical fiction provides a sort of corroboration. Writers of the 1920s were cursed by a burden of unresolved business that understandably distracted them from the passing shows of their own time. This business was the understanding of recent history, in particular the period from the late-Victorian decades through to the end of the Great War. That period was of course the one in which most 1920s authors had spent their childhoods, so its history was both public and personal, while the telling of it could involve any combination of fiction with autobiography, and could be pursued with motives ranging from nostalgic retreat into a mythical 'Edwardian summer' to arraignment of the parental and grandparental generations. The great questions to which readers as well as writers sought answers in the wake of the cataclysm were many and complex: How did we come to this? How could a self-confident civilisation come to wreck itself? What were the hidden seeds of its self-destruction? Were its high-sounding ideals and values only a sham? Were we all blindly deluded, and if so, how? The consuming preoccupation of the decade's fiction and autobiography, and even of some poetry and drama, lay here, in a great collective inquest into the late-Victorian, Edwardian and early-Georgian phases of British life.

This was a literature of hindsight and of Remembrance – an especially significant term of 1920s culture. When Charles Scott Moncrieff set about his English translation (1922–30) of Marcel Proust's *A la recherche du temps perdu*, he chose a new title for the novel-sequence that he knew to be inaccurate, and in the teeth of Proust's own objections: instead of *In Search of Lost Time*, he called it, from a phrase in Shakespeare's 30th sonnet, *Remembrance of Things Past*. It says something about the timely authority of the very term Remembrance that it could tempt Proust's Scottish disciple – himself a war-veteran with a permanent limp – into such perverse infidelity. Remembrance dominated the public culture of Britain through the early 1920s, when every municipal authority, and almost every parish council and workplace, was busy commissioning memorial monuments for its dead, as the local counterparts to the Cenotaph (inaugurated November 1920) in Whitehall. Later, the tenth anniversary of the Armistice sparked a 'boom' in commemorative war literature that included R. H. Mottram's story-collection *Ten Years Ago* (1928), in which one sketch conjures the war memories that run through a typical ex-serviceman's mind during the now customary two minutes' silence.

The decade's literary hindsight is often ironic in its reassessments of pre-War life, especially, as we shall see in Chapter 3, in the war-novels, war-memoirs and other war-dominated autobiographical writings of the late 1920s. Its retrospective impulse often also generates curiously recursive or backward-looping narrative or dramatic structures, some of which we will examine in Chapter 2. For example, Noël Coward's favourite among his own plays was *Bitter-Sweet* (1929), a musical drama that begins in the present day but then takes us back to the Victorian age. In the realm of war fiction, Richard Aldington's *Death of a Hero* begins with a prologue set just after the 1918 Armistice, but then jumps back to 1890 to begin an account of the protagonist's family history, launching this with a version of the paradox we have already encountered:

> A very different England, that of 1890, and yet curiously the same. In some ways so fabulous, so remote from us; in others so near, terrifyingly near and like us. An England morally buried in great foggy wrappings of hypocrisy and prosperity and cheapness. (Aldington 1984: 39)

Aldington's tone here is accusatory and satirical, which is not to be taken as representative of what I am calling the larger literary inquest into the recent past. Other fictional reconstructions of the pre-War world are more fondly elegiac, as in the first part of Woolf's *To the Lighthouse*.

Genres of the Twenties

The new predominance of literary hindsight combined with a widely shared perception of the War as a great watershed to produce some remarkable generic shifts in the novel, profoundly affecting the fortunes of those subgenres that had depended most upon assumptions of continuity and organic development, namely the *Bildungsroman* (education-novel or 'coming-of-age' novel) and the family saga. Both of these fictional models had suddenly become, if not actually impossible, then hard to accommodate within the new post-War awareness of discontinuity. A symptomatic case that has often been noticed is the disjunction between D. H. Lawrence's family saga *The Rainbow* (1915) and its sequel, *Women in Love*: the first novel progresses through time (1840 to 1905) according to the passing and emerging of successive generations; but then the sequel, written and rewritten during the War, seems to arrest this onward movement (or we might say 'freeze' it: one of the principal characters ends up freezing to death) in a series of episodes that appear unrelated to pasts or futures. *Women in Love* also seems obsessed in its imagery with inorganic matter, as if not only the 'smooth road' from past to future but the possibility of narrating organic human development has suddenly become unavailable.

Family sagas and multi-generation family novels were still being written in this decade, but under certain warping and fracturing pressures of historical awareness. The best known, John Galsworthy's *The Forsyte Saga* (1922) has a great gap in its chronology where the War years should be, and Woolf's *To the Lighthouse* is similarly split, the ten-year gap between its pre-War and post-War sections filled in with a summary during which the characters themselves are absent from its setting. Rose Macaulay's family saga *Told by an Idiot* (1923) does cover the War period, but in a strangely perfunctory fashion, as if the leisurely tracing of family fortunes at such a time could not decently be attempted. It is also worth noting that novels of the 1920s that focus upon familial destinies more often present us with doomed dynasties coming to an end: *Women in Love*, *Lady Chatterley's Lover* and Ford's *Last Post* (1928) are significant cases of these last gasps.

The case of the coming-of-age novel is perhaps even more striking. The decade prior to the Twenties had been a golden age of *Bildungsromane*, from Arnold Bennett's *Clayhanger* (1910) to May Sinclair's *Mary*

Olivier (1919), in which Joyce, Woolf, Lawrence and Maugham had all produced memorable examples of the form. Now there came a dearth, at least of really noteworthy education-novels, especially by male authors. Dorothy Richardson's apparently interminable *Pilgrimage* sequence was still in progress, reaching its ninth volume with *Oberland* (1927); Lawrence's Scottish friend Catherine Carswell won critical respect for her first novel, *Open the Door!* (1920); and Rosamond Lehmann made a creditable debut with her coming-of-age novel *Dusty Answer* (1927). More significant for the fate of this subgenre in the Twenties, however, is Virginia Woolf's *Jacob's Room*, which is a kind of anti-*Bildungsroman* in which the hero, Jacob Flanders, keeps disappearing. His ominous surname reminds us that the forward-looking momentum of ambition and summoning destiny that governs this kind of novel had been, for his generation at least, abruptly cancelled. To simplify, the novel of youthful expectation tends in the 1920s to give way to the novel of mature retrospection.

Some peculiarities of the Twenties' configuration of literary genres have already been remarked upon above: the decline of historical fiction, the booms in detective novels and war literature. To those observations we should add a few more about the ways in which the literary culture of this decade favours some kinds of writings over others. The largest general tendency is found in the predominance of comedy, across a range from the theatrical comedy of manners to light satirical verse and the farcical short story. Twenties comedy – in which category I include detective fiction too – is in this book the subject of Chapter 4, in which I examine the curious moral impunities it indulges. At this stage, we may look at this generic drift from the other end, and so notice the almost complete withering away of tragedy. 'Ours is essentially a tragic age,' wrote Lawrence, 'so we refuse to take it tragically.' The general refusal of tragedy is especially significant in the light of the War, which in 1920s literature tends to be treated not according to tragic convention but in various compounds of satire, elegy and even farce. Comedy of many kinds dominated the theatre, leaving (apart from revivals of Shakespeare's tragedies) only a few historical plays by John Drinkwater and Bernard Shaw that deal with the fall of great men or, in the outstanding case of Shaw's *Saint Joan* (1924), the fall of a great teenage girl. The most important feature of *Saint Joan* in this context is that although it treats tragic materials in its main action, Shaw insists upon giving it an openly comic conclusion in its Epilogue on Joan's recent canonisation. To some extent the disappearance of tragedy is masked by the popularity of pseudo-tragic melodrama on the stage (as with Coward's *The Vortex*, 1924) or in fleetingly notorious novels like Michael Arlen's *The*

Green Hat, Margaret Kennedy's *The Constant Nymph* (both 1924) and Radclyffe Hall's *The Well of Loneliness* (1928). Otherwise it was the comic mask that dominated not just the stage but the fiction shelf.

One special genre that flourished with remarkable vitality and originality in the 1920s was literary criticism. Indeed the decade that runs from T. S. Eliot's collection of essays *The Sacred Wood* (1920) through Woolf's *The Common Reader* (1925) to I. A. Richards's *Practical Criticism* (1929) has no rival in earlier or later phases of critical work in English. This body of 1920s writing has proved to be momentous in providing the bases for the later academic construction of literary Modernism, as a current distinguished from others by repeated citation of Eliot's and Woolf's essays. Twenties criticism not only brought about a shift in poetical taste in which Eliot's interest in seventeenth-century verse helped to dethrone the nineteenth-century poets for a generation; it established the basic analytic vocabulary for understanding the novel as a genre with its own formal challenges. Before the 1920s, there had been hardly any noteworthy theorising of the novel apart from Henry James's Prefaces (1907–9) to his reprinted works. Percy Lubbock's codification of Jamesian principles in *The Craft of Fiction* (1921) set off an unprecedented discussion of the elements of novel-construction that ran through the decade, culminating in E. M. Forster's *Aspects of the Novel* (1927) and Edwin Muir's *The Structure of the Novel* (1928). That opening up of the modern world's dominant literary genre to formal analysis would by itself be a creditable record for a decade of criticism, but there were bold new ideas emerging elsewhere in the critical arena too: the provocative essays of D. H. Lawrence's *Studies in Classic American Literature* (1924); new methods of 'close' analysis of poetry offered both in Richards's *Practical Criticism* and in Laura Riding and Robert Graves's *A Survey of Modernist Poetry* (1927); and an absorbing debate about romanticism and classicism carried on between Eliot and John Middleton Murry in the pages of their rival journals the *Criterion* and the *Adelphi* (see Harding 2002: 25–43). Even without considering critical studies of individual writers, we have ample evidence upon which to claim the critical achievements of the decade as the most important of the century.

On the other hand, there is one subgenre in which the 1920s have almost nothing to offer. Love poetry in this decade becomes simply negligible. If a brave anthologist were to attempt a book of Twenties love poems, it would be a slim and largely undistinguished volume, sustained by a few poems of W. B. Yeats and Robert Graves that do not actually express erotic feeling but play upon the ironies of love; perhaps two lyrics by Charlotte Mew could go into it, then some rather light ditties by W. H. Davies, two or three lyrics from C. Day Lewis's *Transitional Poem* (1929) and perhaps three poems from Siegfried Sassoon's unmemorable sequence *The Heart's Journey* (1928). Such a collection could be padded out with perhaps as many as four love poems of the decade by Vita Sackville-West and a similar number of John Drinkwater's sonnets. Otherwise one of the very few convincing love poems in the true sense would be Hugh MacDiarmid's 'Wheesht, Wheesht' (1926). Quite why the voice of Eros falls so silent in the 1920s is a mystery, made more puzzling by the presence of poets who had written significant love poetry before 1920 (Harold Monro, D. H. Lawrence and most famously Yeats) but composed little or none after that date. By diverting their talents into political or satirical verse, these rejoined a larger body of modern poets – John Masefield, Walter de la Mare, T. S. Eliot, Edith Sitwell – who had not shown any interest in love poetry. Newly arriving 1920s poets such as Edmund Blunden, Edwin Muir and Louis MacNeice did nothing to redress that imbalance. The dominant trend of the decade's poetry led away from the erotic and overwhelmingly towards lampoon and lamentation, from Eliot's *Ara Vos Prec* (1920) to Sitwell's *Gold Coast Customs* (1929) and Lawrence's *Pansies* (1929). When erotic passion is addressed at all in 1920s poetry, it is most often held at arm's length as an object of squeamish disgust (as in Aldous Huxley's collection *Leda* of 1920) or of ironic contemplation, as in Herbert Read's 'The Analysis of Love' (1923). A fashion for coolly anaphrodisiac ironies, set by T. S. Eliot, may account for this trend, but only in part; other possible factors await investigation.

Places of the Twenties

The short list that I offered above of notable fictions set in the present-day times of the 1920s was more abbreviated than it might have been, because I excluded stories set overseas, withholding until this point the consideration of geographical displacement, which is the second factor that curtails Twenties literature's engagement with the Britain of its day. There are of course gains as well as losses to be noted here, as British readers were given fictional and non-fictional treatments of an unprecedented range of far-flung locations. E. M. Forster's *A Passage to India* (1924), set in a fictional Indian city, is now the best-known example, but it belongs to an extensive library of exotic novels and stories written by an unusually well-travelled and in some cases self-exiling generation.

Forster and, among others, Rose Macaulay (who had grown up near Genoa) had published novels before the War that were set in Italy, so there is no particular surprise in finding a number of 1920s novels set wholly or partly in various Italian locations, and usually involving groups of English-speaking tourists or expatriates: Aldous Huxley's *Those Barren Leaves* (1925), D. H. Lawrence's *Aaron's Rod*, Compton Mackenzie's *Extraordinary Women* (1928), H. G. Wells's *Meanwhile* (1928) and Elizabeth Bowen's first novel, *The Hotel* (1927). Nor is the novel set in Paris, like Jean Rhys's *Postures* (1928; later retitled *Quartet*), much of a novelty on that account. More notable is a fictional setting in Vladivostok, as in William Gerhardi's *Futility* (1922); or in Hong Kong (Maugham's *The Painted Veil*, 1925); or in Malaya (H. M. Tomlinson's *Gallions Reach*, 1927); or in the Caribbean sea (Richard Hughes's *A High Wind in Jamaica*, 1929); or in Sydney, Australia (Lawrence's *Kangaroo*, 1923); or in Mexico (Lawrence's *The Plumed Serpent*, 1926); or in Cairo, which despite the novella's misleading title is the location for Vita Sackville-West's *Seducers in Equador* (1924). Many of Katherine Mansfield's stories are set in her native New Zealand, while Maugham's tales in *The Casuarina Tree* (1926) locate their action in Borneo, Singapore and Malaya, following on from the South-Sea setting of his story 'Rain' (1921).

In addition to those novels and stories, the 1920s, although not as rich in this genre as the 1930s were to be, produced some memorable travel books, often by the same authors. Aldous Huxley, for example, published essays on aspects of Italy and the Netherlands in *Along the Road* (1925), before embarking on a much more ambitious world tour, written up in his *Jesting Pilate* (1926), that took him from India through Burma, Malaya, the Philippines and Japan to California and then eastward to New York. Lawrence wrote two travel books, *Sea and Sardinia* (1921) and *Mornings in Mexico* (1927), in addition to many essays devoted to Italy, New Mexico and other stops on his world travels. Maugham published his sketches of a visit to China in *On a Chinese Screen* (1922), shortly after staging a spectacular drama, *East of Suez* (1922), set in what was then called Peking.

Huxley, Lawrence and Maugham were especially restless and widely-travelled authors, but they were not alone: Ronald Firbank spent most of his final years, before his death in Rome in 1926, on overseas travels; while Edmund Blunden spent the years 1924–7 as a lecturer at Tokyo University, where he really was a writer among the ruins, most of the university buildings having collapsed in the great earthquake of 1923. 'Abroad', though, was of strong personal and literary significance to many others who had never reached Mexico or Malaya. A special case, indeed the single most recurrent overseas setting for fictional and non-fictional narratives in this decade, and for some poetry and drama, was Flanders, recently occupied by the British sector of the Western Front cutting across the Belgian-French border, and by now the site of pilgrimages to the huge war cemeteries. The plentiful war-poetry, war-fiction and war-memoirs of the 1920s repeatedly returned their readers – many of whose brothers and husbands were buried there – to its unforgotten war-zone. For those who preferred not to dwell on such memories, another favoured location for fiction was an entirely invented one: the imaginary island, Pacific or Mediterranean, adopted by several authors for fabulous tales such as Rose Macaulay's *Orphan Island*, John Buchan's *The Dancing Floor* (1926) and Sylvia Townsend Warner's *Mr Fortune's Maggot* (1927). In the realm of popular romance and adventure fiction, there was a vogue for the Saharan desert, as in P. C. Wren's bestseller *Beau Geste* (1924). The British literary imagination in the 1920s seemed to extend everywhere, and to be only intermittently at home.

Another important consideration of literary locations arises from the somewhat misleading priorities of Modernism as presented in academic syllabuses. A commonly found conjunction of Eliot's 'The Waste Land' with Joyce's *Ulysses* and Woolf's *Mrs Dalloway* may give the impression that Modernism and indeed modern literature more broadly in the 1920s represent a radical turn away from the provincial and rural emphasis of the previous century and towards the metropolis. Considered on an international scale, Modernism does of course have a more than accidental preoccupation with urban experience, especially in German literature and in some major American fiction. In the British case, however, 'The Waste Land' (several parts of which take us beyond London) and *Mrs Dalloway* should not be mistaken for the tip of a large iceberg of metropolitan writing. There were some notable novels of the 1920s set in London, just as there had been in previous decades: *The Forsyte Saga*, Huxley's *Antic Hay* (1923) and *Point Counter Point*, Bennett's *Riceyman Steps* (1923), Radclyffe Hall's *Adam's Breed* (1926), Rebecca West's *Harriet Hume* (1929) and quite a few detective novels by Dorothy L. Sayers and others. There are also some vivid London episodes in a few of Mansfield's short stories, and in novels that are set partly elsewhere, as in Richardson's *Revolving Lights* (1923), Bennett's *Lord Raingo* (1926), Lawrence's *Aaron's Rod*, Woolf's *Jacob's Room*, Ford's *Some Do Not . . .* (1924) and Macaulay's *Crewe Train* (1926; in no sense a Cheshire novel). These are all significant works, but, even if we throw in the Paris of Jean Rhys's *Postures* for good measure, they do not as a corpus amount to a predominance – or even a particularly telling incidence – of metropolitan settings. If we turn from prose fiction to the drama and to poetry, the case for such metropolitanism weakens still further: only a very few poems of the decade are about London scenes: G. K. Chesterton's 'The Old Song' (1922) and Sassoon's 'Observations in Hyde Park' (1926) are rare examples. In the drama, the usual setting is the drawing room of a country house, as in Maugham's *The Circle* and Coward's *Hay Fever* (1925).

It needs to be emphasised that while British publishing was highly centralised in London, the imaginative world of its literature, insofar as its settings were in Britain at all, remained predominantly provincial and strongly rural. Even the Modernist writers were by no means tied to London: Woolf's *To the Lighthouse* is set on a remote island off the Scottish coast, and the action of Mary Butts's Modernist novel *Armed with Madness* (1928) takes place in a country house in rural Dorset, while Wyndham Lewis's *The Childermass* (1928) is not set in a city but in the open terrain of some other-worldly purgatory. Other sophisticated semi-Modernist writers set novels in country-house locations (as with Huxley's first novel, *Crome Yellow*, 1921) and in provincial towns or cities, like the Scarborough of Osbert Sitwell's *Before the Bombardment* and the industrial Birmingham of Henry Green's *Living*.

Further beyond the Modernist camp, one can read through the *Georgian Poetry* anthology of 1922 from cover to cover and not find a single urban poem in it, while there are plenty of bucolic verses, and of course many more that betray no specific location. Georgianism, and its often-noted rustic bias, did not die out with that final anthology, but persisted through the decade in the largely bucolic poetry of Edmund Blunden, W. H. Davies, Walter de la Mare and Vita Sackville-West, among many others. Sackville-West won the Hawthornden Prize for a long poem – it runs to more than a hundred printed pages – called *The Land* (1926), which is modelled upon the *Georgics* of Virgil and *The Seasons* (1726–30) of James Thomson in its celebration of the traditional cycle of the agricultural year.

> I sing once more
> The mild continuous epic of the soil,
> Haysel and harvest, tilth and husbandry;
> I tell of marl and dung, and of the means
> That break the unkindly spirit of the clay
>
> (Sackville-West 1933: 3)

Even Robert Graves, who had repudiated his earlier Georgian phase by the mid-Twenties, shows no interest in the urban scene in the nine verse collections he published in the decade. Older poets who had no direct link with the Georgians – notably Thomas Hardy and A. E. Housman – continued to publish poems of melancholic rusticity.

Even more strongly visible in the 1920s than bucolic poetry was the tradition of provincial or 'regional' fiction inherited from Victorian literature. Arnold Bennett and D. H. Lawrence had both emerged from that tradition, and Lawrence's *Lady Chatterley's Lover* represents an important return to it. The brothers T. F. Powys and John Cowper Powys similarly showed that regionally-centred fiction, in their case of Dorset, could be combined with highly original new styles, as in T. F. Powys's *Mr Tasker's Gods* (1925) and his elder brother's *Wolf Solent* (1928). The form proved congenial also to several women writers living in the provinces, such as Constance Holme of Westmorland (*The Things which Belong*, 1925), Mary Webb of Shropshire (*The House in Dormer Forest*, 1920), Sheila Kaye-Smith of Sussex (*Joanna Godden*, 1921) and the younger Yorkshire writer Winifred Holtby (*Anderby Wold*, 1923). While not exactly singing of marl and dung, some of these writers of both sexes waxed lyrical about the immemorial soil, and unfolded extravagantly gloomy legends of accursed families, as in Webb's *Precious Bane*:

> Sarns mostly have grey eyes – cold grey like the mere in winter – and the Sarn men are mainly dark and sullen. 'Sullen as a Sarn,' they say about these parts. And they say there's been something queer in the family ever since Timothy Sarn was struck by forkit lightning in the times of the religious wars. There were Sarns about here then, and always have been, ever since there was anybody. (Webb 1978: 18)

Writing of this sort later attracted the mockery of Stella Gibbons in her *Cold Comfort Farm* (1932); but that celebrated parody would scarcely have been conceivable had not the novel of rural life been so vigorous and so widely known in the 1920s.

National Literatures and International Authors

While the English provinces maintained their literary visibility, the fortunes of the peripheral nations were much more mixed. On the one hand, what has become known as the Irish Literary Renaissance reached its heyday with the mature work of W. B. Yeats, James Joyce and Sean O'Casey, coincident with their country's political secession as the Irish Free State (1922). On the other, Welsh and Scottish literatures in English were even more than usually submerged under the cultural dominance of England.

Since this book is devoted to literature in Britain, I draw only selectively in the following chapters on works by Yeats (who published through the London house of Macmillan) and by Joyce (who retained his British passport despite entitlement to a new Irish one), and not at all on O'Casey's plays, which – although O'Casey took up residence in England from 1926 – belong very much to the story of Dublin theatre. The Irish-born Bernard Shaw, however, long established as a British resident, is treated as belonging fully to the literary culture of his adoptive country.

Britain entered the 1920s under a prime minister, David Lloyd George, of Welsh origin, but there was certainly no equivalent Welsh leadership in its literature. On the contrary, this decade witnessed the virtual disappearance – before a significant resuscitation in the 1930s – of Welsh writing in English. The London-Welsh poet Edward Thomas had been killed in the War, as had Wilfred Owen, an Englishman of third-generation Welsh descent, while the short-storyist Arthur Machen published little of significance in the 1920s. The best-known Welsh-born poet of the times was the 'Supertramp' W. H. Davies, who lived mostly in London and showed little inclination to speak for or about his native land. The Welsh presence flickered in the realm of the short story, with the first collection of Rhys Davies (1927), a Londoner by residence, although the most important stories of the London-based journalist Caradoc Evans belonged to the previous decade. There were a few other writers who claimed Welsh descent without much experience of Welsh life, among them the English novelist and playwright Richard Hughes and the Dominican-born migrant novelist Jean Rhys. The literary brothers Powys (John, Theodore and Llewellyn) were, despite their surname, only of remote Welsh extraction.

The Scottish case was not so desperate, this proving to be a decade of transition in which an older and partly Anglicised generation faded away but was replaced by the emergence of younger Scottish writers, some of them committed to new aspirations of national literary renewal. The elders who had long ago migrated south to pursue literary careers in England included the playwright J. M. Barrie, whose work in the 1920s failed to match earlier successes, and Arthur Conan Doyle, who was now increasingly distracted from literary pursuits by his new obsession with spiritualism. A little younger and certainly more vigorously prolific was the London-based journalist, historian and popular romancer John Buchan, who produced eight novels in this decade, along with several volumes of military history and biography, and still had time to compile *The Northern Muse: An Anthology of Scots Vernacular Poetry* (1924) before entering Parliament as MP for the Scottish Universities from 1927. Buchan was not just the busiest but the most successful Scottish prose writer of the decade, although more influential in other ways was the Glaswegian-born Cambridge anthropologist J. G. Frazer, who had completed the full version of his *magnum opus*, *The Golden Bough*, in 1915 but found a new generation of readers with a one-volume abridgement in 1922. By contrast, one of the unluckiest failures of the time was Buchan's contemporary, David Lindsay, a Scot by parentage and education, although London-born and by the 1920s resident in Cornwall. Lindsay's extraordinary interplanetary romance and religious allegory, *A Voyage to Arcturus* (1920), found only a few hundred readers, and he was scarcely heard of again until later generations elevated the *Voyage* into the canon of speculative fiction.

Of the more recent Scottish arrivals on the literary scene, several had taken the usual path of migration to London: the poet Edwin Muir had arrived there from Glasgow in 1919, and after some years of travel in Europe published his *First Poems* in 1925. The novelist and journalist Rebecca West (Cicely Fairfield) had resettled in her native London in 1910, having been brought up by her Scottish mother in Edinburgh – the setting for much of the action in her second novel, *The Judge* (1922). Catherine Carswell (*née* Macfarlane) had migrated to London in 1911, before opening her literary career with her Glasgow novel *Open the Door!* in 1920. The minor Scottish poet Charles Scott Moncrieff had settled in London while recuperating from war wounds in 1918, but wrote most of his translation of Proust after emigrating to Italy. Naomi Mitchison (*née* Haldane), a native of Edinburgh brought up mostly in Oxford, had relocated to London in 1919, and published her first novel four years later.

Much of Scotland's literary talent, then, was located south of the Border. But there were important signs in this decade of a more credibly indigenous literature emerging from the home country itself. Nan Shepherd, a teacher in Aberdeen, and Neil M. Gunn, a customs officer in Inverness, published their first novels in the late 1920s. At this stage of what eventually became known as the Scottish Renaissance, though, the most important emerging figure was that of C. M. Grieve, a Borderer of Dumfriesshire origin now working as a journalist in Montrose. In his own journal, the *Scottish Chapbook* (1922–3), and in other periodicals, Grieve, evidently inspired by the recent flourishing of Irish writing, lamented the provincial sentimentalism of Barrie's generation and called for a new Scottish literature reconnected both to its roots in the late-medieval poets Dunbar and Henryson and to the wider modern world. In creative practice, Grieve made his appearance in the 1920s under the pen-name Hugh MacDiarmid with a succession of verse collections, among which his long poem *A Drunk Man Looks at the Thistle* (1926; discussed further in Chapter 1 below) stands out. The Scottish Renaissance in its achieved form, marked by the arrival of Lewis Grassic

Gibbon and the mature work of Gunn, is a phenomenon of the Thirties and after; during the Twenties it was almost a one-man show.

The migratory displacement or 'uprooting' of Scottish and Welsh authors of the time is especially noticeable. Even MacDiarmid himself moved to London in 1929, at the start of an unhappy four-year exile. These cases, though, belong to a larger trend within which Irish writers (most famously James Joyce in Paris, where Samuel Beckett joined him in 1928) and English writers (Lawrence, Firbank, Huxley, Ford and many more) are increasingly found to be self-exiled emigrants, while the British scene becomes more noticeably peopled by immigrants and incomers: Eliot from the USA, Mansfield from New Zealand, Michael Arlen from Bulgaria and the poet W. J. Turner from Australia are only a few such cases. This pattern is not a sudden new development of the 1920s, but rather an acceleration of tendencies noticed in the late-Victorian period of Henry James, Joseph Conrad and Olive Schreiner. By the 1920s it was reaching a point at which customary nineteenth-century models of 'national' literatures were being stretched beyond credibility: the locations of a given writer's birthplace, education, residence, language, preferred fictional 'setting' and readership could no longer be assumed to be in organic alignment. It was not only authors who were dislocated, but readers as well: some British writers, including D. H. Lawrence, P. G. Wodehouse and Sylvia Townsend Warner were finding more receptive audiences in the United States than in Britain itself. It already made more sense to regard such writers, and others of international reputation (Shaw, Conrad, Yeats, Joyce, Woolf, Maugham, Ford) inorganically; that is to say, less as fruits of a particular soil than as transnational figures writing in an international language.

Twentyish Figures: Character-types of the Decade

Our quest for the 'Twentyish' features of the decade's writing has so far led us to review certain considerations of time, place, genre and more intangible attitudes (disillusionment, Remembrance) in defining the distinctive features of 1920s literature. Among those writers of the decade who sought to capture the contemporary scene – and, as we have noted above, these were not plentiful – several set out to embody their own sense of the times in representative modern character-types. Some of these types are minor specimens of new fads: following the arrival of the crossword-puzzle in British newspapers in 1924, for example, we witness the cameo appearance of the Crossword Addict as the latest type of eccentric, as with Rome Garden in Macaulay's *Crewe Train*, the manservant Bunter in Sayers's *Lord Peter Views the Body* (1928) and Sidney Quarles in Huxley's *Point Counter Point*. The Motor-cyclist appears as a new Twenties figure too, for example in Macaulay's *Crewe Train* and in Sayers's story 'The Fantastic Horror of the Cat in the Bag' (1928). Some other types are generically specific mutations, such as the Silly-ass Detective best known in the form of Lord Peter Wimsey in Sayers's novels and stories. Far more important and more frequently encountered are versions of contemporary femininity rendered as the Modern Girl (or 'Flapper', as journalists preferred) and the Spinster, with the twin categories sometimes overlapping.

The Modern Girl is in some respects continuous with the earlier 'New Woman' type of the 1890s and Edwardian periods. Indeed the New Woman of that generation is still present in some Twenties novels that are set in those years, notably in the 1920s instalments of Dorothy Richardson's *Pilgrimage* sequence, just as the Suffragette of 1912 vintage can still be found too: for instance Valentine Wannop in Ford Madox Ford's *Parade's End* tetralogy. The fully contemporary Modern Girl of the 1920s usually smokes cigarettes and regards herself as men's equal, much as the New Woman had, but she is less likely to be found discussing serious social and political issues, and more likely to be engaged in such dissipations as swearing and dancing to gramophone records. She appears most often as an educated single woman, but there are also young-married versions of the type – like Myra Viveash in Huxley's *Antic Hay* and Fleur Mont in Galsworthy's *Swan Song* – and young-widow counterparts too, such as Iris Storm in Arlen's *The Green Hat* and Lucy Tantamount in Huxley's *Point Counter Point*. The most Twentyish new feature – although by no means found in all Modern Girls in 1920s literature – is a cool nonchalance about sexual morality, which in some cases is followed through in active promiscuity, as with Jennifer Baird in Lehmann's *Dusty Answer*, and indeed all the Huxley and Arlen characters just mentioned. The Modern Girl emerges as a figure of open contention in Sayers's crime novel *The Unpleasantness at the Bellona Club*, in which the type is maligned by one prejudiced character for 'all this jazzing and short skirts and pretending to have careers' (Sayers 1968b: 71), and on the other hand defended by Wimsey as he begins to understand the character of Ann Dorland, a suspect in the murder case, and to justify her sexual curiosity as essentially healthy.

The figure of the Spinster had a special significance in the 1920s, not only within the context of women's growing involvement in education and the professions, but especially against the background of the 1921 census, which had revealed, unsurprisingly, a post-War imbalance between male and female populations. A tasteless (and numerically exaggerated) remark by Lord Northcliffe about the problem of two million 'superfluous' women provoked a national controversy in which some contenders promoted the idea of exporting spinsters to the colonies to breed a new generation of empire-builders while others defended the spinster as a valuable member of society. Spinster characters appear significantly in such short stories of the early 1920s as Katherine Mansfield's 'The Daughters of the Late Colonel' (1921) and Aldous Huxley's 'The Giaconda Smile' (1921) and in May Sinclair's novella *Life and Death of Harriett Frean* (1922), while a special 'period' subgenre of the novel became noticed as 'the Spinster Novel'. This kind of novel either explored the plight of the dutiful daughter who is trapped by domestic obligations to parents, as in Radclyffe Hall's *The Unlit Lamp* and F. M. Mayor's *The Rector's Daughter* (both 1924), or followed a heroine along a path of independence through work, as in Sheila Kaye-Smith's *Joanna Godden* (1921) and Winifred Holtby's *The Crowded Street* (1924) (see Joannou 1995: 77–101). Dorothy L. Sayers's detective novel *Unnatural Death* (1927) is especially concerned with spinsterhood: its third chapter, entitled 'A Use for Spinsters', makes mocking reference to the 'superfluous women' controversy and introduces Wimsey's talented assistant Miss Climpson, who is able to investigate feminine spheres to which Wimsey cannot easily gain access. The most imaginatively original of the Spinster Novels of this decade is Sylvia Townsend Warner's *Lolly Willowes* (1926), in which the title character spends many years enduring the routine family duties of a maiden aunt before breaking out into her own independent life in devilishly perverse fashion.

On the masculine side of the cast-list, the salient period type is the ex-soldier, who often carries the physical or mental scars of his recent Great-War service. The best-known and the most debilitated is Sir Clifford in Lawrence's *Lady Chatterley's Lover*. Other fictional veterans include the traumatised Septimus Warren Smith in Woolf's *Mrs Dalloway* and the similarly disturbed Clarence in Mary Butts's *Armed with Madness*, although there are cases of apparently undamaged ex-servicemen too, including Calamy in Huxley's *Those Barren Leaves*. Detective fiction in this decade seems especially determined to include such types. Christie's detective Hercule Poirot is a war-refugee rather than an ex-serviceman, but his English assistant Captain Hastings carries a wound from his time at the Front. More striking as an example of damaged post-War heroism is Sayers's detective, Lord Peter Wimsey, who, on his first outing in *Whose Body?* (1923), suffers a severe bout of hallucinations in which he imagines himself again under enemy bombardment in the trenches; at this point it is revealed that his valet Bunter had been Wimsey's sergeant during the War. The most Twentyish of novels, in these terms, are those that include both a war-veteran and a Modern Girl or Spinster among their principal characters, in some cases managing to pair them off. Thus in John Galsworthy's *To Let* (1921), the modern girl Fleur Forsyte marries the ex-soldier Michael Mont. Christie's *The Murder on the Links* opens with Captain Hastings encountering a Modern Girl (we know at once that she is modern because she swears in public), and ends with him engaged to be married to her. Ford's *Parade's End*, being set mostly before 1919, gives us wartime equivalents for this pairing, in which serving warrior meets suffragette. The most Twentyish cast-list of all is that of Sayers's *The Unpleasantness at the Bellona Club*, in which Wimsey as usual plays the combined role of Veteran and Silly-ass Detective, this time investigating both another ex-serviceman afflicted with shell-shock and a Spinster, Miss Ann Dorland, of modern artistic tastes (her bookshelves show that she reads Woolf, Mansfield, Galsworthy, Lawrence and of course crime novels too); some of the most important action takes place amid a group of ex-soldiers during a Remembrance Day commemoration.

Antinomies of the Twenties: Tradition and Experiment

Although we may sometimes address the literary 1920s in terms of some general mood of disillusionment or post-War despair, there is a better chance of understanding the period if we set aside any single prevailing *Zeitgeist* in favour of a recognition that the literary world was constantly self-divided. The most commonly adopted model by which the internal tensions of the decade's literature have been presented is one in which a radical new tendency to Experiment does battle with the doomed rearguard of Tradition. The academic discourse of literary Modernism in recent times has tended to preserve that heroic myth in triumphalist versions that too easily gloss over the real complexities of literary diversity and debate in the 1920s.

It was generally assumed at the time that one of the more important tensions within the literary sphere concerned the apparent challenge to Tradition offered by some newcomers who were held to be gathered under the banner of Experiment. This was no doubt why the City Literary Institute in London invited T. S. Eliot, Edmund Blunden, Edith Sitwell and several other writers to address its students on this topic in the early months of 1929, publishing the lecture series as *Tradition and Experiment in Present-day Literature* (1929). The notable consensus that emerged from that exercise was that Tradition and Experiment are not, after all, antagonistic principles or diametrically opposed directions. One of the invited lecturers, Ashley Dukes, told the Institute audience that 'properly considered, tradition is no more than the fruit of successful experiment'; another, R. H. Mottram, confirmed that 'the tradition of the English novel is experiment'; yet another, Edmund Blunden, pointed out that 'Experiment itself seems obliged to seek materials and implements from the stores of tradition'. By the time Edith Sitwell addressed it, that audience would not have been at all puzzled to hear her declaring that 'the great poet is, in almost every case, both a traditionalist and an experimentalist' (Williams 1929: 99, 1, 56, 75). The final guest in this series, T. S. Eliot, did not trouble to iterate the same point, as his critical essays had already insisted that immersion in Tradition was a prerequisite of true literary originality.

We must not expect to find, then, any clear separation between camps of traditionalists and experimenters. In part this is because there were various kinds of experiment, and more than one kind of tradition as well. The literary trend that we call Modernism was not dedicated, as is too often assumed, to overthrowing or discarding Tradition as such, but rather to finding alternative traditions from which to work in new conditions. The Modernist quest for usable traditions most often involved some by-passing of Romantic and Victorian canons and a retrieval of earlier writers as rediscovered models. Ezra Pound had attempted to renew poetry from sources in the medieval troubadour tradition, and T. S. Eliot was more influentially proposing a different line of inheritance from Dante, Elizabethan dramatic verse and the seventeenth-century 'metaphysical' poets. Wyndham Lewis defended a broadly 'Greek' tradition in the arts against nineteenth-century heresies. Hugh MacDiarmid attempted to seize the mantle of Robert Burns from the bourgeois banqueters of Burns-Night dinners, and held up the early sixteenth-century poet William Dunbar as the source from which a revived Scottish tradition could be refashioned.

Other semi-Modernist and non-Modernist writers sought to recover the literary ideals of the eighteenth century, in more than one form: Lytton Strachey adopted the tradition of the French Enlightenment, while Edmund Blunden worked within the line of post-Augustan English verse. It was still even possible for 'experimental' writers of the Twenties to work from selected nineteenth-century models: Virginia Woolf owed much to the example of Walter Pater, Katherine Mansfield was clearly a disciple of Anton Chekhov, James Joyce had hailed Henrik Ibsen as his master, and D. H. Lawrence wrote within a 'modern' tradition deriving from Thomas Hardy, Herman Melville and Leo Tolstoy in his fiction, and from Walt Whitman in his verse (his book *Studies in*

Classic American Literature also involves the construction of a tradition to which he could commit himself following his rejection of England). Non-Modernist writers were of course even more comfortable working within various nineteenth-century traditions: Arnold Bennett's fiction, for example, derives from the French realist school, as does W. Somerset Maugham's, while E. M. Forster's takes its bearings from Jane Austen, and in the realm of verse, most of the 'Georgian' poets follow the example of William Wordsworth. Tradition of some sort, then, is always audible in 1920s writing. What is new is not any radically anti-traditional revolt but the sheer variety of traditions being remade and rediscovered.

Experiment too is a concept that disintegrates upon closer examination. We might assume on the basis of some simplified accounts of Modernism that the most important recent discoveries in the 1920s were free verse and the 'stream-of-consciousness' style in prose fiction, and yet these developments are of quite restricted significance within any broad review of Twenties writing. Beyond the important cases of Dorothy Richardson, Ford Madox Ford and James Joyce, we do not find the stream-of-consciousness method much used. The more frequent adoption of free verse since the heyday of Imagism in 1914 has its importance too in the poetry of T. S. Eliot, D. H. Lawrence, Edith Sitwell and a few others, but the larger story of Twenties verse is that most of the decade's leading poets – including W. B. Yeats, Thomas Hardy, Robert Graves and Walter de la Mare – stayed loyal to 'traditional' metres. Hugh MacDiarmid's *A Drunk Man Looks at the Thistle* is an indicative case of a long poem that is in some respects Modernist in affiliation but that employs free verse only in a few of its later passages, the rest being composed as a medley of ballad-like quatrains, couplets, triplets and rhyming quintets or sestets. Even where free verse is employed by Twenties poets, no guarantee of poetic quality comes with it: there are truly lamentable free-verse productions to be found, even from the pens of recognised authors, notably Osbert Sitwell and D. H. Lawrence.

If we go looking for innovative literary experiment in the decade's writing, there is plenty to be discovered, but we need to look well beyond the apparently radical disruptions of style involved in stream-of-consciousness prose or in free verse. In Chapter 2 of this book I argue that a far more important kind of Modernist experiment – although some non-Modernist writers partake of it too – involves the creative use of anachronism and related disorderings of the reader's time-sense. Among other kinds of innovation, MacDiarmid's most significant experiment had little to do with his sparing use of free verse, but was found in his use of a 'synthetic Scots' that combined Standard English syntax with elements of the spoken Lowlands vernacular and with words dug up from an etymological dictionary. The easiest but gravest mistake we can fall into about Twenties literary experiment, though, is to assume that the Modernists had any monopoly upon it. Writers of a 'traditionalist' bent were experimenting all the time: Thomas Hardy, for instance, was still devising new and untried stanza-forms in his old age. W. B. Yeats was still exploring the effects of half-rhyme that he had begun using a decade before; and interesting variants upon the same device were found in the posthumous *Poems* (1920) of Wilfred Owen. The Poet Laureate of the time, Robert Bridges, was a 'Victorian' author who had begun publishing verse in the 1870s, but this did not prevent him from making a new departure in the Twenties. In his 1925 collection *The Tapestry* he employed a 12-syllable line with no regular number of stresses, thereby founding the modern tradition of syllabic verse in English; he also experimented with a reformed system of spelling, notably in *The Testament of Beauty* (1929; discussed further in Chapter 1). Meanwhile, Noël Coward's use of informal and sometimes slangy speech in his plays was an experiment of far-reaching consequences for English drama. The art of biography was being transformed by Lytton Strachey's use of novelistic devices, inaugurated with his *Eminent Victorians* (1918) and continued in *Queen Victoria* (1921) and *Elizabeth and Essex* (1928). Experiment and striking innovation were not confined to highbrows, either: the remarkable narrative coup pulled off by Agatha Christie in *The Murder of Roger Ackroyd* (1926) provoked a debate among detective writers about how far the rules of their game could be stretched; and Ben Travers devised a new form of 'bedroom' farce, distinctively British in its presentation of sexual attraction as essentially terrifying.

Generations of the Twenties

There are other antinomies that shape the internal tensions of the decade's literary scene, among them the clash between upholders of 'classical' ideals (notably T. S. Eliot and Wyndham Lewis) and partisans of the Romantic tradition (John Middleton Murry, D. H. Lawrence and others). The most extensive kind of internecine literary conflict, however, was generational. As we have seen already in the case of Richard Aldington, some writers who had suffered badly in the War took that as a licence to engage not only in normal immature derision of their elders but in slandering entire generations of 'Old Men' or 'Old Fools' as guilty – so their blood-libel would have it – of deliberately driving their own sons into pointless slaughter. Such an accusation might reasonably have been levelled against Kaiser Wilhelm and his political advisors, but hardly against the over-40s of Britain as a whole. However, the war-veterans of the 1920s, and many of their non-combatant contemporaries, were not inclined to be reasonable about the terrible fate of their own generation or about what they regarded as the comfortable exemptions of the middle-aged and elderly; and so they felt little compunction in treating everyone who had been above military age in 1914–18 as members of an indifferent and indeed murderous gerontocracy.

The enraged finger-pointing at the bloodthirsty Old Men that we find in certain writers – notably Siegfried Sassoon, Osbert Sitwell, Richard Aldington and sometimes D. H. Lawrence too – is only the most lurid feature of a wider generational antagonism that deformed the culture of 1920s Britain. Mutual incomprehension between the Young and the Old is one of the most recurrent topics of the period's literature. A symptomatic example among many is the young widow Lucy Tantamount in Aldous Huxley's *Point Counter Point*, who dismisses her elders in general with the observation that 'they don't happen to belong to our civilization. They're aliens' (Huxley 1994e: 134). Virginia Woolf in the earliest version (1923) of her famous essay, 'Mr Bennett and Mrs Brown', refers in passing to 'the respectful hostility which is the only healthy relation between old and young' (Woolf 1988: 384), and although she is indeed more respectful than Lucy Tantamount, Woolf manages in this essay to enforce an alienating dividing-line between her literary generation of 'Georgians' and Arnold Bennett's generation of 'Edwardians', presenting this as a sharp, fundamental 'break between one generation and the next' (Woolf 1988: 387). Woolf was in fact only fifteen years younger than Bennett, so the 'Edwardian' tag here is for her an important device by which she can consign her antagonist to a closed episode of the pre-War past, while she and her contemporaries claim possession of the present day. Those fifteen years of age dividing Bennett (and John Galsworthy and the slightly older H. G. Wells) from Woolf (and James Joyce and the slightly younger D. H. Lawrence) would in normal conditions not amount to any great gulf between Old and Young or even between generations strictly defined. In the Twenties, though, normal conditions did not apply, and even smaller age-differences could divide writers into seemingly separate and hostile 'generations'.

The abnormal conditions of 1920s generational antagonism were those that had been provided by the War. When the narrator of Aldington's *Death of a Hero* declares 'I hold a brief for the war generation' (Aldington 1984: 155), he addresses a late-Twenties readership for whom the term needed no explanation. My readers, however, may benefit from a gloss upon it, which I offer here in simplified form. A more accurate version would have to allow for volunteers who had falsified their ages in order to join up (Ford Madox Ford had been one of those middle-aged warriors), and for panic measures that had exposed men in their forties to conscription in the last months of the War. Setting aside those considerations, a workable definition of the 'war generation' would be all those born between 1875 and 1899. When we come to 'map' those dates of birth onto the cohorts of authors active in the Twenties, we soon find that the literary world, like all other walks of life, falls into three demographic divisions: the pre-War generations, the war generation and the post-War generation. The clearest way to represent the place of any given author in this succession is to take a particular date – and for convenience I have picked 31 December 1920 – and to represent the age (given in brackets below) that the author had attained at that point.

Thus, among the prominent writers mentioned in this book, those who belonged to the pre-War generations included Thomas Hardy (80), Robert Bridges (76), Bernard Shaw (64), Joseph Conrad (63), Arthur Conan Doyle, A. E. Housman (both 61), J. M. Barrie (60), May Sinclair (57), Rudyard Kipling, W. B. Yeats (both 55), H. G. Wells (54), Arnold Bennett, John Galsworthy, C. E. Montague (all 53), W. H. Davies (49), F. M. Mayor, John Cowper Powys (both 48), Walter de la Mare, Ford Madox Ford, Dorothy Richardson (all 47), G. K. Chesterton and W. Somerset Maugham (both 46). The post-War generation does not show up on the literary scene until the late Twenties. At the end of the year 1920, its still prospective literary cohort included Richard Hughes (20), Rosamond Lehmann (21), Evelyn Waugh (17), C. Day Lewis, Christopher Isherwood (both 16), Henry Green (15) and Louis MacNeice (13).

Demographically considered, the single most important fact of 1920s literature is that, for all the respect either accorded to or pointedly withheld from the senior figures listed above, it is dominated by the war generation, and increasingly so as the decade rolls on. This was the decade in which writers who had been born in the last quarter of the nineteenth century either came to artistic maturity or made their first literary appearance. It would be tedious to list them in full, but the maturing writers who had emerged in the previous decade or earlier included John Buchan (45), John Masefield (42), E. M. Forster (41), Lytton Strachey (40), Rose Macaulay, P. G. Wodehouse (both 39), James Joyce, Virginia Woolf, Wyndham Lewis (all 38), D. H. Lawrence (35), Siegfried Sassoon, Ronald Firbank (both 34), Edith Sitwell (33), T. S. Eliot, Katherine Mansfield (both 32), Richard Aldington, Rebecca West (both 28) and Robert Graves (25). Among the newly emerging talents of the 1920s were Radclyffe Hall (40), R. H. Mottram (37), Edwin Muir (33), Agatha Christie, Jean Rhys (both 30), Hugh MacDiarmid (28), Dorothy L. Sayers, Sylvia Townsend Warner (both 27), Aldous Huxley (26), Edmund Blunden (24), Naomi Mitchison (23), Elizabeth Bowen and Noël Coward (both 22).

It will be obvious from this roll-call that I am defining the war generation purely by date of birth and not by experience of military combat itself, otherwise the above list would be reduced to only six names: Lewis, Sassoon, Aldington, Graves, Mottram and Blunden – although Buchan, Masefield and MacDiarmid had also served in medical or intelligence roles. As a literary cohort, the war generation was dominated not by ex-servicemen but by writers whose wartime experience had been non-combatant: women, and men who had been exempt as medically unfit (Masefield, Lawrence, Firbank, Eliot, Muir, Huxley, Coward) or as conscientious objectors (Strachey) or as Irish (Joyce), or who had relocated beyond the reach of the conscription laws (Forster, Wodehouse). The national stock of able-bodied men had been severely depleted by the War, and the literary war generation that survived into the 1920s was especially lacking in them: of those who had been deemed fit for military service, some were by now traumatised (Aldington, Blunden, Graves) or damaged by sexually-transmitted disease (Lewis). No eugenically-minded observer at the time could have regarded such a group as reliable breeding stock.

Further demographic analysis of this literary cohort reveals that of the nineteen war-generation male writers named in the previous paragraph, five were homosexual and a further eight were by the end of the decade either childless or separated from mothers of their children, which leaves only six (Buchan, Masefield, Joyce, Mottram, Muir and Huxley) who carried paternal responsibilities, although Wodehouse, a doting stepfather, should be counted too. Of the dozen war-generation women writers named above, six were spinsters (until Rebecca West's marriage in 1930), while of the six married women three were childless; only four of the twelve were bringing up children. In summary, only a third of the leading war-generation writers of the 1920s were themselves active parents. These statistics may go some way towards accounting for the general readiness of Twenties writers to take the side of the child-figure against the parent-figure, often caricatured as preposterous or malign, in their representations of generational conflict, and perhaps even for the adolescent note of sullen petulance which is so often heard in the writings of the decade. These problems of generational caricature and hostility, though, will be revisited at greater length in Chapter 3.

Insecure Boundaries and Textual Revisions

It would not be entirely perverse for readers to ask whether it is even worth attempting to fix literary history into decade-long slices at all: why so cruelly apply the shears of calendric pedantry to the always-continuous fabric of literature's rich tapestry? On this point, I can hardly do better than to quote the editor of this series and his collaborator on a related project: 'Ending a literary history at the end of one century and the beginning of a new one is arbitrary, but at least it has the virtue of being *transparently* arbitrary' (McHale and Stevenson 2006: 273). Substituting 'decade' for 'century' here, the same justification applies. The seemingly non-arbitrary alternative is to tell the story of what always amounts to a single dominant movement or line of development, following its course across decade-boundaries from origin to exhaustion. That procedure has the benefit of organic coherence, but its covert arbitrariness lies in the occlusion of rival or alternative lines and movements that are not only contemporary with but could serve to explain the specific character of the chosen dominant movement. In the case of the 1920s, that dominant movement is inevitably Modernism, of which we have heard probably too much in the last forty years or so, some of it 'contextual' in various valuable ways, but little enough devoted to the specifically literary contexts of non-Modernist contemporary writing. I approach the arbitrary temporal frame of 1920–9, then, not as a regrettable straitjacket (nuns fret not at their convent's narrow room, as Wordsworth says) but as a positive opportunity to bring into clearer focus those features that writings of supposedly distinct groupings in this decade have in common.

The division of modern literary history into decades has further justifications, and indeed virtues. It has a certain mnemonic value that has been tried and tested in similar realms of cultural memory, notably those of popular music, cinema, fashion, design and architecture; one that helps us to navigate through complicated evolutions of taste, although often at the price of oversimplified models of context. It is likely to stay with us as a habit, which also comes at a price. In the particular case of the 1920s, and despite the incoherences that I have discussed above by contrast with the more sharply-defined case of the 1930s, it has another kind of justification. It might be going too far to claim that arbitrary divisions between one period and another are exactly what Twenties culture was all about, but a slightly more cautious version of that case has been sketched out in this Introduction and will be developed further in Chapter 3.

A well-known Twentyish instance of periodising by stark discontinuity will bear repetition here. Readers of T. S. Eliot's journal the *Criterion* found in it, in July 1924, Woolf's essay 'Character in Fiction' – an expanded version of 'Mr Bennett and Mrs Brown', subsequently reprinted under the original title – and read her provocative assertion that 'on or about December 1910 human character changed' (Woolf 1988: 421). Her daringly arbitrary choice of a particular month for such a transformation is still something of a puzzle, but the specification of the year in which Edward VII had died (in May, not December) and George V had acceded certainly helped to entrench that division between Edwardians and Georgians upon which she insisted. That the new king had acceded in a year ending with a zero makes it also a decade-marker, and by no means the first, references back to 'the Nineties' being by that time commonplace.

Let us now take another of Woolf's famous declarations, one that is in some ways more baffling. It was in 1925, and on 23 April to be precise, that readers could first go into a bookshop, pick up a freshly-printed copy of her latest book, *The Common Reader*, and find in its essay on 'Modern Fiction' Woolf's thoughts about Life: 'Life is not a series of gig-lamps symmetrically arranged; life is a luminous halo, a semi-transparent envelope [. . .]' (Woolf 1994: 160). We might wish to quarrel with the halo or with the envelope metaphors, but in our own times we are likely to concur with the initial dismissal of gig-lamps, all the more enthusiastically for not knowing what on earth a gig-lamp might be. Readers of the 1920s had the advantage over us there, having grown up with gig-lamps all around them. In fact these objects were lights affixed either side of a gig, which was a light one-horse carriage commonly used both privately and as a public taxicab. A series of gig-lamps symmetrically arranged would have been a sight that a young lady would expect to greet her as she emerged from a theatre or from a ball at a country estate; an image, in short, of well-ordered leisure – only it was no longer applicable in 1925, when a Modern Girl stepping out of a West-End show would expect to find a row of motor-taxis waiting to speed her home, and would rather be seen in a semi-transparent envelope than climb into a slow-moving antique designed for her grandmother's generation. Grandmother might still in 1925 have been going to church in a gig, but Woolf's image is essentially a 'period' snapshot of pre-War days, designed to suggest that orderly views of Life belong to that lost 'Edwardian' world before everything became nebulously uncertain and unpredictable. The gig-lamps, then, are decidedly unTwentyish, but then so too (and here my unlikely digression through horse-drawn transport returns us to my main point) is much of the essay in which they appear. 'Modern Fiction' is a reworking of an essay initially entitled 'Modern

Novels', that had been published in the *Times Literary Supplement* in April 1919, complete with luminous halo and semi-transparent envelope – but not with the gig-lamps, these being added in 1925. This leaves us with the question whether 'Modern Fiction' is a Twenties text at all, or just a revised work of the Teens. It is by no means the only such doubtful case.

Having embarked upon a literary history framed by arbitrary decade boundaries, I am under an obligation to be transparent, or at least more than semi-transparent, about the degree to which those boundaries prove to be unreliable when successive versions of one work slip over them, or when curious time-lags and delays seem to place a work in the 'wrong' decade. My usual guiding principle has been to allot a work to the 1920s period if its date of first publication falls within the decade, regardless of date of composition. Thomas Hardy's three verse collections of the period all contain some poems written – but not published – several decades before, as the title of one volume (*Late Lyrics and Earlier*, 1922) indicates, but these are still 1920s poems. The same applies to a number of works composed before 1920 but published rather later: several of Mansfield's stories, Housman's poems, along with D. H. Lawrence's *Women in Love*, for instance. Most of Wilfred Owen's posthumously published *Poems* (1920), although composed before late 1918, are in my view works of the Twenties, because that is when the reading public first set eyes upon them; but a few of those poems that had first appeared in periodicals in 1918 and 1919 are not. Again, most of the poems that still appear in collected editions of T. S. Eliot's verse as the Poems of 1920 are, with the exception of 'Gerontion', actually poems of 1919 by date of their first appearance in magazines, so in this book I pass over them. For similar reasons, most of the essays in his collection *The Sacred Wood* (1920) are overlooked because they first appeared in 1917–19.

In some more difficult cases, a lot depends on what we mean by 'publication': Bernard Shaw's play *Heartbreak House* first appeared in book form in 1919 but was not staged in Britain until 1921, so the play (although not the Preface) could fairly be assigned to either decade. I make only passing mention of Dorothy Richardson's *Pilgrimage* sequence (1915–38), regarding that, perhaps unfairly, as essentially a work of wartime Modernism to which the sequels add nothing particularly Twentyish. Far more complicated is the publishing history of T. E. Lawrence's *Seven Pillars of Wisdom*: an expensive edition was issued for private subscribers in 1926, followed the next year by a severely abridged version under the title *Revolt in the Desert*, but not until 1935 was a reasonably full version released to the public; so I have disregarded it as a work that belongs to the 1930s. Other aspects of the rather porous boundary between the Twenties and the Thirties will be held over for discussion in Chapter 5, which is devoted to that transitional phase and to other extensions of 1920s literature.

The logic of my exclusions, then, involves an attempt to reconstruct a body of texts that were available to readers in the decade itself. For this reason I make hardly any use of private documents such as diaries and letters of the time, because in almost all cases (Katherine Mansfield, who died in 1923, is an exception), these were not published until much later and so were invisible to 1920s public culture. Other works written in the 1920s but not published until long after, as with much of the poetry of Ivor Gurney, are set aside on the same principle. I have not pressed that principle so far, though, as to insist that any given work should have been easily available to the reader in a normal bookshop or library in the 1920s. I bring in essays from small-circulation magazines such as Edgell Rickword's *Calendar of Modern Letters* (1925–7), and more importantly I include certain novels that were either legally suppressed (*The Well of Loneliness*) or had no British publisher for fear of such suppression (*Ulysses*, *Lady Chatterley's Lover*). These were illicitly available, in that any British resident who was sufficiently determined to read them – and plenty were at least curious to see what all the fuss was about – could usually arrange for a friend, or their local pornography dealer, to smuggle a copy in from Paris.

A full reconstruction of the literature actually encountered by readers in this decade, however, now meets particular difficulties in the form of special textual histories of revision. It is necessary here to alert readers to the fact that several of the 1920s texts that we read today are not as they first appeared. One of the most important single poems of the decade, which since 1963 we have come to know as 'The Parable of the Old Man and the Young' by Wilfred Owen, was available in the 1920s only in a version that had the crucial last line missing and the title misspelt: very significantly misspelt, too, as 'the Old Men'. Graves's *Good-bye to All That*, as it was titled in 1929, has for many decades now been read in its heavily revised 1957 version, under the unhyphenated *Goodbye* form of the title, the advantage of the revised text being that it restores many self-censored phrases and passages, the disadvantage that it cuts the original opening and much of the material about Graves's life in the 1920s. Where I quote from this book, I do so from the 1929 text. Another such case is Aldington's *Death of a Hero*, in which since 1965 we have benefited from an unexpurgated text in place of the asterisk-peppered version that readers of 1929 had before them. Again with Waugh's *Decline and Fall*, the text we read today is the 1961 revision in which a few self-censored phrases are restored. Maugham's novel *The*

Painted Veil has also featured an ending silently amended by its author after the reviewers of 1925 ridiculed the original version of its last sentences. Yeats's *A Vision* has long been read only in its expanded 1937 version. In such cases I have tried as far as possible to avoid quoting material amended after 1929.

In a similar spirit, my aim here is to present the literature of the 1920s broadly on its own terms, as understood in its own time. This does mean that the now-customary quest for premonitions of twenty-first-century values, or for flickers of 'transgression' in literary works of the period, will not be pursued in the following chapters. I can only trust that the omission of such exercises will not strike my readers as too crushing a disappointment.

Notes

1. Notable exceptions are David Ayers's *English Literature of the 1920s* (Ayers 1999) and John Lucas's *The Radical Twenties* (Lucas 1997). Ayers's study, despite its comprehensive title, examines a selection of prose fiction, and does not cover poetry or drama. Lucas's book, although wide-ranging, concentrates upon retrieving forgotten currents of socialism and feminism in the writings of the decade.
2. Some historiographic exceptions that do treat the 1920s alone are listed among the Works Cited at the end of this book: see Branson 1975, Melman 1988, Montgomery 1957 and on 1920s theatre Trewin 1958.
3. In contrast to Robin Skelton's *Poetry of the Thirties*, which has remained almost continuously in print since its appearance in 1964, Sydney Bolt's useful anthology *Poetry of the 1920s* (Bolt 1967) seems not to have been reprinted at all.
4. The coinage is not mine but, in the second sense recorded by *OED2*, that of Robert Graves and Alan Hodge in 1940 (Graves and Hodge 1971: 122).
5. Lawrence had already used the phrase 'Writers among the Ruins', thus capitalised, to characterise the pessimistic attitude he attributed to Joseph Conrad and others unnamed, in a letter of October 1912, to Edward Garnett (Boulton 1979: 465). His partial readoption of the phrase amounts to a vindication of Conradian attitudes that in pre-War days Lawrence had dismissed.

Chapter One

A Literature of Ideas

You would not enjoy Nietzsche, sir. He is fundamentally unsound.
P. G. Wodehouse, *Carry on, Jeeves* (1925)

The literature of the 1920s has a certain reputation for abstemious self-purification and withdrawal from the busy world of controversy. In simplified comparisons with neighbouring decades, it is presented as less political than the literary scene of the Thirties, less reform-minded than the Edwardian age, and certainly less propagandist than the various patriotic effusions of the war period. Writers of the 1920s, it is generally held, withdrew into a sanctuary of aesthetic isolation, cultivating pure artistic forms and avoiding the snares of public debate. There is a censorious version of this story that arose in the 1930s, according to which the prior decade's literary culture is charged with frivolous abstention from political purposes. On the other side, in academic vindications of Modernism we may often hear the affirmative case that in the 1920s a generation of serious artists had at last liberated literature from the old burdens of moralistic preaching, didactic hectoring and opinion-mongering, and so had achieved a more 'impersonal' or at least less rhetorical kind of literary effect. Such apologetics draw upon a very important body of critical writing by leading Modernist authors, a corpus that calls for some brief summary at this point.

The principal sources in this context are Henry James's Prefaces (1907–9) to his reprinted novels, and the codification of Jamesian principles in his disciple Percy Lubbock's *The Craft of Fiction* (1921); the final diaristic section of James Joyce's novel *A Portrait of the Artist as a Young Man* (1916), in which Stephen Dedalus writes of the author removing himself from his work like God from his creation; the essays of Virginia Woolf in *The Common Reader* (1925) and elsewhere; the critical writings of Ford Madox Ford on James and on Joseph Conrad; the essays of T. S. Eliot in *The Sacred Wood* (1920) and *Homage to John*

Dryden (1924); and a few remarks by W. B. Yeats and Ezra Pound that repudiate the didactic and rhetorical bias of Victorian poetry. There is indeed in this selected body of writing a shared tendency to deplore not only didactic moralising in literature but more specifically the intrusive habits of those novelists (Thackeray in particular) who interpret their characters for us in overt commentary. For James as for Ford, Lubbock and Joyce, a novel should be artistically self-contained, giving the reader the impression of being 'shown' its fictional world rather than being 'told' about it by an opinionated guide. Pursuing a slightly different but still compatible argument about poetry, T. S. Eliot's influential essays regard a poem as 'autotelic', that is to say lacking ulterior motives. Above all, poetry was not for Eliot a vehicle for the expression of ideas, of 'philosophies' or of authorial personality, but a medium into which those contributory elements disappear, transformed into an independent and 'objective' work.

The Modernist critical consensus summarised so far covers the realms of prose fiction and poetry. In relation to drama, some of Eliot's essays point in the same direction, notably his 1919 essay on *Hamlet* and its failure to 'objectify' Shakespeare's – and Prince Hamlet's – feelings. But if we turn from dramatic theory to contemporary practice in the Twenties, we find a parallel tendency among dramatists who were not even remotely associated with Modernist experiment. W. Somerset Maugham is now remembered, if at all, primarily as a writer of short stories, but in the 1920s he was also known as one of the most successful playwrights of the day. Maugham was convinced that his duty was to entertain audiences rather than to foist ideas upon them in the manner of the Edwardian social-problem play. Accordingly we find in his dramatic work a relatively pure devotion to established conventions of comedy and melodrama, unburdened by any intellectual programme or social purpose. The same is true, and more emphatically, in the case of Noël Coward, the most distinctive new playwright of the decade: his best early work, notably *Hay Fever* (1925), is exceptionally pure comedy of manners, constructed in perfect symmetrical patterns of repetition and contrast. The 'period' novelty of Coward's plays lay partly in their atmosphere of decadent frivolity, but more significantly in their informal style of dialogue, which replaced the conventional stiffness of stage rhetoric with light banter. It was not until he staged his patriotic pageant of modern British history, *Cavalcade* (1931), that Coward employed drama, to the great surprise of his admirers, in the service of public responsibility and wrote in the higher rhetorical register required. The new note sounded in *Cavalcade* helped to highlight retrospectively the 'irresponsible' tone of Coward's work in the 1920s, and indeed in the context of English theatre it serves as a landmark indicating a more general, albeit too simple, contrast between the aesthetic Twenties and the politicised Thirties.

So far we have considered the positive basis for regarding the literature of this decade as distinctively self-insulated from opinion or public controversy. The remainder of this chapter, however, is devoted to qualifying, unpicking and at times overturning that view. I contend here that an argumentative, intellectually combative spirit runs through the decade, and that it is barely subdued by the efforts of a minority to maintain an impassive aesthetic integrity above its clamour. Those efforts, indeed, can be accounted for only by recognising the continuing strength of the disputatious culture they were resisting. Surveying the current state of literary criticism in 1923, T. S. Eliot concluded that the critical scene, which ought to be marked by 'quiet cooperative labour' was instead 'no better than a Sunday park of contending and contentious orators', in which critics traded upon the vehemence and eccentricity of their opinions (Eliot 1975: 69). As we shall see, this description could fairly be extended beyond criticism and across the larger literary arena of the decade. Much as he might have longed for a calm, orderly and collaborative spirit in the literary culture of his time, Eliot himself was increasingly swept up into the adversarial position-taking he deplored. In fact in the same essay, 'The Function of Criticism', he launched his long-running dispute with John Middleton Murry (a personal friend and literary mentor), openly taking sides on behalf of 'Classical' principles against Murry's Romantic-Protestant trust in the supremacy of the 'Inner Voice'. For Eliot, the Inner Voice was the voice not only of political 'Whiggery' but of 'vanity, fear and lust' (Eliot 1975: 71). The culmination of this controversy came in 1928 with Eliot's declaration that he now regarded himself as a 'classicist in literature, royalist in politics and anglo-catholic in religion' (Eliot 1928: ix). The battle-lines of political and religious antagonism that we associate with the literary world of the 1930s had been marked out in the previous decade.

Eliot's constant suspicion of Protestantism and its cultural consequences provides a useful vantage-point for considering the place of ideas and controversy in 1920s writing. Eliot's position derives in part from the earlier, less aggressive classicism of the Victorian poet-critic Matthew Arnold, the author of *Culture and Anarchy* (1869), for whom the literary tradition represented a kind of balanced sanity that was needed to restrain the anarchic self-assertive individualism of British intellectual life. Eliot felt more urgently that the stabilising centrality of artistic and religious Tradition must be upheld against a contemporary tide of disputatious eccentricity.

The Inner Voice: Gyres and Ganglia

Eccentricity was on constant display in the decade's literary scene, most luridly in that Protestant-Romantic tradition of which Eliot was so wary, and within which an array of private heresies, cranky mysticisms, pseudo-religious fads and fraudulent cults had flourished since the late nineteenth century. One of the most important apparent consequences of the Great War was that church or chapel attendance among younger people (except in Roman Catholic communities) went into a noticeable decline through the Twenties (Stevenson 1984: 360–2). Literature may be said to have reaped some benefit from that trend, to the extent that – as Matthew Arnold had predicted – it replaced religious belief in the hearts and imaginations of the spiritually hungry. If so, it paid a certain price in thralldom to mystical gibberish, homespun faith-healing and spiritual charlatanism, as writers and readers went whoring after strange gods or attending to inner voices unconstrained by fact or by earthly probabilities.

Lady Rothermere, wife of the press baron who owned the *Daily Mail*, was a woman of considerable wealth who in the early 1920s decided to fund two pet projects of hers. The first of these was a new literary review, the *Criterion*, with T. S. Eliot as editor; its first issue appeared in October 1922, carrying Eliot's major poem 'The Waste Land', and it remained an important cultural forum until the late 1930s. The second beneficiary of her largesse was the Gurdjieff Institute for the Harmonious Development of Man, a curious commune established in a dilapidated priory at Fontainebleau outside Paris, directed by G. I. Gurdjieff, a charismatic Russian mystic and dance-teacher of obscure Armenian-Greek origins (his date of birth remains a mystery) whose disciples – about a hundred of them – busied themselves there with agricultural labour and regular sessions of 'oriental' dancing. Lady Rothermere had come under the influence of Gurdjieff's leading spokesman P. D. Ouspensky, and taken Eliot along to hear his lectures in London on the Fourth Dimension and similar arcana. The Gurdjieffian gospel was a vague call for the restoration of a lost inner harmony to be achieved not through harsh ascetic self-discipline but by easier methods of awakening from the alleged somnambulism of everyday existence. Among Gurdjieff's prominent disciples was Alfred Orage, a Fabian-socialist exponent of Nietzschean philosophy who had been editor of the influential weekly literary journal *The New Age* since 1907 until in September 1922 he threw up the literary life to spend the rest of the decade preaching the new revelation. Shortly after his resignation, he persuaded his literary protégée Katherine Mansfield (also known to Eliot, as the wife of J. M. Murry), who was at the time severely ill with tuberculosis, to join his pilgrimage to Fontainebleau, which is where, after a few weeks of residence in unheated rooms, she died in January 1923.

It would probably be unfair to charge Gurdjieff or Orage with actually killing the author of *The Garden Party and Other Stories* (1922), although that accusation has sometimes been made. She was by the time of her induction into the Gurdjieff cult already too ill to continue writing, which means that we find no trace of the doctrine in her work. On the contrary, her stories are enlivened by a distinctly sceptical and ironic spirit, and nowhere marked by occultist preoccupations. The strange death of Katherine Mansfield illustrates only the personal exposure of writers to the cults of the day, and very little of their intellectual susceptibility.

On the other hand we may take two major cases of literary eccentricity in which the peculiar beliefs and hobby-horses of the authors clearly do show up in their writings. Two of the very maddest books of the decade, both issued from major modern authors within the Protestant-Romantic tradition, were W. B. Yeats's *A Vision* (1926) and D. H. Lawrence's *Fantasia of the Unconscious* (1923). The former was a culmination of Yeats's enduring occultist interests, dating from his studies of William Blake's Prophetic Books and his enrolment into the Hermetic Order of the Golden Dawn in the late 1880s. Having married a young English occultist, George Hyde-Lees, in 1917, Yeats had spent much of the next three years engaged in 'automatic writing' experiments with her, during which various ghostly 'instructors' from the Other Side disclosed fitful glimpses of an elaborate body of arcane knowledge. Yeats then worked this material up into a comprehensive system in the early 1920s, using antinomies derived from Blake and methods of human taxonomy familiar from astrological charts. The baffling result in *A Vision* (a misnomer, its data being auditory and written revelation) is a grand schematic design in which all of human history and every conceivable personality-type appears neatly packed into a series of diagrams aligning them with the twenty-eight phases of the lunar cycle. This is all of course lunacy, in almost the strict sense, and lunacy of an obsessively tidy kind that reduces the variety and complexity of human life to a set of explicable archetypes, and ultimately to a geometry.

The master-pattern of *A Vision* is given by the gyre: a sixteenth-century term for a spiral, as in the shape of a whirlpool or vortex, rendered geometrically as a cone. Yeats arranges the entire human universe according to the pattern made by two intersecting gyres, each with its apex meeting the other's base. The purpose is to represent cycles of antithetical force in which the originating energy from the apex eventually exhausts itself at the base, which provides the weakened ground from which the contrary movement asserts itself in reverse. All human impulses at the level of individual temperament, and all forms of civilisation too, thus find themselves growing to a stage at which they collapse and then grow backwards. After much poring over such diagrams, Yeats concluded that there were exactly twenty-six types of human character, not just the twelve provided by the orthodox Zodiac; and that the rise and fall of civilisations, religions and artistic movements could all be mapped onto double-conical charts covering periods of approximately two thousand years, with shorter pseudo-lunar phases discernible within them.

As a literary performance, *A Vision* is enlivened now and again by an eloquent paragraph, or by a startling observation on ancient sculpture or nineteenth-century poetry. But on the whole it is a tediously repetitious procession through permutations of obscure Blakean jargon, mitigated by what is, given the universal scope of Yeats's scheme, a surprisingly tentative exposition, many a sentence beginning 'I imagine . . .' rather than making any stronger claim to truth. The only reason this book still earns a place on the shelves of literary scholars is that knowledge of its arbitrary propositions is required in order to understand fully some of Yeats's greatest poems as well as several lesser ones of this period. When the speaker of 'Sailing to Byzantium' (1928) implores the Byzantine sages to 'perne in a gyre', we may get the sense of 'gyre' from a large dictionary, although we have to guess that the verb 'perne' – Yeats's own coinage – means something like 'rotate'. In the more formidable case of 'The Second Coming' (1921), though, the dictionary that glosses 'gyre' in the poem's opening line helps us not at all with the enigmatic closing lines:

> The darkness drops again; but now I know
> That twenty centuries of stony sleep
> Were vexed to nightmare by a rocking cradle,
> And what rough beast, its hour come round at last,
> Slouches towards Bethlehem to be born?
>
> (Yeats 1990: 235)

From references to the Sphinx, described but unnamed in earlier lines, some readers in the early 1920s could guess that the Second Coming foreseen here is not the promised return of the Christ but an impending rebirth, figured by the Egyptian monument, of a pre-Christian era that will invert the values of the last two thousand years. It took the appearance of *A Vision* to confirm such guesses, and to account for the invented 'myth' that the poem follows.

The fact that many of Yeats's poems of this decade refer us outside of themselves to a private mythology or intellectual system, as many of his earlier poems had pointed to a private circle of friends, indicates that in his case – and it is a major case – no thorough aesthetic detachment of the poem from ideas, opinions and personalities was attempted, let alone achieved. T. S. Eliot's ideal model of a depersonalised art, announced in his essay 'Tradition and the Individual Talent' (1919), required something that for Yeats, as for his precursor William Blake, was neither desirable nor possible: 'the more perfect the artist, the more completely separate in him will be the man who suffers and the mind which creates' (Eliot 1975: 41). The magnificence of Yeats's poetry has little to do with such separation or with the Modernist dream of the artist disappearing behind or into the achieved perfection of the work. His art is defiantly imperfect in those terms, putting on display the 'man who suffers', his creative mind saddled with personal self-questioning and with ideas of the crankiest kind.

D. H. Lawrence's eccentric opinions and personal hobby-horses obtrude in various ways throughout his writings, but *Fantasia of the Unconscious* exhibits some of the oddest examples. The book offers itself as a tract on child development, written in opposition to the new Freudian wisdom, but its discussion often veers off into education, sexology, tree-worship and cosmology, and repeatedly into a schematic physiology of the nervous system, derived from long-outdated nineteenth-century sources (Heywood 1987: 104–23). In contrast to Yeats, Lawrence turns his back on the spirit-world, violently repudiating the dominance of spiritual life over bodily energy; and leads us inside the human body in search of a polar balance between the twin 'nerve centres' of the upper body (the cardiac plexus and the thoracic ganglion) and those of the lower body (the solar plexus and the lumbar ganglion), the brain being a pestilential irrelevance. His argument is that the idealism of modern civilisation has disastrously overcultivated the upper body, seat of sympathy and love, at the expense of the lower body, the seat of pride and independence. This is no longer a traditional quarrel between head and heart, but a tension in the unconscious somatic world below the neck, between breast and belly and more ominously between feminine love and masculine pride.

As for practical recommendations, Lawrence, who had no children himself, demands that all schools be closed so that children do not become infected with ideas. Children under ten years of age are to be kept at home; thereafter they should be trained in practical crafts and in gymnastics, not in book-learning: '*The great mass of humanity should never learn to read and write – never*' (Lawrence 1971b: 87). He further recommends that children be protected from the insidiously bullying demands of maternal sympathy, and given a sound thrashing from time to time, for the good of their spinal posture:

> The vibration of the spanking acts direct upon the spinal nerve-system, there is a direct reciprocity and reaction, the spanker transfers his wrath to the great will-centres in the child, and these will-centres react intensely, are vivified and educated. (Lawrence 1971b: 50)

Other forms of education are to be avoided as poisonous, especially sex-education: 'The mass of mankind should *never* be acquainted with the scientific biological facts of sex: *never*' (Lawrence 1971b: 113). Lawrence's anti-educational proposals presuppose a new anti-democratic social order supervised by a wise minority of people who are capable of withstanding the dangers of mental consciousness. The values of such a new order are to be service, obedience, leadership and unquestioned authority: 'it must be a system of culminating aristocracy, society tapering like a pyramid to the supreme leader' (Lawrence 1971b: 182). These authoritarian principles are replicated at the level of marital relations too, when Lawrence advises husbands to batter the modern self-consciousness out of their wives, making them 'yield once more to the male leadership' (Lawrence 1971b: 191).

Looking beyond such proto-fascist and phallocratic arguments, we find even more startling assertions in Lawrence's *Fantasia*, especially in the chapter entitled 'Cosmological'. Here Lawrence flatly denies all scientific explanations for the origins and physical formation of the sun and the moon, insisting that since all apparently inert matter is generated from organic life, both are created and renewed from the 'life-emission' – or equally the death-emission – of people and animals: 'The sun is materially composed of all the effluence of the dead' (Lawrence 1971b: 153). It follows, for Lawrence if not for his bemused reader, that without man and his solar plexus the sun would die out, just as the moon's light is sustained by the human lumbar ganglion. After this, the jocular folk theory that the moon is made of cheese begins to look almost scientifically respectable by comparison.

Fantasia of the Unconscious is a minor work, and should not be elevated to any commanding position in Lawrence's oeuvre as a definitive credo. It shows repeated signs of hurried composition, digressive padding and merely flippant obstinacy, in which Lawrence seems well aware that his provocations will be greeted as mere 'bosh and abracadabra' (Lawrence 1971b: 14). It is worth remembering too that the obsession with male leadership that mars this and other writings of the early 1920s was something that Lawrence had partly put behind him by the time he came to write *Lady Chatterley's Lover* (1928). At the same time the *Fantasia* is not a work of marginal irrelevance either. Its obsessions and its quack-physiological jargon feed into Lawrence's other writings of the decade. In *Studies in Classic American Literature* (1924), for example, Lawrence interrupts his discussion of Edgar Allan Poe to tell us 'It is love that causes the neuroticism of the day. It is love that is the prime cause of tuberculosis' (Lawrence 1971c: 73). He follows up that assertion with an explanation involving excessive vibration of the ganglia. Later in the same essay Lawrence's insistence that sexual intercourse should take place strictly in darkness obtrudes as he denounces the 'evil thing that daytime love-making is' (Lawrence 1971c: 81). Turning to R. H. Dana's *Two Years Before the Mast*, he resumes his earlier defence of parental spanking in a sustained justification of the flogging of sailors, as a sure tonic for jaded ganglionic nerves. An essay on Hawthorne in the same volume digresses into an extended warning against the modern educated woman:

> these women-doctors, these nurses, these educationalists, these public-spirited women, these female saviours: they are all, from the inside, sending out waves of destructive malevolence which eat out the inner life of a man, like a cancer. (Lawrence 1971c: 99)

On a more cheerful note, Lawrence looks forward here to the passing-away of such she-devils and to a new age of female submission to the dark phallic principle.

The physiological preoccupations of the *Fantasia*, along with its nebulous jargon of quickening dark rays and fecundating nuclei, are found echoed not only in the critical writings of Lawrence but in his novels and tales too, where the accursed dominance of the brain ('mental consciousness') and the heart (love and benevolence) over the oppressed spine and loins is a constant theme. Sir Clifford Chatterley, paralysed from the waist down from injuries sustained in the Great War, appears as a crude personification of a whole civilisation that has lost its vital lower body. Other representative characters – notably Hermione Roddice, Gerald Crich and the artist Loerke in *Women in Love* (1921) – are repeatedly analysed in terms of their controlling mental 'will', their sexualities presented as cerebral and thus pervertedly voyeuristic. Meanwhile the novel's hero, Rupert Birkin, complains about the importance attached to love as a supreme value, seeking instead a new individualistic kind of equilibrium with his lover Ursula Brangwen, who is at first indignant at this. Ursula's climactic discovery comes to her while caressing Birkin's thighs on a hearth-rug in a country inn:

> She had discovered something, something more than wonderful, more wonderful than life itself. It was the strange mystery of his life-motion, there, at the back of the thighs, down the flanks. It was a strange reality of his being, the very stuff of being, there in the straight downflow of the thighs. (Lawrence 1998: 325)

This is not so much an erotic experience as an intellectual-mystical recognition of the lower body as the very stuff of being, an insight that converts Ursula from her prior attachments to upper-body values of love and sympathy.

In a similar fashion, the Irish widow Kate Leslie, the protagonist of Lawrence's much darker novel of phallic supremacy set in Mexico, *The Plumed Serpent* (1926), arrives at a true spinal awareness that has been lost since the days of the Flood:

> Sometimes, in America, the shadow of that old pre-Flood world was so strong, that the day of historic humanity would melt out of Kate's consciousness, and she would begin to approximate to the old mode of consciousness, the old, dark will, the unconcern for death, the subtle, dark consciousness, non-cerebral, but vertebrate. When the mind and the power of man was in his blood and his back-bone, and there was the strange, dark intercommunication between man and man and man and beast, from the powerful spine. (Lawrence 1983: 451–2)

The special energy of the lower body in Lawrence's fiction is frequently and repetitiously described as 'dark', as 'electric', or as 'suave'. Although he tries with such diction to invoke the throbbing of the primal blood, Lawrence's language in such passages is noticeably and somewhat desperately abstract, clogged with Latinate iteration, this being the index of his inescapably intellectual anti-intellectualism.

We shall have occasion later to return to this doctrinaire side of Lawrence's writing; but first we should review the role of ideas in 1920s literature within a larger context, one that takes us from the eccentricities of the Inner Voice to the more identifiable traditions of thought deriving from the nineteenth century.

Heavy Food

Viewed from the standpoint of intellectual history, literature in the early twentieth century is marked by the continuing absorption and reworking of the great challenges of the previous century's thinking that we associate principally with the trinity of Darwin, Marx and Nietzsche. A new modern world-view, or – in Nietzsche's phrase – a transvaluation of all values, was slowly taking shape around concepts of natural selection, class struggle and the death of God, with imaginative writers often engaged in the task of re-imagining the world according to those new lights. Some drew their intellectual inspiration from pioneers of the literary-artistic world (Richard Wagner, Leo Tolstoy, Gustave Flaubert, Henrik Ibsen), others from figures whose names are now less familiar, from philosophy and sociology (Auguste Comte, Herbert Spencer, Henri Bergson), from the new science of anthropology (E. B. Tylor, J. G. Frazer), or from the pseudo-science of anthropometrics (Francis Galton). The impressions made upon literature by this mixed intellectual diet are of course highly varied, both according to sometimes eclectic combinations of influence and according to differing modes of appropriation or adaptation. Some writers absorbed aspects of the new thinking more or less 'silently' into the larger presuppositions or attitudes implied by their work, while others became convinced advocates of one intellectual trend or another, sometimes even using their literary talents for purposes of open advocacy.

In this context, it is best to approach the ideational side of 1920s literature through a preliminary comparison with the situation in the Edwardian period. The literary scene before the Great War had often resembled a debating chamber or Sunday park of orators, in which a good deal of public noise was being made by dramatists and novelists who were eager for social reform of various kinds. Some of them gravitated towards the Fabian Society of socialist intellectuals, in which Bernard Shaw was a leading figure and H. G. Wells for a while a dissident member. From the other side of the debating-hall the enthusiasms of an ascendant Liberal progressivism were challenged by writers of a Catholic persuasion, notably Hilaire Belloc and G. K. Chesterton. The dramatist and novelist John Galsworthy busied himself with campaigns to improve prison conditions (as reflected in his play *Justice* of 1910) and the conditions of zoo animals. Bernard Shaw, a well-known platform speaker, adopted a whole range of pet causes from anti-vivisectionism and vegetarianism to the rational reform of English spelling and of women's clothing. These and other writers also lent support to the cause of women's suffrage, while Rudyard Kipling in his notorious poem 'The Female of the Species' (1911) argued for the other side. Literary journals such as A. R. Orage's *New Age* opened their columns to debates about Nietzsche, Tolstoy and other figures of the new thinking, while poets dabbled in 'pagan' or otherwise post-Christian values, encouraged in part by the Nietzschean revolution in ethics. Feminist writers of both sexes speculated about an imaginary prehistoric matriarchy while projecting a sturdier future for 'the race' achieved through healthy motherhood and 'Eugenics', which meant selective breeding and the sterilisation of the 'unfit'.

Something of the changed mood of the 1920s can be caught in Virginia Woolf's essay 'Character in Fiction' (1924), where she observes that reading novels by Galsworthy leaves the reader with a sense of incompletion, in that their aims lie outside themselves in the world of social reform: 'In order to complete them it seems necessary to do something – to join a society, or, more desperately, to write a cheque' (Woolf 1988: 427). For her, the novel or other literary artwork should be complete in itself. T. S. Eliot, who shared broadly the same view, wrote in *The Sacred Wood* (1920), in reference to the imaginative impact of anthropological discoveries, that 'If we are to digest the heavy food of historical and scientific knowledge that we have eaten we must be prepared for much greater exertions' (Eliot 1950: 77). Eliot's favoured metaphors for the process by which art transmutes its materials involved abdominal labours of excretion or childbirth, so here it is likely that he is calling for an intellectual and aesthetic self-discipline by which the 'heavy food' not just of anthropology but of later nineteenth-century science and thought more generally could be purified into genuine art. From his perspective or from Woolf's, the unsatisfactory quality of the Edwardian literary scene was that it had too openly masticated its philosophical or socio-political meals without having absorbed them into its bloodstream.

The purpose of this chapter is to show the extent to which the Edwardian agenda of intellectually contentious writing survived and even refreshed itself through the 1920s despite the misgivings of a few advanced Modernist objectors. There was no wholesale Modernist 'revolution' on this front, although a selective reading of the critical essays mentioned at the start of this chapter might give the impression that there had been. In the first place, the Modernists themselves were not always shy about entering public socio-political controversy, as is confirmed by such works as Woolf's feminist classic *A Room of One's Own* (1929) and Wyndham Lewis's irascible *The Art of Being Ruled* (1926), and by Eliot's numerous anti-Liberal editorials in the *Criterion*. Some of the surviving 'Edwardian' liberals carried on as before with their variously humanitarian, utopian, or post-Nietzschean musings, either in non-fictional form (Wells's *A Short History of the World* (1922) was a bestseller) or in works of fiction (Wells again, in his 1923 utopian romance *Men Like Gods*), while still coming under assault from Chesterton in his *Eugenics and Other Evils* (1922) and *The Superstitions of the Sceptic* (1925). At this point we can take a closer look at one lavish exhibition of Edwardian-style opinion-mongering.

Shaw: *Back to Methuselah*

As we have noted already, what had once been the Ibsenite 'New Drama' of topical social issues in the Edwardian period had largely given way after the Great War to a theatre dominated by comedy and other light genres (musical revue, melodrama, or detective thriller). Yet in the 1920s there were still some tendentious plays that confronted audiences with issues of contemporary public debate. Galsworthy's *The Show* (1925), for instance, tackles the question of journalism and its ethical responsibilities. W. Somerset Maugham's play *The Sacred Flame* (1929), unusually for this master of modern comedy, starts off with a detective mystery and ends up with a strongly implied endorsement of euthanasia. Ernest Hutchinson's *The Right to Strike* (1920) deals with the trade-unionist topic its title suggests, while Clemence Dane's *A Bill of Divorcement* (1921) focuses upon the specific issue of divorce on grounds of insanity. These were exceptions, however, that tended to confirm the rule.

The most energetic champion of Ibsen in the pre-War period, though, had never been a practitioner of soberly realistic social-issue drama at all. Bernard Shaw had been well-known for introducing such topics as prostitution and poverty into his plays, but these had always been cast in the form of intellectual comedy in which discussion and paradoxical rhetoric had taken precedence over plot or character. So Shaw's theatre of ideas was left relatively unaffected by the decline of the old New Drama. In 1921 Shaw launched his most ambitious work to date, the published text of *Back to Methuselah*, a sequence of five plays that he regarded as unperformable on stage but which still constituted, on his own view, his grand masterpiece, or in Wagnerian terms his *Ring* cycle. In fact, to Shaw's surprise, this sequence was staged after all, in both New York (1922) and Birmingham (1923), taking over twelve hours to perform and losing large sums of money for the theatres concerned. Aside from that endurance test for audiences (Arnold Bennett failed it by falling asleep), *Back to Methuselah* was published and read as a work of dramatic literature in book form, including, as was habitual with Shaw, a lengthy Preface.

Shaw's putative masterpiece is forbiddingly subtitled 'A Metabiological Pentateuch', which is one way of conceding that it incorporates another eccentric pseudo-science that has mistaken itself for a religious revelation. Shaw's personal religion of the Life Force had been evolving for some time since he had offered an early version of it in his play *Man and Superman* (1903). By the time of *Methuselah* he had made of it an elaborate doctrine, and felt that he could offer his pentateuch in all seriousness as a new bible for the twentieth century, and as a gospel of hope amid the cynicism and much-discussed 'disillusionment' of the post-War years. The temporal span of the five-play sequence is biblical, taking us all the way from Adam and Eve in the Garden of Eden to a projected superhuman world some thirty millennia into the future. Its imaginative mode, though, is that of science-fictional fable, oddly compounded with elements of political satire. As science fiction, its founding speculation is that humanity can – and indeed must, if reason and sanity are to prevail – attain an optimal individual lifespan of about 300 years. The sequence shows the results of such an enhanced longevity arriving by means of unexpected mutation, bringing with it conflict and comical misunderstanding, between the new 'long-livers' and the doomed breed of immature 'short-livers'. Thus in Part IV (*Tragedy of an Elderly Gentleman*) we witness what looks to us like an old man being condescended to by a young-looking – but in fact older – woman of the superior long-lived human strain, and frustrated by her inability to understand his now antique vocabulary ('decency', 'married' and so forth). Prior to this, in Part II (*The Gospel of the Brothers Barnabas*, set in 1921) we have had the 300-year lifespan predicted as the only hope for humanity by Conrad and Franklin Barnabas, a biologist and a theologian respectively, their paired professions signifying Shaw's presumptive synthesis of science and religion. The prophetic brothers argue that a human being who lives only seventy years is incapable of mature responsibility, whereas one who expects to live to 300 will have a more far-sighted sense of obligation to the future. The point is pressed home by the introduction of two politicians who are obvious caricatures of the wartime Liberal prime ministers Herbert Asquith and David Lloyd George (the latter being still in office when *Methuselah* appeared): the petty opportunism of their scheming in response to the Barnabian 'gospel' exposes the disastrously myopic leadership inevitably produced by a democracy of short-livers.

The ultimate goal of human evolution, although by its nature unrepresentable, is outlined in Part V, *As Far as Thought Can Reach*, which is set in 'AD 31,920'. By this point sexual reproduction, inaugurated by Adam and Eve in Part I as an escape from the burden of immortality, has at last died out along with other physical processes such as the eating of food, so that human beings are now hatched from eggs, in a form resembling a young adult of earlier eras. They enjoy a brief 'childhood' occupied with such infantile pursuits as art, music and romantic infatuation (there are still males and females, for no apparent reason), before joining the serene gerontocracy of the Ancients, whose lives are spent in blissful solitary contemplation. According to the Marxist political theory that Shaw had absorbed back in the 1880s, the advent of communism involves the withering away of the State, which indeed seems to have happened by the year 31,920, in which there is no visible government apart from the moral authority of the nearest Ancient. More surprising is that Shaw envisages beyond that not just the evolution but the withering away of the human body itself. The final frontier for the Ancients, who are still vulnerable to accidental death, is true immortality, which will mean casting off the tyranny of physical form. As one of them predicts, 'The day will come when there will be no people, only thought' (Shaw 1939: 306). The long story of humanity, then, appears to be one in which the happy ending is disembodiment, or the final disappearance of Body into Spirit.

Shaw seems genuinely to have believed that *Back to Methuselah* offered a timely remedy for post-War despair, a condition that figures in the sequence itself as the deadly disease of 'discouragement'. Against that depressive and often cynical mood of the times he pits an irrepressible Life Force that propels us all, whether we recognise it or not, ever upward to utopian sublimation. His gospel of Creative Evolution is essentially a religious affirmation that life has a purpose and a higher goal. This is why much of Shaw's Preface to the sequence is devoted to the attempted demolition of Darwinism as a false doctrine in which Nature is reduced to an accumulation of mere accidents. Shaw's preferred model of evolution he derived from the French biologist Jean-Baptiste Lamarck (1744–1829), as reinterpreted by the English writer Samuel Butler. In the Lamarck–Butler scheme of things, life-forms evolve because they unconsciously will themselves to do so: thus the giraffe acquired its long neck by yearning and persevering. Shaw clung fast to the notion of willed or purposeful evolution simply because the Darwinian alternative struck him as too demoralising to accept. Although it seems to peer positively into a distant future of human self-perfection, *Back to Methuselah* is, as its title revealingly suggests, a backward-looking work that belongs intellectually to the debates of the 1870s and more generally to the earnest atmosphere of Victorian idealism that Shaw himself had once so mischievously challenged. Quite apart from the grandiose folly of its sheer scale, the play-sequence was spectacularly out of tune with its time: the prevailing cultural mood of the 1920s being oversexed and dismissive of the older generations, this was not a propitious time to propose that the ultimate goal of human existence was a sexless gerontocracy. Untimely or not, the Shavian gospel expounded in *Methuselah* is remarkable for the mechanical equation it assumes between longevity and wisdom. It is as if Shaw had never heard of senile dotage, or simply – and perhaps understandably at the age of sixty-five – refused to contemplate it.

The Advent of Freud

Shaw had been in his idiosyncratic fashion a major synthesiser and interpreter of nineteenth-century thought. In the 1920s, though, the intellectual landscape was being reshaped by what can properly be described as the new thinking of the twentieth century, with Freud and the larger movement of psychoanalysis at the head of its agenda. Boosted by the growing awareness of wartime shell-shock, psychoanalysis was seized upon eagerly by intellectuals of both scientific and literary kinds as a powerful new key to the understanding of human motivation and development. Its central concepts – the Unconscious, repression, the dominance of the sexual motive, the Oedipus Complex – rapidly became matters of table-talk among the educated classes. Some writers greeted Freud's ideas as a liberating revelation (for example the novelist John Cowper Powys in his *Psychoanalysis and Morality*, 1923), while others, including D. H. Lawrence in *Psychoanalysis and the Unconscious* (1923), responded with alarm and suspicion. Hardly any writer, though, could remain ignorant of these ideas. Indeed, some acquaintance with Freudianism was obligatory for anybody keeping abreast of modern thought in the 1920s.

The huge significance of this recent and supposedly scientific revelation lay in the value it assigned to the open discussion of sexual impulses of all kinds. As widely understood in its most simplified form, psychoanalysis was believed to effect the cure of neuroses simply by bringing forgotten or repressed sexual material out into the open through dialogue. Put crudely, talking about one's sexual history or about the coded sexual contents of one's dreams was inherently healthy, whereas failing to discuss them was morbid. This principle was speedily adopted as a matter of historical pride among the self-consciously modern spirits of the time, enabling them to dismiss with knowing complacency the civilisation of their grandparents: a new condescending myth of 'the Victorians' grew up in which those generations could be condemned not just as inflexibly moralistic or chauvinistic but as grotesquely and damagingly blind to the central facts of life. To be modern in the 1920s meant being 'frank', at least in private conversation.

The broader impact of these developments upon literary culture in this decade is beyond the scope of this chapter. We are concerned here with the place of ideas in 1920s literature, and in this instance with writers' appropriation and treatment of the Freudian doctrine. Here a notable difference emerges between British literary adoptions of Freud and the European pattern. In France and elsewhere, the most visible and spectacular exploitation of psychoanalytic ideas came with the launch of the

Surrealist movement by André Breton in 1924. The Surrealists ignored Freud's attempts to assist the Ego, and seized upon the Unconscious as an armoury for their 'revolutionary' irrationalism. They eventually attracted a few British disciples in the 1930s, but before then the nearest equivalent to their techniques was the kind of verbal free-association found in the poems of Edith Sitwell, notably in her *Façade* sequence of 1923, although Sitwell had no sympathy for Surrealism as such. For the most part, British literary Freudianism was orthodox in its devotion to rational explanation of motive and cause. It took two forms, biographical and fictional. In the first, the pioneer was Lytton Strachey, the celebrated author of *Eminent Victorians* (1918) and *Queen Victoria* (1921) and the brother of Freud's authorised English translator James Strachey. His last major work, *Elizabeth and Essex* (1928), offers a new explanation for the political crises in the latter phase of Elizabeth I's reign brought on by her adoption of the Earl of Essex as a favourite. The problems surrounding the virgin queen are traced back to her upbringing and the profound political insecurities of her childhood, as Strachey claims that 'it so happened that, in Elizabeth's case, there was a special cause for a neurotic condition: her sexual organization was seriously warped' (Strachey 1950: 20). The subsequent tradition of 'psychobiography', in which the pattern of the subject's life is explained according to Freudian principles of causation, begins here.

In the realm of prose fiction, the rapid acceptance of Freudian explanatory logic in readers' and writers' understanding of human character may be illustrated by the success of W. Somerset Maugham's short story 'Rain' (1921), a widely acclaimed tale from which Maugham made a small fortune by selling the film rights. 'Rain' presents a dramatic clash set on a South-Sea island between a prostitute, Sadie Thompson, and a crusading Christian missionary, Mr Davidson, as observed by the narrator, a worldly-wise physician. Davidson attempts to get Sadie expelled from the island, but as that official process unfolds, he is surprised by her apparent conversion to his faith, and thus obliged to help in her salvation by spending time with her in private prayer. Meanwhile we learn from the missionary's wife that he has been dreaming of the mountains of Nebraska, which the doctor-narrator happens to remember are shaped like women's breasts. On the day of Sadie's scheduled expulsion, Davidson is found dead with a razor in his hand, his throat slit. No explanation of this suicide is offered, because Maugham trusts his readers to decode the dream-symbolism and so to follow the Freudian logic of repression: the missionary zealot has, we are to understand, succumbed to sexual temptation during the supposed prayer-sessions, and has been unable to face the shame of Sadie's victory. 'Rain' is a very modern kind of moral fable that deliberately inverts 'Victorian' notions of religion and sex, in effect warning against attempts to purify human nature. The most remarkable thing about it is that Maugham feels no need to spell this out explicitly, confident as he is that his readers already share in the tale's psychoanalytic assumptions.

A book review by Virginia Woolf, published in the previous year, helps to confirm the rapid recent adoption of a common Freudian wisdom among readers and writers of the time. Her article 'Freudian Fiction' (1920) assesses J. D. Beresford's new novel *An Imperfect Mother*, finding its treatment of the protagonist's erotic incapacity (he is thwarted by excessive devotion to his mother) too predictable and too close to becoming a kind of medical case-history (Woolf 1988: 195–7). It is worth noting that Freud's own published case-histories, of Dora, the Wolf-Man and other patients have often been admired for their powerful literary qualities, following as they do a narrative logic akin to the detective story. Woolf's worry is clearly that the complexity and unexpectedness of human behaviour would be crudely simplified by the new Freudian fiction, and forced to exemplify a settled medical doctrine. Woolf's worries about psychoanalysis and its impact on fiction indeed extended further than this. Even after 1924, when she became, as co-director of the Hogarth Press, the official English-language publisher of Freud's writings, Woolf abstained from studying them, for fear that such contact might somehow blight her own sources of creative invention.

Sinclair: *Life and Death of Harriett Frean*

Woolf's apprehensions about the emergence of a programmatic Freudian fiction in which characters are reduced to didactic case-studies were soon borne out by the appearance of May Sinclair's novella *Life and Death of Harriett Frean* in 1922. Sinclair was an established novelist of the generation prior to Woolf's, and had been among the earliest literary converts to psychoanalysis, having helped to establish London's first analytic practice in 1913. Her best and most recent novel, the semi-autobiographical *Mary Olivier* (1919), had been a sensitively realistic coming-of-age novel notable for its treatment of a mother–daughter conflict in which the protagonist's intellectual ambitions are stifled by her mother's manipulative hypochondria. With *Harriett Frean*, though, Sinclair took a turn towards a much more simplified kind of narrative.

As the title suggests, Sinclair's novella covers the entire life of its title character from infancy in the 1840s to her death nearly seventy years later, and at a brisk pace that allows no expansion or enrichment of character. Harriett is something of a cartoon figure with only two characteristics: pride in being her father's daughter, and devotion to a 'beautiful' code of self-abnegation. We are first shown her being brought up to suppress her own needs, as her parents train her by insidious moral blackmail to live a life of noble self-denial according to a familiar model of Victorian femininity. In late adolescence, Harriett has a best friend, Priscilla, who becomes engaged to a young man called Robin. The pivotal event of the story is Robin's declaration of his love for Harriett, and Harriett's rejection of his otherwise welcome devotion, solely on principled grounds of loyalty to her friend. Harriett spends the rest of her life unmarried, privately congratulating herself on the beautiful nobility of this decisive refusal. The marriage of Robin and Priscilla, meanwhile, does not go at all well: Priscilla turns into an embittered invalid, the basis of her paralysis later being revealed as hysterical. After Priscilla dies, Robin marries her nurse Beatrice, and he in turn degenerates into peevish invalidism. Harriett herself withdraws from life, expelling any disturbances to her solitude: her servant Maggie gets the sack because her baby cries; then as an indirect result of this dismissal, the baby dies. Harriett eventually contracts cancer, the same disease that killed her similarly self-sacrificing mother; and in her terminal delirium she confuses her tumour with Maggie's baby.

In case the reader has not already taken the strong hints that these afflictions have resulted from Harriett's own refusal of Robin's love, Sinclair introduces at a late stage of the story a younger character, Robin's niece Mona Floyd, whose sole function is to serve as the *raisonneur*, that is to say the mouthpiece of the author's verdicts upon her characters. We are by this stage in the 1890s, and Mona is clearly a 'New Woman' of that period, her name echoing that of Mona Caird, a noted feminist novelist of the time. Mona announces that she has become engaged to a man who had recently been her best friend's fiancé. Harriett cautiously reveals that she had once faced the same dilemma, but had made exactly the opposite choice, 'because I was brought up not to think of myself before other people' (Sinclair 1922: 145). At this, Mona denounces the selfish folly of Harriett's choice, which has put her own conception of moral beauty above the true welfare of Robin, Priscilla, Harriett herself and ultimately Beatrice too, blighting all their lives. As Mona explains, both Priscilla and Robin had become miserable and ill from their awareness of having – with Harriett's encouragement – entered into a loveless marriage. Referring to her uncle, Mona adds:

> 'Of course he hated you, after what you'd let him in for.' She paused. 'You don't *mind* my telling you the truth, do you?'

... Harriett sat a long time, her hands folded on her lap, her eyes staring into the room, trying to see the truth. She saw the girl, Robin's niece, in her young indignation, her tender brilliance suddenly hard, suddenly cruel, flashing out the truth. Was it true that she had sacrificed Robin and Priscilla and Beatrice to her parents' idea of moral beauty? Was it true that this idea had been all wrong? That she might have married Robin and been happy and been right? (Sinclair 1922: 147)

Mona's interpretation of the story's central events is laid before the reader here as a 'truth' to which there is no credible riposte. Although the larger logic of the story has a recognisably Freudian basis, in that neurotic paralysis afflicting the principal characters ensues from a perverse sexual self-denial, the specific lesson that Mona is brought in to teach us has a more Nietzschean flavour, addressing as it does the covert selfishness underlying pseudo-altruistic conduct. Mona does appear cruelly hard in her verdict on Harriett's disastrous error, dispatching it as simply wrong, according to her new modern morality, and as unworthy of any sympathetic understanding. The narrative voice of the tale is similarly implacable in its treatment of Harriett, entering her mind only to show up its blindness from the secure height of doctrinal certainty. *Life and Death of Harriett Frean* illustrates a modern ethical position with powerful conviction, but its generic form of moral fable is strangely old-fashioned, in that it grants readers no discretion to draw their own conclusions.

Tendentious Fiction and Narrative Preaching

According to the Modernist critical consensus summarised at the start of this chapter, the obligation of the modern novelist was to withdraw discreetly from the encounter between the reader and the novel's events, giving us the impression that we 'see' the characters in action rather than be 'told' about them. There should, then, be no audible voice of guiding narrative interpretation – and above all no moral interpretation – that would tell us what to make of the actions and conversations to which we are witness. If opinions were articulated in a novel, these would be attributable only to characters in some specific dramatic context, while the presiding narrative voice held aloof from them in neutral or potentially ironic distance. Such at least was the purist position derived from Henry James.

For the most part, this consensus held good in the 1920s. Novelists of course had pet ideas and opinions of their own, but were usually careful to put these into the mouths of their characters rather than propound them directly. They did not begin their works with aphorisms in the manner of Jane Austen ('It is a truth universally acknowledged . . .') or of Leo Tolstoy ('All happy families are alike'). The opening paragraph of D. H. Lawrence's *Lady Chatterley's Lover* is unusual in making a general assertion ('Ours is essentially a tragic age . . .') outside the context of any fictional frame. At least it is unusual as an opening move. When we look more closely at the fiction of this decade, we find that in much of it the old habits of the opinionated and 'intrusive' narrator in fact died hard. The temptation to address the reader directly 'over the heads' of the fictional characters was still felt by novelists, and was by no means always resisted.

This attenuated survival of the opinionated narrative voice was not a simple matter of old-fashioned novelists failing to catch up with the new wisdom of Modernism. The novelists dismissed by Virginia Woolf as 'Edwardians' indeed show far more self-discipline in this respect, in their works of the 1920s, than Woolf herself does: Arnold Bennett's *Riceyman Steps* (1923), for example, keeps us focused upon what its characters are observing and thinking, and never directly betrays what Bennett thinks of anything. No more does John Galsworthy in his second sequence of Forsyte novels from *The White Monkey* (1924) to *Swan Song* (1928) make general pronouncements on the world, although his characters often do. Two of Woolf's experimental novels of this decade, on the other hand, mix the modes of fiction and essay, alternating the description of characters and fictional events with general observations on life, delivered in the essayistic present tense. The first, *Jacob's Room* (1922), offers plentiful examples, as the already oblique and fragmentary story of Jacob Flanders is suspended in favour now of a short essay on the importance of letter-writing ('Let us consider letters . . . ') (Woolf 1992a: 125), now of a travelogue-like account of the Parthenon at Athens. Amid these shifts of genre Woolf throws out maxims on her own account, which are relevant to her own sceptical approach to her art, but not directly justified by the story at hand, as with the repeated observation that 'It is no use trying to sum people up' (Woolf 1992a: 37, repeated 214). In the more light-hearted novel *Orlando* (1928) Woolf at first fictionalises the narrative voice, making it a parody of a pompously authoritative biographer; but after a while she abandons that game and slips back into her essayist's voice in numerous more or less flippant 'asides' to the reader on general matters beyond the scope of her story. Woolf's more admired works of this phase, *Mrs Dalloway* (1925) and *To the Lighthouse* (1927), are artistically purer in this respect, sticking closely to the thoughts of their characters and holding the essayistic voice at bay.

Woolf's example helps to show that there was in practice no strict Modernist orthodoxy that could exclude the ventilation of 'raw' ideas in the novel. This should not really surprise us if we bear in mind the major French example of Marcel Proust, whose *A la recherche du temps perdu* (1913–27) treats us on almost every other page to generally applicable aphorisms and miniature essays on the perversities of the human heart, often readily detachable from their fictional contexts. Proust is indeed clearly the inspiration for several of Woolf's own aphoristic observations in *Orlando* on time, memory and identity. Apart from Woolf herself, some other novelists who were not Modernists but were associated closely or loosely with her Bloomsbury Group show a similar readiness to address us in their own voices. E. M. Forster does this rather less often in *A Passage to India* (1924) than in his novels of the Edwardian period, but the habit still persists. At one point we are told, on the authority of the narrator, that 'Most of the inhabitants of India do not mind how India is governed.' A later chapter begins with the assertion that 'Most of life is so dull that there is nothing to be said about it.' More controversially, we hear later that

> Suspicion in the Oriental is a sort of malignant tumour, a mental malady, that makes him self-conscious and unfriendly suddenly; he trusts and mistrusts at the same time in a way the Westerner cannot comprehend. It is his demon, as the Westerner's is hypocrisy. (Forster 1989: 126, 145, 276)

Novelists speaking in their own voice take the same risks as criminal suspects upon arrest: anything they say may be taken down and used in evidence against them, as this little observation has been, by those keen to convict Forster for 'orientalist' deviations.

Another such case, and in many ways a more perplexing one, is the fiction of D. H. Lawrence. As the homiletic opening of *Lady Chatterley* indicates, Lawrence was far less inclined than other novelists to keep his ideas to himself. Many of the characters in his novels and stories hold strong views, sometimes tending to violent prejudice, but these come to us mostly through dialogue or reported introspection. At times, though, in his accounts of a character's thoughts, the fictional frame slips away as though Lawrence has forgotten it, and the narrator takes over with a short sermon on a similar theme. In *Women in Love* (1921), for instance, Lawrence discusses the philanthropy of the mine-owner Thomas Crich, in the chapter 'The Industrial Magnate', showing how it has introduced what is clearly for Lawrence a false notion of equality into the minds of the colliers. At this point the text switches from the narrative past tense into the present tense appropriate for the declaration of general truths, and we are told that 'Mystic equality lies in being, not in having or doing', and then treated to further authorial assertions on the necessity of hierarchy in human life (Lawrence 1998: 234). Again in the later chapter entitled 'Moony' we find Rupert Birkin reflecting upon the sight of an African statuette and thinking further about the processes of racial degeneration that he believes are now besetting the West. Twice this train of thoughts flips from Rupert's own rumination in the past tense to what can only be Lawrence's own endorsement of it in the present tense: 'There is a long way we can travel after the death-break . . .', and 'Is our day of creative life finished? . . .' (Lawrence 1998: 263). Artless slippages of this kind from story to homily become habitual with Lawrence throughout the Twenties, and tend to betray the impatient preacher wresting control from the storyteller. The tendency is most visible in *Kangaroo* (1923), a novel that is all but capsized by its essayistic digressions. Its sixteenth chapter ('A Row in Town'), for instance, begins with a brief mention of one of the characters but then abandons the story to launch into a ten-page essay in Lawrence's own voice on the evils of democracy, with much solemn comment upon ganglionic telepathy among insects.

Ideas can of course be aired and debated in fiction without having to be articulated directly by a voice that we take to be the author's, in the fashion we have considered so far. They may be propounded, for instance, by a fictitious narrator who appears before us laden with definite opinions about life in general and about the characters of the story in particular. Richard Aldington's *Death of a Hero* (1929) is a clear example of this method, presented as a narrative written by a personal friend of the deceased protagonist, George Winterbourne. At an early stage we recognise that this narrator has his own distinct interpretation of his characters' various motives, and will not hesitate to tell us exactly what is wrong with them, as here in his account of Winterbourne's mother:

> She was a mistress of would-be revolutionary platitudes about marriage and property (rather like the talk of an 'enlightened' parson), but, in fact, was as sordid, avaricious, conventional, and spiteful a middle-class woman as you could dread to meet. Like all her class, she toadied to her betters and bullied her inferiors. But, with her conventionality, she was, of course, a hypocrite. (Aldington 1984: 17)

From this narrator we are not to expect any judicious neutrality in recounting the tale of how Winterbourne came to die in the Great War. What we get instead is the bracing partisanship of satire, along with a good many opinions on the sex-war, the British class system and the evils of journalism. There is a convincing dramatic reason for the narrator's disposition, though: he is still revolted by the enormous waste of the War, and by those he deems responsible for it.

More often, however, ideas were put into the mouths – or the unspoken thoughts – of non-narrating characters within the story. As always, it was open to the novelist to favour one of these voices, usually the protagonist's, with more sympathy or implied authority than the rival voices within the story, and thus to 'slant' the book so as to endorse the author's preferred set of values, beliefs, or ideas. Even in such an artistically impartial Modernist novel as Woolf's *To the Lighthouse* such biases show through, as the values of Mr Ramsay are openly satirised while those of his wife and of the artist Lily Briscoe are not, although the novel never goes so far as to promote a body of ideas. With other notable novels of the time, though, covert endorsement of one character's declared ideas is a more prominent issue. The continuing critical debate over Lawrence's *Women in Love*, for example, still revolves around the degree to which the ever-argumentative Rupert Birkin acts as a mouthpiece for the author's own desperate misanthropy. Birkin's sermons on the death of Western civilisation and the inadequacy of love do encounter some answering resistance from his friends Gerald Crich and Hermione Roddice, but both those characters are so relentlessly maligned by the narrative voice that we must regard their ideas as discredited from the start; which leaves us with the intermittent protests of his lover Ursula Gudrun. Some readings of the novel would claim that Ursula's scepticism towards what she calls Birkin's Sunday-school preaching is finally 'silenced' by her submission to his magnetic loins, while others draw attention to the novel's final page, which shows the couple still locked in unresolved debate. For all that, the imaginative power of *Women in Love* takes it well beyond the status of fictionalised tract, and the same could just about be said of the more openly didactic novels *Kangaroo* and *The Plumed Serpent*.

Lawrence's critical essays on fiction always abhor didacticism in the novel, but as a practising storyteller he is constantly tempted to ignore his own precepts. A similar inconsistency is to be found in the decade's literary culture more generally, the Olympian or merely Shakespearian detachment of the true artist being much easier to recommend than to practise. Novelists still wrote in order to win their readers round to their own view of the world, often enough to their own ideas about some social or political question that mattered to them. Forster's *A Passage to India*, for example, clearly treats the thoughts of its more sensitive, liberal-minded characters (Fielding, Aziz, Mrs Moore) with greater respect than those of its satirised bigots (Heaslop and others), and thus attempts to win us to Forster's ideal of humane sympathy crossing the barriers of race and religion. Radclyffe Hall's landmark story of lesbianism, *The Well of Loneliness* (1928), is another novel-with-a-purpose, a prose melodrama that clearly aims to win public sympathy for an outcast minority. John Galsworthy's *The Forsyte Saga* (1922, expanded to trilogy length from his earlier *The Man of Property* 1906) pursues an openly liberal-feminist agenda that condemns the upper-middle-class 'Victorian' values of Property and Respectability as cruelly destructive of Love and Art, the values associated with Galsworthy's more sympathetically-drawn characters.

The subgenre in which we might expect to find socio-political ideas tested in fiction is the Condition-of-England novel, a form dating from the 1840s and briefly revived in the Edwardian period in H. G. Wells's *Tono-Bungay* (1909) and Forster's *Howards End* (1910). However, it is a significant failure of 1920s literary culture that it did not respond to the severe economic recession and industrial turmoil of 1920–2, nor to the unprecedented crisis of the May 1926 General Strike, with any such work of convincing fictional interpretation. Some novelists did attempt fairly ambitious fictional diagnoses of the times and of their class conflicts, but the results were either insipid, as in the case of A. S. M. Hutchinson's *If Winter Comes* (1921); or imaginatively and intellectually indolent, as with Galsworthy's second Forsyte trilogy *A Modern Comedy* (1924–8), a miserably inferior sequel; or risibly blinkered, as we find with Warwick Deeping's bestseller *Sorrell and Son* (1925). The last novel takes a significant social type of the period, a demobilised military officer fallen on hard times, and follows his struggle to safeguard his beloved son Kit both from the modern woman (including Kit's grasping mother) and from the envious 'bolshie' spirit of the lower orders. There were novels of class conflict in the decade: J. D. Beresford's *Revolution* (1921), for instance, is notable for its clairvoyance in predicting a coming general strike, which evolves into a failed insurrection. There were novels later about the real General Strike of 1926, of which the most convincing is Ellen Wilkinson's *Clash* (1929). The nearest thing we have to a generally diagnostic Condition-of-England novel, however, is Lawrence's *Lady Chatterley's Lover*, which is of course a generic hybrid with erotic romance.

The Condition-of-England novel had always been more convincing in dramatising class conflicts than in resolving them; and *Lady Chatterley's Lover* is no exception. At the end of the novel, the gamekeeper Mellors sends Connie Chatterley a letter in which he offers his ideas about 'the only way to solve the industrial problem'. The solution is for the coalminers to stop complaining about their low wages and instead to revitalise their lower bodies:

If only they were educated to *live* instead of earn and spend, they could manage very happily on twenty-five shillings. If the men wore scarlet trousers as I said, they wouldn't think so much of money: if they could dance and hop and skip, and sing and swagger and be handsome, they could do with very little cash. (Lawrence 1990: 312)

As a considered response to the General Strike and to the long-running conflict in the coal industry that led up to it, this is hardly impressive.

Longer Philosophical Poems: Bridges and MacDiarmid

So far, we have looked at a range of idea-mongering fictions and an important case of didactic drama in Shaw's *Methuselah*. The realm of poetry might seem to be more resistant to the expression of intellectual controversy or of opinion. Even those poems of Yeats that draw upon his private scheme of occult cosmology tend rather to presuppose it in their background rather than actively propound it. In fact the general redirection of poetry in the 1920s away from erotic feeling and towards satire did open several opportunities for opinionated verse, for example in G. K. Chesterton's 'Songs of Education' sequence (1922), in several of Sassoon's poems and most persistently in D. H. Lawrence's *Pansies* collection (1929), the title of which is not primarily botanical but a pun on *pensées* or thoughts. Here, though, we shall consider two of most extraordinary experiments in verse from the decade's later years, each of which in its own way is a sustained exercise in philosophical poetry: Robert Bridges's *The Testament of Beauty* (1929) and Hugh MacDiarmid's *A Drunk Man Looks at the Thistle* (1926).

Bridges's didactic poem unfolds a considered philosophical and aesthetic position across four books, amounting to 4,374 lines. Seemingly inspired by the classical example of the *De Rerum Natura* of Lucretius, Bridges nonetheless sets out a modern, or at least post-Darwinian account of the place of beauty in the natural and human worlds, seeking a scientifically credible justification both for art and for the superior claims of 'vision' – meaning artistic inspiration – over those of abstract reason. Ranging freely and unsystematically over the realms of zoology, botany, anthropology and moral philosophy, Bridges expounds a philosophically Monist position in which body and spirit, and thus Nature and Art, are to be regarded as inseparable. His larger argument proposes that a properly cultivated appreciation of Beauty is capable of raising human awareness from its animal basis in egotism ('Selfhood', the title of Book II) and sexuality ('Breed', that of Book III) towards a balanced moral Wisdom ('Ethick' in Book IV) that is naturally derived but spiritual and ultimately religious. The attempt to build a modified idealism upon a materialist foundation draws upon *The Life of Reason* (1905–6) and other works by Bridges's younger friend the Spanish-American philosopher George Santayana, although Santayana was obliged to point out politely that he could barely recognise his own more pessimistic scepticism in the English Poet Laureate's version, notable for its quasi-Christian optimism.

To any reader unfamiliar with Bridges's verse experiments of the mid 1920s, *The Testament of Beauty* immediately presents two disorienting features of style. The first of these is the idiosyncratic but deliberate modification of English spellings according to a system that Bridges curiously regarded as a simplification of standard orthography in the interests of the reader's ability to read the poem aloud. In a few cases, such as the distinction between the pronoun 'that', spelt normally in its unstressed relative form but appearing as 'thatt' when stressed in its demonstrative function, there is a case to be made for such oddities as guides to pronunciation, but for the most part the effect strikes readers as one of distracting eccentricity. The second feature is the poem's unusual metre. In response to what he felt were the essentially inartistic liberties of modern free verse, Bridges had devised, on the basis of his earlier technical analyses of Milton's prosody, a verse line that he liked to regard as a loose 'alexandrine', that is, a twelve-syllable line in which no set number of stresses is to be expected. Thus discarding the predominantly iambic rhythm of the English verse tradition (although allowing himself the occasional variant decasyllable), Bridges makes the line, commonly end-stopped, rather than the 'foot' the primary unit of his metre.

Whatever we make of its merits as a philosophical utterance, *The Testament of Beauty* is the first major exercise in English syllabic verse, inaugurating a significant tradition that was later to be developed by W. H. Auden and Thom Gunn, among others. The advantage of this very loose metre for a long philosophical poem is that it allows the poet the free use of a polysyllabic abstract and technical diction that would be impossibly ungainly within iambic measures. The disadvantage is that it always risks slipping into a pedestrian expository prosiness. The following passage from Book IV illustrates both sides of that coin, along with other typical effects of style:

> From Universal Mind the first-born atoms draw
> their function, whose rich chemistry the plants transmute
> to make organic life, whereon animals feed
> to fashion sight and sense and give service to man,
> who sprung from them is conscient in his last degree

> of ministry unto God, the Universal Mind,
> whither all effect returneth whence it first began.
> The Ring in its repose is Unity and Being:
> Causation and Existence are the motion thereof.
> Thru'out all runneth Duty, and the conscience of it
> is thatt creativ faculty of animal mind
> that, wakening to self-conscience of all Essences,
> closeth the full circle, where the spirit of man
> escaping from the bondage of physical Law
> re-entereth eternity by the vision of God.
>
> (Bridges 1929: 136–7)

The metre here shows a typical dependence upon, as well as departure from, the reader's almost inevitable iambic expectations: the first and fifth lines here are iambic hexameters, from whose regularity the other lines seem to unwind. Bridges's use of the archaic -*eth* inflection, we may note in passing, was a device that he thought necessary to prevent readers confusing plural nouns with verbs; which shows a perverse distrust of our ability to parse according to the syntax.

Bridges's verse in the *Testament* comes to life more convincingly in its digressive passages of narrative and of natural description, some of them resembling Wordsworthian revelations or 'spots of time', than in the intermittent critique of Aristotle. One striking anecdote appears amid Bridges's defence of pleasure against ascetic moralists:

> whence pleasure with them,
> instead of being an in-itself absolute good
> as nature would have had it, and which man would wish
> to be always present and with his perfection increase,
> came to be bann'd as the pollution of virtue;–And so,
> when the young poet my companion in study
> and friend of my heart refused a peach at my hands,
> he being then a housecarl in Loyola's menie,
> 'twas that he feared the savor of it, and when he waived
> his scruple to my banter, 'twas to avoid offence.
>
> (Bridges 1929: 149–50)

The Jesuit priest ('housecarl in Loyola's menie') and young poet here remembered for his initial refusal of tempting fruit was Gerard Manley Hopkins, Bridges's long-mourned contemporary whose works – also experimental in metre – had appeared under Bridges's editorship in 1918.

Bridges's long poem, if brought up against MacDiarmid's *Drunk Man* for comparison, looks sedate to the point of complacency beside the much younger poet's work. *A Drunk Man Looks at the Thistle* is a 'philosophical' poem in an altogether different manner not only poetical but philosophical: the playfully mythological and provocatively combative style of Nietzsche's writings is an important influence upon it. (Among the incidental benefits of MacDiarmid's adoption of an adapted form of Scots dialect for the poem rather than Standard English is that it permits him to rhyme *teach ye* with *Nietzsche*.) In Nietzchean terms, the poem is distinctly Dionysian in its unpredictable energies and – as the title indicates – its primary conceit of intoxication, whereas Bridges's *Testament*, for all its defence of imaginative pleasure against dry reason, is governed by an essentially Apollonian aspiration to harmonious order. Bridges's poem can fairly be described as didactic, but MacDiarmid's – much the shorter work at 2,684 lines – takes the entirely different generic form of an extended dramatic monologue, into which various semi-independent lyrics are interwoven. Its dramatic situation, loosely reminiscent of Robert Burns's 'Tam O'Shanter' (1791), is that the speaker has spent a whisky-fuelled evening with friends at a pub before staggering homeward; while his wife Jean awaits his return, he settles down to rest on a moonlit hillside and unburdens his reeling mind to the nearest specimen of the national weed, sometimes turning to address the moon.

MacDiarmid introduced his poem to the world as a 'gallimaufry', that is, a jumble or hotchpotch. In structure, it is a medley of brief lyrics and satires, incorporating a few translations of modern Russian and German poems in a meandering and inconclusive sequence. The task of ordering these elements into their final published form was one that the poet delegated to his friend F. G. Scott, who has been rebuked by students of *A Drunk Man* for misplacing various sections and stanzas that would appear to belong elsewhere in the sequence. This disorderly construction is partly covered, though, by the poem's drunkenness, which also helps to motivate and indeed excuse several of its other features. The inebriated speaker is a dramatic 'mask' that allows MacDiarmid in sober daylight to disclaim responsibility for the poem's perceived excesses of lampoon, obscenity and meandering incoherence while of course allowing them to stand. A long poem composed of fragments uncertainly connected, *A Drunk Man Looks at the Thistle* knowingly invites comparison with T. S. Eliot's 'The Waste Land', to which indeed it directly alludes in jocular rivalry (at lines 345–9). It shares with that poem a few incidental features such as macaronic rhyming, sometimes obscure allusion, lamentation of cultural decline and an element of semi-Expressionist distortion, but for all that, it differs in that it has an underlying consistency provided by its single voice, which Eliot's poem denies us, and by a relatively stable symbolic design in which the thistle and the moon are the principal figures.

As a philosophical poem, *A Drunk Man* proceeds not according to any logical exposition but by inventive elaboration of symbolism. It has no settled system of thought to offer, but a symbolic manner of playing with contrary principles, and of exhibiting its own self-contradictions. It is a philosophical poem in the special sense that Melville's *Moby-Dick* or Dostoevsky's *Brothers Karamazov* are philosophical novels. Its speaker addresses fundamental enigmas of life and death, love and sex, religion and nation, art and drink, revolving these all around the Thistle:

> A' the uncouth dilemmas o' oor natur'
> Objectified in vegetable maitter
>
> (MacDiarmid 1987: 84)

MacDiarmid's symbolism is elastic, allowing the shifting moods – appropriately pugnacious, ribald and maudlin – of the drunken speaker to magnify or diminish the Thistle's meanings according to the occasion. At times the Thistle transforms into a crucifix or a gravestone, at times it becomes an octopus, a candelabrum, or even a Melvillean white whale. Its ready-made status as national emblem gives the speaker occasion to bewail the cultural deprivations of his country and its linked curses of Calvinism and sobriety, or to rail against its fake Burns-Night patriots. At moments of depression, 'this vile growth' is no more than a wretched weed suggestive of the barren condition of Scottish culture, but then at moments of elation it can become something like a resurgent tree of knowledge:

> The thistle yet'll unite
> Man and the Infinite!
>
> (MacDiarmid 1987: 40)

In similar fashion, the speaker himself expands and contracts, at one moment a pitifully confused sot, at the next a reincarnation of Burns himself, or a Scottish messiah who can transmute the wine of '*in vino veritas*' into whisky. In the dizzyingly unsteady vision of this poem, nothing is at rest.

Sozzled though he must be, this speaker is never to be mistaken for the stage-stereotype Scotsman of whom MacDiarmid despaired. He is a man of broad mind as well as broad dialect, who can dwell with sympathetic humility on his wife's virtues (without actually getting up to rejoin her), then lunge from theology to Russian literature before meditating – in 1920s Freudian fashion – upon the fragility of the intellect itself in the context of

> the physical basis
> O' a' life's seemin' airs and graces
>
> (MacDiarmid 1987: 48)

Although very simple in its verse-forms, which stay close to the popular traditions of vernacular ballad and song, this is a 'difficult' poem, especially for readers who are not easily familiar with Lowlands speech, but even for those who are, because MacDiarmid's diction reaches beyond the vernacular into recondite archaism and into phrases brought in from other regions. The poem was conceived as an exhibition of the lost lexical treasures of Scots, its true rival being not so much 'The Waste Land' as the then almost-finished *New English Dictionary* (1928; later retitled the *Oxford English Dictionary*), the brainchild of another Scot. Both kinds of reader have work to do, assisted by the poet's glosses, in tackling *A Drunk Man*, but they are repaid with unique imaginative agilities and intoxications.

Aldous Huxley and the Novel of Ideas

In his Preface to *Back to Methuselah*, Bernard Shaw refers to 'the professional classes whose recreation is reading and whose intellectual sport is controversy' (Shaw 1939: 58). This class had provided the principal audience for Shaw's own discussion-plays in the pre-War and wartime periods; and it clearly lived on through the 1920s, still hungry for intellectual controversy in literary form. H. G. Wells's novel *Meanwhile* (1928), for example, both represents that chattering class in its cast and caters to its appetite for talk, curiously transposing the crisis of the 1926 General Strike into endless after-dinner conversations in an Italian holiday home. Controversy-hunters were now entertained most successfully by the young novelist Aldous Huxley, whose first comic novel, *Crome Yellow*, appeared in 1921. Huxley was very much a 'period' phenomenon of the decade, regarded at the time by many observers as a leading voice of the new post-War generation, even in that sense as the prose counterpart to T. S. Eliot's poetry. Descended from the Arnold–Darwin–Huxley clan of English intellectuals, he was formidably well-educated and well-connected, personally known to most of the major figures in the literary scene from Lawrence to Eliot, and was more literate in science than any novelist of his time, his brother Julian Huxley being a leading biologist and populariser of scientific discoveries. From *Crome Yellow* through *Antic Hay* (1923) and *Those Barren Leaves* (1925) to *Point Counter Point* (1928), Aldous Huxley offered a fictional diet of satirical comedy in a formula that has frequently and fairly been called the discussion novel or novel of ideas.

Huxley's early novels assemble casts of eccentric characters, mostly artists and intellectuals, in order that they should talk. In *Crome Yellow* and *Those Barren Leaves* the odd characters are gathered in an English country house and an Italian coastal summer-palace respectively, each presided over by a gushing literary hostess (the model for each being Lady Ottoline Morrell). The unity of place – although in the latter novel there are excursions to the seaside and to Rome – tends further to replace action, beyond a few erotic dalliances, with conversation. In *Antic Hay*, by contrast, the characters are seen scurrying around London on various fruitless quests, but end up visiting one another in order to talk. The first few chapters of *Point Counter Point* are taken up by conversations held in and around a large house-party, after which something resembling a sub-plot eventually develops, culminating in the assassination of a prominent English Fascist; but still it is the talk that predominates, much of it done by Mark Rampion, a character transparently based upon D. H. Lawrence himself. One minor character in that novel is said not only to have been born into conversation but even to have 'married into conversation' too (Huxley 1994e: 85).

The kind of talk we hear in an early Huxley novel is distinctive in its coherence and erudition. When these highly educated characters open their mouths, they deliver themselves of long perfectly-formed paragraphs complete with arcane historical references, biblical or literary allusions, Latin tags and accurately recalled quotations, sometimes from the original French. These are in effect miniature essays, often exhibiting heterodox opinion, as when Mr Scogan the philosopher in *Crome Yellow* defends the aristocracy as the necessary guardians of eccentricity. The vocabulary of these speeches is recondite and polysyllabic: most of the twentieth chapter in *Crome Yellow* is devoted to a discussion of the single word *carminative*; the conversations of *Those Barren Leaves* sparkle with such lexical curios as *geodesic*, *capripede*, *alembicated*, *atrabilious* and *omphaloskepsis*, while the characters' private musings include *anopheles* and *coenobite*, and the narrator throws in *amphisbaena* for good measure. What these characters talk about covers an impressive range: ancient and modern history, the arts (from drama and music to advertising), theology, moral philosophy, natural science (especially physiology), anthropology, psychology (especially sexology), language, travel, politics and sociology. As a newly arrived member of Mrs Aldwinkle's set in *Those Barren Leaves* tells himself after listening to his fellow-guests, 'what a classy conversation!' (Huxley 1994f: 148).

The conversationalists of Huxley's early novels are fully up to date with the latest thinking: with Einsteinian Relativity, with Freud and the Oedipus Complex, with the philosophy of Wittgenstein and the politics of Italian Fascism. They can even talk the talk of Lawrentian trouser-philosophy. The protagonist of *Antic Hay*, Theodore Gumbril

Jr, dreams of making a fortune by patenting a design for comfortably pneumatic trousers. His friend the financier Boldero advises him on how to advertise the benefits of this new commodity:

> '[...] we'll have to talk very scientifically about the great lumbar ganglia – if there are such things, which I really don't pretend to know. We'll even talk almost mystically about the ganglia. You know that sort of ganglia philosophy?' (Huxley 1994b: 113)

Boldero certainly knows enough of it to be able to summarise Lawrence's critique of modern life in terms of the overdevelopment of the thoracic ganglia. The joke here is that such quack physiology is so readily co-opted into the mystifications of sales-talk.

Intellectually sophisticated talk dominates these books, then, but it is not their only medium for ideas. The characters' private speculations are reported too, in various forms including narrative summary, interpolated autobiography (as in Part II of *Those Barren Leaves*, narrated by the cynical poet Francis Chelifer), or notebook entries (the novelist Mary Triplow keeps one in the same novel, as does her fellow-practitioner Philip Quarles in *Point Counter Point*). Ideas are sometimes even aired directly by the narrator too, more often in *Those Barren Leaves* than in the other three novels, although an assertive aphorism on the narrator's part, such as 'man's greatest strength lies in his capacity for irrelevance' (Huxley 1994b: 143), is a rarity. What distinguishes the Huxleian novel of ideas from tendentious fiction, indeed, is a careful reluctance to promote any single 'philosophy'. Huxley prefers to assemble a cast of characters each of whose intellectual perspectives is to be seen as partial, distorted by his or her own obsessions, and to let them argue it all out, the narrative voice remaining impartial. Having said that, we are to some extent guided in our assessment of such debates by the presence of a more thoughtful Huxley-like character (Gumbril Jr in *Antic Hay*, Calamy in *Those Barren Leaves*, Philip Quarles in *Point Counter Point*) who articulates a need for some synthesis within which all the multiple perspectives could be reconciled. All the novels end without such a synthesis having been outlined, let alone attained.

Huxley's early novels are notably self-conscious works, not only in that they present various self-portraits of the excessively intellectualised and emotionally deficient writer – as Huxley saw himself, under the growing influence of his friend D. H. Lawrence – but also in their overt concern for the uses of poetry and fiction in the modern age, if indeed they have any uses left, which several of the characters doubt. The most striking example of this self-consciousness comes in *Point Counter Point* with the adoption, inspired by the French example of André Gide's

Les Faux-Monnayeurs (1925), of the reflexive *mise-en-abyme* device in which a novelist within the novel considers the problems of writing the kind of novel in which he is a character. Here Philip Quarles in his writer's notebook sketches out various ideas for a planned novel, including this observation:

> Novel of ideas. The character of each personage must be implied, as far as possible, in the ideas of which he is the mouthpiece. In so far as theories are rationalizations of sentiments, instincts, dispositions of soul, this is feasible. The chief defect of the novel of ideas is that you must write about people who have ideas to express – which excludes all but about .01 percent of the human race. Hence the real, the congenital novelists don't write such books. (Huxley 1994e: 297)

Two points should be observed about Quarles's jotting here. The first is that the idea that theories are rationalisations of instincts or sentiments is itself one of the most challenging implications of the modern German intellectual tradition that runs from Schopenhauer through Nietzsche to Freud. It puts the supposed autonomy of Reason, philosophy and poetry at the mercy of Will and ultimately of biology, while relativising all values. In Huxley's fiction the consequence is a preoccupation with the vulnerability of Mind both to comical trumping by sexual impulses and to tragic obliteration by physical decay and death. The comedy of Huxley's novels is often sunny and exuberant, but it has its sombre undertones, particularly in the later death-shadowed parts of *Those Barren Leaves* and *Point Counter Point*.

The second notable feature of Quarles's thoughts about the novel of ideas is their modesty in relation to 'real' novelists. Huxley thought of himself as an essayist with no genuine inventive talent for fiction; and here he confesses indirectly through Quarles that his human range is much narrower than in the novel proper. As an objection to these novels – and it has been raised in those terms by hostile critics – this is only a weak case. It is true that his books are peopled almost exclusively by caricatures of an impossibly sophisticated intellectual elite, yet Huxley never mistakes this social bubble for the wider world. When Mrs Aldwinkle in *Those Barren Leaves* declares that her endless chattering about Art is 'the only life', Huxley immediately launches into a global survey of the system of wage-slavery that at that very moment condemns thousands of labourers to drudgery in sustaining the privileged hostess's idle way of life (Huxley 1994f: 56); and her guest the puritanical Labour leader Mr Falx keeps coming back to the same point. In other novels Huxley is careful to provide intruders into the leisured elite, who provide such reminders from outside it: the Marxist-Leninist tailor Bojanus in *Antic Hay* and the left-wing physiologist Illidge in *Point Counter Point*.

Huxley's early novels may present the superficial appearance of being merely coterie fiction. The *roman-à-clef* mode that bases characters upon identifiable celebrity intellectuals of the day tends to 'date' them for readers of a century later, as do many of the contemporary cultural allusions. For all that, they remain lastingly entertaining and provocative. They also give us a unique, although comically distorted, insight into the intellectual preoccupations, moods and fads of the decade. Commentators who compared the atmosphere of these books with that of Eliot's 'The Waste Land' were partly right, in that a characteristic post-War weariness is heard in their characters' various kinds of cynicism, bored hedonism and shared sense of futility. *Antic Hay*, for example, concludes with the image of the physiologist Shearwater exhausting himself on a stationary exercise bicycle, pedalling furiously to nowhere. But what Eliot's poetic lamentation cannot show us is something that Huxley more readily captures about the life of the mind in the Twenties. It appears most clearly in an early conversation in *Those Barren Leaves*:

> 'I don't see that it would be possible to live in a more exciting age,' said Calamy. 'The sense that everything's perfectly provisional and temporary – everything, from social institutions to what we've hitherto regarded as the most sacred scientific truths – the feeling that nothing, from the Treaty of Versailles to the rationally explicable universe, is really safe, the intimate conviction that anything may happen, anything may be discovered – another war, the artificial creation of life, the proof of continued existence after death–why, it's all infinitely exhilarating.'
> 'And the possibility that everything may be destroyed?' questioned Mr Cardan.
> 'That's exhilarating too,' Calamy answered, smiling. (Huxley 1994f: 35)

Huxley helps to remind us that the 'disillusioned' mind of the 1920s was not always overcome with ennui or depression, and that the same profound uncertainties that plunged some into nostalgic gloom spurred others into lively curiosity and positive intellectual excitement.

Chapter Two

Mixing Memory and Desire: Modernism and Anachronism

> In me, past, present, future meet.
> Siegfried Sassoon, *The Heart's Journey* (1928)

We have already noted that the 1920s are to some extent a lost decade in literary history; but it would in one respect be idle to complain of that, given that so many significant writers of the period itself appeared to be throwing the calendar away and opting out of orderly, official linear history in favour of perspectives that seemed to them mythic or otherwise timeless, perspectives according to which ten years here or there might matter little. In part this inclination arose from a generalised disdain for optimistic 'Victorian' conceptions of Progress that stood discredited by the barbarities of the Great War. Chronologies and periods, then, especially if associated with some imaginary onward march of history, now seemed much less important than whatever could be conjured of the permanent or the eternal in art and life. Accordingly we find in Twenties writing various distinctive sophistications and manipulations of temporality, often devoted to stopping the clocks or mingling the past with the present moment. In resolving that it was high time to forget, abandon or suppress Time or its conventionally ordered presentation, the innovative writers we consider here were embarking on a most paradoxical enterprise. The same is true of this chapter, which proposes that such writers were most truly 'of their time' in their imaginative efforts to lead readers out of that time.

The critical claim from which this argument proceeds is that what we please – often misleadingly – to call Modernism in British writing of the 1920s attained its most important achievement not in relatively superficial and intermittent devices such as stream-of-consciousness prose or free verse but in its productive disorderings of the time-sense, especially in narrative fiction but also in non-narrative poetry. The great Modernist discovery, in effect, was the literary potential of anachronism and anachrony, variously exploited. (Anachronism confounds distinct historical times, while the literary device of anachrony recounts events out of their original sequence.) Although it is within the Modernist current that the most important experiments with literary temporality arise, we shall find sympathetic preoccupations and equivalent disorderings of the literary time-sense in works by authors of a more 'traditional' bent.

Woolf: Mrs Dalloway

One powerful exploitation of narrative anachrony will strike any reader who encounters the abrupt opening of Virginia Woolf's novel *Mrs Dalloway* (1925), which introduces us to its title character first by reference to her intentions for the immediate future, but then by means of distant memories seemingly 'triggered' by her present situation.

> Mrs Dalloway said she would buy the flowers herself.
> For Lucy had her work cut out for her. The doors would be taken off their hinges; Rumpelmayer's men were coming. And then, thought Clarissa Dalloway, what a morning – fresh as if issued to children on a beach.
> What a lark! What a plunge! For so it had always seemed to her when, with a little squeak of the hinges, which she could hear now, she had burst open the French windows and plunged at Bourton into the open air. How fresh, how calm, stiller than this of course, the air was in the early morning; like the flap of a wave; the kiss of a wave; chill and sharp and yet (for a girl of eighteen as she then was), solemn, feeling as she did, standing there at the open window, that something awful was about to happen; looking at the flowers, at the trees with the smoke winding off them and the rooks rising, falling; standing and looking until Peter Walsh said, 'Musing among the vegetables?' – was that it? – 'I prefer men to cauliflowers' – was that it? He must have said it at breakfast one morning when she had gone out on the terrace – Peter Walsh. He would be back from India one of these days, June or July, she forgot which, for his letters were awfully dull; it was his sayings one remembered; his eyes, his pocket-knife, his smile, his grumpiness and, when millions of things had utterly vanished – how strange it was! – a few sayings like this about cabbages.
>
> (Woolf 1992b: 3)

This opening captures much of Woolf's purposes both for this novel and for her experimental fiction of the 1920s more generally. It is resolutely psychological in emphasis, inviting the reader very quickly to set aside the practical activity of the fictive present moment (preparations for a party, it turns out – hence the flowers and door-removal) and to focus instead upon the mental processes of the protagonist. Although Clarissa

Dalloway is seen here clearly to be responding in part to her immediate circumstances – it is a sunny June morning and her mood is elated – the most striking feature of her thoughts is their orientation to incidents, apparently inconsequential, of the quite remote personal past. We learn soon after this opening passage that Clarissa is now in her early fifties and living in Westminster as the wife of a politician, but she is recalling moments of her life when she was eighteen years old in her original family home, Bourton.

The motivating link between the 'now' and the 'then' of Woolf's opening to *Mrs Dalloway* appears at first to be a symbolic connection between the opening of doors today and the opening of French windows some thirty years before, conflated in Clarissa's mind: 'a little squeak of the hinges, which she could hear now'. But other cues for reminiscence emerge too: she has been receiving letters from Peter Walsh about his imminent return, which understandably brings him to mind, stirring up memories of a conversation with him long ago. As the novel unfolds over the course of a single day in Clarissa's life, we come across further reasons for her to be dwelling upon her past: Peter actually shows up on the same day, throwing her mind back to the reasons why she did not marry him but her present husband Richard Dalloway MP; and then we encounter Clarissa's 17-year-old daughter Elizabeth, who serves as a living reminder of the protagonist's younger self.

In this analysis so far, though, we are at risk of treating the past and the present as clearly separable realms, which is exactly what Woolf does not want us to do here. *Mrs Dalloway* repeatedly insists otherwise, both thematically and in its prose style too. For Woolf, there is in real human consciousness no purely present moment that could be disentangled from past or future, every apparently immediate impression being mediated through memory or desire, recollection or expectation, just as every summoning of a past moment or projection of a future state is in turn coloured by the mood of the present. This interpenetration of supposedly separate temporal realms is central to Woolf's fictional project. Its philosophical and literary backgrounds lie first in the work of the French philosopher Henri Bergson (1859–1941), who had questioned the misleading divisions of conventional 'clock' time and called attention to the much more fluid real experience we have of living in time; and secondly in the work of the major French novelist Marcel Proust (1871–1922), himself an ardent Bergsonian, whose novel-sequence *A la recherche du temps perdu* (1913–27) meditates at length upon the vagaries and perversities of human memory and desire, and offers a model of 'involuntary memory' by which a trivial incident may open up vistas of a character's earlier life.

The signature of these principles and influences is felt in the syntax and the grammatical tense-shifts of Woolf's prose. Although Woolf rarely attempts to emulate the famously intricate mazes of Proust's syntax, in which multiple subordinate clauses can 'fold' past and future times into the same sentence, she produces some similar effects of time-warping in her own writing. So in this opening passage of *Mrs Dalloway* she interrupts a sentence cast in the pluperfect ('For so it had always seemed . . .') with a clause in the simple past, calculated to slip us back into the fictional present ('which she could hear now'), before setting the next long sentence in the simple past, which then becomes complicated by projections of a future ('feeling . . . that something awful was about to happen'). Woolf's favourite stylistic device of self-interruption is the qualifying clause beginning with a present participle, often employed to emphasise the simultaneity of thought and action: 'feeling as she did, standing there at the open window, that something . . .' ; or again on the following page, 'Such fools we are, she thought, crossing Victoria Street'. In fact in the opening passage the piling on of successive present participles gives us the effect, within a remembered episode of the remote past, of a continuously 'present' and thus incomplete impression:

> . . . feeling as she did, standing there at the open window, that something awful was about to happen; looking at the flowers, at the trees with the smoke winding off them and the rooks rising, falling; standing and looking until Peter Walsh said, 'Musing among the vegetables?'

The texture, then, of Woolf's prose testifies to an insistence upon the permeability of past with present, and of action with reflection. Its textual presentation too, echoes that ambition, in that the novel is, unusually, not segmented by chapter divisions.

In structure and theme, too, *Mrs Dalloway* is a time-preoccupied novel. Originally entitled *The Hours*, its action is punctuated by the striking of the hours by Big Ben, while Clarissa's thoughts are often coloured by awareness of her post-menopausal 'time of life' in contrast with her daughter's late adolescent bloom. As in Proust, the fallibilities, hesitancies and curious selectivities of human memory ('was it that?' 'June or July, she forgot which') figure prominently too. The temporal scheme of the narrative's design is unusual if certainly not original, deriving as it does from James Joyce's *Ulysses* (1922): as in Joyce's epic, the action is confined to the events of a single June day in a modern city as observed by two principal characters and by a host of passers-by, while the thoughts – memories, observations, daydreams, hopes, fears, fantasies – of the principal and even minor characters are certainly not restricted by 'the hours' of that day, but roam freely beyond it.

The adoption of the diurnal time-limit to the action, resembling one of the 'unities' of classical and neoclassical drama, amounts in one sense to a repudiation of the major tradition of the novel of preceding centuries, in which typically the 'Life and Adventures' of a heroine or hero would be traced over several years of action. By strong contrary implication, the 'Day in the Life of' temporal scheme proclaims the redundancy of the old novel of adventure (duels, quests, elopements and all the rest) in the name of the new novel of psychology. It shows that there is potentially more to be found in the mental life of one unadventurous or even average character within a few hours than in a lifetime of heroic 'exploits' in the traditional manner. Such a claim, though, can be upheld only insofar as the examined mental life transcends the time-limited sphere of practical action, so that the represented day turns out to expand into recollected pasts and imagined futures that far exceed the immediate registration of action and impression. In this way the diurnal frame serves not as a restriction so much as an 'occasion': the exaggerated confinement of time in the action, familiar in drama but not in the novel, calls forth a compensating expansion of time in the psychological realm, in the forms of memory and aspiration.

Another way of putting this would be that the artifice of the time-limited action in *Mrs Dalloway* as in *Ulysses* obliges Woolf and Joyce to provide their characters with past lives – and to some extent future destinies – in a way that dramatises their activity of recollection within the fictional 'present' time of active memory, desire and impression. So what we know of these characters' pasts is what they are now selectively recalling in response to unexpected cues, not what some omniscient narrator has summarised for us by way of prelude, nor what a traditional kind of first-person narrator has arranged in linear order as an autobiographical account. The narrative principles involved here are not in themselves especially modern, but draw, like the unities of time and place, upon an ancient precedent: the opening of the classical epic (of which *Ulysses* is an extended travesty) in the middle of the action (*in medias res*), to be followed by a retrospective account of earlier events. *Mrs Dalloway*, then, can open in such an abrupt fashion because the knowledge needed by the reader about Clarissa's history and circumstances will be provided piecemeal as we follow her actions and conversations, both by the narrator's interjections and by the protagonist's own reported trains of reminiscence.

Woolf's deliberately experimental quest in the 1920s for a new kind of fiction is most often understood through the critical mediation of her polemical essays 'Modern Fiction' (1919; revd 1925) and 'Mr Bennett and Mrs Brown' (1923; revd 1925), both of which deplore the 'materialist' descriptive conventions employed by such senior 'Edwardian' novelists as Arnold Bennett and H. G. Wells. These often-quoted essays have had the effect of distorting our view of Modernist fiction and its purposes, in that they encourage us to think of Modernist fiction as primarily a reaction against Victorian and Edwardian realism. This view is mistaken on two counts: first, Woolf and her Modernist contemporaries were not rejecting realism but re-animating its commitment to everyday life while redefining it in more psychological terms; and second, her impatience with older narrative conventions went much further than a reaction against an older generation and its practice: she was questioning centuries-old ingredients of storytelling, not just the relatively recent ones. When Woolf asks, after reading yet another conventionally constructed novel, 'Is life like this? Must novels be like this?' (Woolf 1994: 160), she invokes a central realist principle of lifelikeness, which such novels fail to meet. Her experimental but still broadly realist ambition was to produce novels that felt more like life being lived, the fluidity and evanescence of its experiences artistically captured on the page. What she thought she could dispense with for such a fiction was not realism at all; it was plotting. Imagining a writer liberating himself from the expected routines of novel-writing, Woolf predicted that 'if he could base his work upon his own feeling and not upon convention, there would be no plot, no comedy, no tragedy, no love interest or catastrophe in the accepted style' (Woolf 1994: 160). No element on that list is in the least peculiar to Arnold Bennett or to the tradition of nineteenth-century realist fiction he inherited. Woolf in fact imagines here a discarding of much older elements of storytelling, stretching all the way back to epic, romance and folktale.

Like her other extended narrative fictions of the 1920s, the anti-novel *Jacob's Room* (1922), the unorthodox family novel *To the Lighthouse* (1927) and the mock-historical romance *Orlando* (1928), *Mrs Dalloway* is deliberately plotless. Its action does include one sensational event – a suicide – and two socially significant incidents – the return of Peter Walsh and the arrival of the prime minister at Clarissa's party – but otherwise consists of unremarkable social encounters, observations of street life, domestic routine and a great deal of private rumination. It is this private rumination or self-communion of the characters, including several minor players chosen as if at random from the streets of Westminster and then forgotten, that dominates the book. Instead of a plot in the old manner, involving such stock devices as babies exchanged at birth, long-lost heirs to family fortunes, or intercepted love-letters, we encounter a medley of seemingly inconsequential thoughts passing through the minds of major or minor characters; these characters being connected to one another not through plotted intrigue but simply by virtue of being in roughly the same place at the same time. Some of the leading characters in *Mrs Dalloway* are indeed linked by familial prehistories or long-standing friendships, but most of the minor figures earn their place in the narrative solely upon the basis of *simultaneity*: that is to say, they happen to be in the same street or park at the same time as a character whose thoughts we have just been overhearing. A remarkable set-piece exercise early in the novel introduces us fleetingly to a succession of characters, at first in Regent's Park, then further east in the City and in Greenwich, who are all looking up at the same aeroplane engaged in a sky-writing stunt. Nothing else links these people apart from this coincidental 'moment' of observation, which cannot truly be called shared or communal, as it is shown to be an aggregation of private glimpses.

Strong causal links between one event and the next being absent or withheld in this narrative, we are left to make sense of the novel's elements according to more tenuous association by proximity, simultaneity, or thematic echo. As the title implies, Clarissa Dalloway is the central character in the story, but she is shadowed by an important secondary figure, a 30-year-old ex-soldier named Septimus Warren Smith, who is suffering from hallucinations attributable to shell-shock following his War service. Septimus and Clarissa never meet in *Mrs Dalloway*, as they surely would in an orthodox double-plotted novel. The sole connection between them is another coincidence: the eminent psychiatrist Sir William Bradshaw has been assessing the condition of the shell-shocked Septimus, and he later shows up as a guest at Clarissa's party, apologising for his late arrival caused by Septimus's suicide. Momentarily, then, the death of the secondary character casts its shadow over the festivities of the principal, but that is all that connects them in causal terms.

To construct a novel as the 'Day in the Life' of two different characters who never meet is to invite – such is our readerly demand for cohesion – some way of comprehending them together, whether as ego and alter-ego or as a contrasting pair. Interpreters of *Mrs Dalloway* have strained variously to establish either some reliable thematic opposition (female/male, older/younger, sane/mad, manic/depressive) to hold them as a pairing or on the other hand some identity that the two share (victimised outsider to the always-monolithic Patriarchy, for instance). Many such interpretative frames are possible, none fully convincing. In the context of Modernist temporality within which we are considering the novel here, it is worth observing how differently Clarissa and Septimus experience the relation between past and present. For the delusional traumatised Septimus, the past appears vividly 'present' in the figure of his beloved comrade Evans, killed in the war but resurrected in hallucination. Clarissa habitually interrupts her impressions of the present day with memories of past experiences, but she is able to hold these memories at a slight interrogative distance ('was that it?'), to interweave them through the present moment rather than collapse them entirely into it. For Septimus the past is either obliterated (he imagines that he has committed a terrible crime, but cannot remember what it was) or terrifyingly immediate, as with his sightings of the dead Evans. The advantages of mature sanity enjoyed by Clarissa, for whom the past is neither all lost nor altogether overwhelming, are those of her generation: unlike Septimus, who would have been twenty-one years old at the War's outbreak, Clarissa has a pre-War adulthood and married life to reflect upon, in most respects continuous with her post-War life. As we shall see in the next chapter, the war veteran in the Twenties is especially prone to the radically discontinuous Before/After conception of the relation of past to present, although non-combatant writers were able to 'borrow' that model too, as Woolf herself was to do in *To the Lighthouse*.

Ford: *Some Do Not . . .*

While Woolf pitches the reader straight into the anachronic mazes of her protagonist's blended impressions and memories, another outstanding Modernist novel published in the previous year leads us more gently into an even more complex narrative labyrinth. This is *Some Do Not . . .* (1924), the first and longest novel in Ford Madox Ford's great 'Tietjens' tetralogy that came eventually to be reprinted as *Parade's End* (1950). The chronological design of this novel comprises two parts, the first set near the town of Rye over the course of a long weekend – which proves to be a momentous one for several leading characters – in June 1912. The second part is set in London over a few hours – from lunchtime until 3.30am that night – of a similarly significant day in August 1917. Yet these temporal restrictions are overcome and indeed overwhelmed by an anachronic narrative that, still more persistently than Woolf or Joyce, constantly retrieves rich prehistories, often ironically pointed, for each of these moments and each of the characters involved in them. Ford's story not only traces thematic and verbal echoes between the 1912 weekend and the 1917 day, thus linking and contrasting the pre-War and wartime phases; it also delves back into family histories, then again into tellingly selected episodes of the five-year gap between the two parts. Several characters in Part II, for example, remember certain events that took place on the eve – 3 August 1914 – of the War's outbreak, each from a partial perspective but within a chapter that allows us to connect these jigsaw pieces into a fuller picture.

The story begins with the description of two middle-class British men seated in a railway carriage heading from London to the Kentish coast at the start of what turns out to be a golfing weekend. It comes to us in the third person, but increasingly adopts the viewpoint first of the protagonist, Christopher Tietjens, a talented young government statistician, and then of his Scottish friend and colleague Vincent Macmaster. The opening pages pursue a number of brief backward loops into their remote and more recent connections as schoolfellows and room-mates; then we are led back four months to the time at which Tietjens's wife Sylvia had eloped with a lover; then to an earlier point of 'today's' events, at which a letter from her had arrived requesting a resumption of the marriage. Before the train journey concludes, we have time for the two characters to discuss the prospects of a European war: Macmaster regards it as impossible, Tietjens declares it inevitable. By the end of the first chapter, we know, because we are in the realist fictional tradition, where we are geographically (Ryeward bound), socially (among the English governing elite) and historically (June 1912). We have also learned, thanks to the retrospective leaps by which their prehistory has been filled in, a good deal about these contrasting characters and their positions: not only that Tietjens is in the classically comic position of the cuckold but also that Macmaster is among the few who know of this private torment and has helped to cover it up for the sake of his friend's reputation. Macmaster himself is in the equally comical position of considering the acquisition of a wife to adorn his nascent literary career, his daydreams of which weave the future into this temporal fabric. We have also learned by this point that the story will proceed by shifts of viewpoint and by shifts in time.

Primed in this way, we are prepared for the second chapter to take us to a German spa where Sylvia exposes her unscrupulous nature (she lured Tietjens into marriage while pregnant by another man) to her own scandalised mother and to a priest of her Catholic faith. The third and fourth chapters form a sequence that we are also by now trained to follow without too much bewilderment, as the story here takes the form of a 'review' of the next day's events in the Macmaster–Tietjens golfing trip, starting at the end of the day as Tietjens stays up late, then recounting the odd adventures of that day first from Macmaster's limited viewpoint and then more fully from Tietjens's own. As we follow the narrative further, we find each chapter thereafter to be shaped by the same recursive pattern, typically opening with a character in a moment of revealing pressure or clarification, then reaching back into the relevant memories that illuminate this moment's significance before returning – often after folding in further recollections in the minds of other characters – to the dramatic present.

As we proceed, Ford's prose style becomes ever more experimental in its more frequent passages of interior monologue, at times presented in that disjointed notation of fragmentary thoughts known as the 'stream-of-consciousness' technique, which comes riddled with ellipses (the unusual ellipsis in the book's title serves as fair warning of that). The intricacies of time-shifting become more pronounced too, so that we are not surprised to overhear one side of a telephone conversation, then to hear it again from the other end, synchronised within another character's recall over 100 pages later. By that point, however, we are convinced that such devices are not introduced as disorientation for disorientation's sake, but always in the interest of character and its dramatic unfolding in plot. Ford shows a stronger interest in character, especially character in its contexts of social history, than Woolf's aesthetic permitted, and a far craftier dedication to the resources of plot, even in its sense of intrigue and conspiracy. The hero of this novel, it turns out, is an endlessly enigmatic and contradictory character, and one who is much plotted against.

In its persistent narrative recursion, *Some Do Not . . .* can fairly be described as a backward-looking novel, albeit very 'advanced' in its technical accomplishment. Indeed it is a historical novel set in the recent past. Fittingly, its protagonist is a backward-looking man who feels that he does not belong to his own times ('what I stand for isn't any more in this world', he remarks (Ford 2010: 289)), and so he serves Ford's historically critical purposes by scrutinising those times from a self-consciously outmoded set of values. Christopher Tietjens, a younger son of the Yorkshire landed gentry, is a Tory of the old school – in fact the eighteenth-century school, a believer in order, tradition, continuity, service and monogamy, who reveres French civilisation of the *dix-huitième* and vainly hopes that the coming war will be fought 'for the eighteenth century against the twentieth' (Ford 2010: 287). As a government official, he serves Liberal masters whom he regards as unprincipled to the point of corruption. Although brilliant and talented in a scarcely believable range of fields from statistics to horsemanship, he is devoid of any personal ambition, his calm integrity serving to highlight the nepotism, double-dealing and careerism that surround him. Tietjens's character is developed through an extensive pattern of contrasts with those around him: with the cynical selfishness of his wife Sylvia, with the obsequious careerism and literary pretensions of his friend Macmaster, with the radicalism of Valentine Wannop, a suffragette activist and pacifist who to her own surprise falls in love with him. The larger pattern of the novel sets the impending fall of the brilliant Tietjens off against the rise of the mediocre sycophant Macmaster, although our interest is increasingly directed towards the love–hate triangle emerging from the rival claims of the scheming wife Sylvia and the virginal would-be mistress Valentine.

Ford puts before us an impossible hero, a man so overladen with admirable qualities and so beset by enemies and doubters that we are perversely challenged not to believe in him. He sometimes appears, especially when chastely paired with the miraculous maiden scholar-athlete Valentine, to be a figure of Romance, too perfect to be accommodated within the novel's emphatically realist frame. One of his unbelievable qualities that carries a special significance is that he has – at least until he suffers shell-shock while serving on the Western Front – an encyclopaedic memory, a precise recall of obscure facts and figures that makes him invaluable to his political masters; it also justifies the memory-driven narrative method of the novel and consolidates his position as a backward-looking man. *Some Do Not . . .* and its sequels in the *Parade's End* sequence are often admired for their ultra-modern narrative methods and techniques, and yet the most startling of this book's challenges is its most antiquated: an old-fashioned virtuous hero whose very presence shames the social and political world he grudgingly inhabits. In a novel marked by matchlessly sophisticated anachronic narration, Ford provides a provocative further twist to our time-sense by providing us with a hero who is a living anachronism.

'The Waste Land': Eliot's Exhumations of the Dead

Having considered two important cases of anachrony in fiction, we may turn now to anachronism, the imaginative power of which is exploited as never before in the decade's most important single poem, T. S. Eliot's 'The Waste Land' (1922). Whereas *Mrs Dalloway* and *Some Do Not . . .* give us experiments with time-consciousness and memory within the otherwise secure frame of third-person narrative, albeit interspersed with passages of interior monologue, 'The Waste Land' is a much more disorienting work, both because it does not offer us a single or continuous narrative or lyric voice and because we often do not know from what time the multiple voices of the poem emerge, nor to what times they refer. With Woolf we can at least assume that Clarissa Dalloway is thinking, in June 1923, of some experience she had back in about 1890, as with Ford we will know one of his characters in 1917 is recalling what happened in 1912. With Eliot in this essentially dramatic poem we often do not know who is speaking any given line at all, or whether we are at some points meant to be in the sixteenth century or the twentieth.

This chapter's title is taken from the poem's famous opening lines, and it helps in reminding us why April is the cruellest month: because it belongs emotionally to two times at once, the past of memory – most probably in this context unwelcome memory – and the future of desire, here inverted as anxious apprehension. The present springtime that breeds lilacs out of a 'dead land' appears as a phase of painfully ambiguous awareness by comparison with the comforting forgetfulness of winter. At this point we appear to be within the realm of anachrony and its psychological equivocations, but what is to come turns out to be a more unnerving exercise in anachronism. The opening seven lines have the appearance of being spoken from under the ground by a chorus of the dead, or more specifically the unwillingly reanimated dead. The poem's opening part (lines 1–76) is entitled 'The Burial of the Dead', but its focus is instead disturbingly upon the return of the dead, perhaps even as exhumation. As 'The Waste Land' unfolds over its five sections, this vernal motif of resurrected life recurs insistently. Indeed resurrection thematically and recurrence formally work all the while to reinforce one another, especially in their literary forms of quotation and pastiche.

Before we explore the power of Eliot's anachronism further, two points about the opening of 'The Waste Land' and its unorthodoxies are worth bearing in mind at this stage. First, Eliot was not yet at the time of the poem's appearance the Christian poet that he became a few years later, so the theme of resurrection carries a full undogmatic range of meanings, some of them more macabre than spiritually affirmative. Second, although a poem responding to springtime with uneasy dread rather than joy does stand outside customary expectations, it is still fully within the poetic tradition, and not at all a subversive revolt against it. The lyric speaker whose grief or lovesickness excludes him from participation in the vernal joy of all other creatures is a familiar topos in medieval poetry and in that of later times too. Indeed, only a month before the first appearance of Eliot's poem, A. E. Housman had provided a fresh variant upon just this tradition in his 'Spring Morning' (Housman 1989: 114). Eliot did not invent the poetry of April gloom; he rediscovered it as a prior tradition and reanimated it.

Taking those observations into account, we can attempt another look at the peculiarly charged anachronistic devices of 'The Burial of the Dead'. Despite the bewildering shifts among identified and unidentified speakers in this part of the poem – Marie the German aristocrat, a desert prophet, a Wagnerian sailor, the hyacinth girl, Madame Sosostris, a

London commuter and more – we can discern, to paraphrase an earlier poem of Eliot's, an insidious intent to lead us to an overwhelming question; a question that takes more than one form. At lines 19–20 we hear a new voice in semi-Biblical idiom, asking

> What are the roots that clutch, what branches grow
> Out of this stony rubbish?
>
> (Eliot 2001: 5)

Setting aside the problem of our not knowing what place or what era we and the unknown speaker occupy at this point, the nature of the question at least is clear enough, asking what kind of growth can be expected to emerge from the nearly barren terrain indicated.

A little later, the question takes a new twist in the startlingly anachronistic closing passage of 'The Burial of the Dead' (lines 60–76), from the line 'Unreal city'. Here we meet a crowd of commuters walking across the Thames at London Bridge into the financial centre ('the City') where Eliot himself worked as an employee of Lloyd's bank. Lines quoted from Dante's description of Limbo then invite us to regard the commuters no longer as time-bound citizens of modern London but as eternal types of the Lost or Unredeemed. As the 'dead sound' of the church bell tolling nine o'clock indicates that modern office-work is a form of living death, we focus upon an encounter between two individuals within that crowd: an anonymous speaker and a man named Stetson whom he accosts as a former companion he recalls from 'the ships at Mylae':

> 'That corpse you planted last year in your garden,
> Has it begun to sprout? Will it bloom this year? [. . .]'
>
> (Eliot 2001: 7)

Here the overwhelming question takes unnerving and menacing shape as an interrogation of the post-War world. First, though, it must be anachronised: the Mylae alluded to is the ancient Sicilian town in whose bay the navies of Rome and Carthage clashed in 260 BCE. Stetson and his questioner, however, are plainly in London at a time when Mylae had disappeared from the maps, having long since been renamed Milazzo. The modern encounter would have been of a very familiar kind in 1922: two men in an urban crowd recognise each other as demobilised former comrades last seen perhaps in Flanders or even in a naval battle. Yet the speaker's recollection of ancient Mylae universalises the occasion, suggesting that all such post-war encounters throughout history are in a sense versions of the same archetypal event. The *Odyssey* of Homer, after all, is a story of post-war disorientation in which Odysseus meets his former comrade Achilles in the underworld; and Eliot had lately been reading instalments of Joyce's *Ulysses*, an extended anachronistic travesty of that story, its events and characters transposed into a modern urban setting. The phrase 'bloom this year' may even be taken as an acknowledgement of *Ulysses*, by a pun on its anti-hero's name (Mr Leopold Bloom) and allusion to its recent publication in book form (1922).

Eliot goes further, though, in strangely transforming that commonplace experience of lately demobilised servicemen. In his sinister interrogation of Stetson, the unnamed speaker not only assumes unlikely recent knowledge of Stetson's domestic habits but also springs upon him what sounds like an accusation of foul play. Of course at this point the realistic presentation of a street encounter has given way to an entirely different literary mode, that of ominous symbolism: the corpse of last year inevitably calls to mind the dead of the Great War, as the putative sprouting represents the emergence of a post-War life rooted in death. Paraphrased from this and other versions in the poem, the overwhelming question repeatedly posed by 'The Waste Land' amounts to asking whether life after the Great War can be other than a kind of living death, a ghastly resurrection of corpses – as with the commuters whose trudging resembles that of Dante's lost souls in Limbo – rather than a genuinely new vernal growth or rebirth. For some readers, especially the poem's numerous Christian commentators, 'The Waste Land' returns a conclusively damning answer in its representations of infertile sexual encounters, and so flatly condemns modern life as a spiritual desert awaiting the rains of baptismal grace. For others, a more riddling or sybilline 'answer' is offered in the great paradox of the poem's language and style, in which by direct quotation, misquotation, artful parody and ventriloquism the dead poets of the past – Dante, Shakespeare, Marvell, Goldsmith, Baudelaire and others – are reanimated and 'assert their immortality' through the living poet whose raiding of tradition is just what makes him most modern. (Eliot 1975: 38) This is the provocatively anachronistic paradox previously announced in Eliot's critical essay 'Tradition and the Individual Talent' (1919), in which he had claimed that 'the historical sense involves a perception, not only of the pastness of the past, but of its presence' (Eliot 1975: 38).

It has sometimes been suggested in this context that 'The Waste Land' is in its highly original fashion a kind of elegy for the War dead. There is in the very broadest terms a plausibility to this claim, although it would be safer to say that the poem offers itself more warily as an inadequate substitute for an elegiac performance, the full consolations of that traditional lyric genre being unavailable in modern conditions. Some of Eliot's adapted quotations come from Jacobean examples (Shakespeare,

Webster) of the simpler kind of mourning poem known as the dirge. There are certainly some important features of the poem, however, that echo the pastoral elegiac conventions descending from ancient Greek practice and resumed in John Milton's 'Lycidas' (1638) – a poem concerning death by water. Prominent here are the themes of resurrection and vegetation, which commentators too often see as derived directly from the anthropological works of James Frazer and Jessie L. Weston. Knowledge of Frazer's work on fertility cults and vegetation rites involving gods drowned only to be reborn, and of Weston's reading of the Grail legends in those terms, certainly strengthens our grasp upon the poem, but may also distract us from its purely poetic antecedents. In pastoral elegy, plant life (such as flowers plucked to adorn a hearse) and the cycle of death and rebirth it suggests is a conventional fixture, and so are addresses to rivers, images of nature blighted by loss, lamentations upon the corrupted times, references to departed nymphs, sudden changes in tone and interruptions by differing voices. All these features are reworked in 'The Waste Land', although in sometimes travestied forms. On the other hand, the ceremonially calming cathartic qualities of elegy are distinctly lacking, the mournful mood being left unresolved.

If 'The Waste Land' is any kind of elegy, it is a contorted one in which some elements of elegiac tradition, including the figure of the elegised, go understated while others loom much larger: here a special prominence is granted both to the lamentation of contemporary corruptions and the 'pathetic fallacy' by which the natural world withers in sympathy with human griefs. In this latter connection, the memorably parched and arid landscapes invoked in the poem have indicated to most readers a clear metaphorical projection of some psychological or spiritual desiccation that is the poem's underlying referent. It does not contradict that equation to bring in here an unusual consideration of the poem's immediate historical context. As readers in 1922 would have recalled, but we are now less likely to know, the year 1921, during which much of the poem was composed and assembled, was one of severe and prolonged drought in England, by some measures the worst since records had begun in the eighteenth century, culminating in a record-breaking heatwave in early October. Eliot's recuperative holiday at Margate followed on immediately both from his nervous breakdown and from that heatwave; after that he wrote more of the poem at a clinic in Switzerland, which had also been affected by severe drought. Stumbling across cracked earth and longing for water were not merely symbolic representations of some inner state; they had recently been the notably extreme shared conditions of English and Swiss life. By an inspired poetic opportunism, then, Eliot charges the unseasonal discomfort of the preceding year with the ancient resonances of curse and blight derived from the myths of Oedipus and of the impotent Fisher King, and from legends of the early Church's desert hermits. In such a way past and present, the ancient and modern worlds are both freshly illumined and reinterpreted one by the other, and so anachronism performs the miracle of transmutation ('Those are pearls that were his eyes': Eliot's favourite Shakespearian image of transmutation is itself transmuted in turn by its new context) that for Eliot is the true power of art.

In his occasionally facetious explanatory 'Notes' attached to 'The Waste Land' in the bound editions following the poem's first magazine appearances, Eliot gives us some intriguing clues to his method of poetic transmutation, especially in relation to his amalgamations of human figures. He suggests that such figures as the one-eyed merchant, the Phoenician sailor and Shakespeare's Ferdinand of Naples should be understood as melting into one another, while 'all the women are one woman, and the two sexes meet in Tiresias' (Eliot 2001: 23). One of the many significances of Tiresias, the man-woman and blind seer whom we encounter in the poem's third part, is that his contradictory doubleness embodies that principle by which so many of the poem's figures become versions of one another – and of other figures from myth and literature – throughout 'The Waste Land'. Thus in 'The Burial of the Dead' the commuters and the lost souls of Dante become one; the hyacinth girl is a version of Hyacinth in Greek myth, a beautiful boy killed but reborn in the form of a flower; Madame Sosostris the clairvoyante who cannot see clearly appears as a comic version of the tragic seer Tiresias; and the drowned Phoenician sailor, who reappears in the fourth part too, is not wholly indistinct from other drowned characters we meet later, including Shakespeare's Ophelia. So later in the poem the sexually exploited typist of the third part is a modern version of the mythical Philomel (violated in life but inviolate in voice, once transmuted to a nightingale), who has further counterparts in the lamenting Thames-daughters, who are in turn versions of Wagner's Rhine-daughters.

The dream-like blending – known to Freudian dream-analysts as 'condensation' – of characters is echoed still more potently in this context of anachronism by the similar blending together of cities and of the historical phases of civilisation that they represent. Modern London is of course the primary 'setting' of the poem, but it refuses to be set. Rather it dissolves at several points into the London of Elizabethan times, while also being offered as a version of Thebes, the accursed city of Oedipus where Tiresias has 'foresuffered all' that he witnesses in the English metropolis. Elsewhere London seems to recapitulate Carthage, the ancient city of Phoenician mercantile power thrice destroyed by

Rome but reborn as a centre of fleshly temptations in the time of St Augustine. Just as Rome can be called 'the Eternal City' and its old enemy Carthage can emerge perpetually from its own ashes, so in this poem London is still London, but at the same time it is all other great cities before it, the last in a series of 'fallen' civilisations named in the poem's final part: Jerusalem, Athens, Alexandria, Vienna, London. The reappearance of the Theban prophet Tiresias as a witness to the conditions of modern London invites us not only to recognise London as a repetition of Thebes, but also to see Eliot's vision of modern life as a resumption of Tiresias's prophetic role. Prophecy is to be understood here not as a matter of fortune-telling as with the commercial mumbo-jumbo of Madame Sosostris, but as an imaginative ability to read the signs of the times through the lens provided by other times. In this sense Modernist anachronism at its most ambitious becomes prophetic.

Yeats and the Artifice of Eternity

The literary method that we are calling anachronistic was one for which Eliot himself had another name. In '*Ulysses*, Order and Myth', an essay of 1923 written in defence of Joyce's novel and its reworking of Homeric material, he calls it the 'mythical method', and recommends it as an alternative to customary narrative methods because it provides a way of 'making the modern world possible for art' – that modern world in untransmuted form being merely an 'immense panorama of futility and anarchy'. 'In using the myth,' Eliot wrote, 'in manipulating a continuous parallel between contemporaneity and antiquity, Mr Joyce is pursuing a method which others must pursue after him' (Eliot 1975: 177–8). More is involved in these observations than just a recommendation for the adoption of new literary techniques. Eliot's unusual imperative phrasing (others *must* pursue Joyce's method) seems to be motivated by the alarming turbulence of recent European and world history in a new age of wars, revolutions, pandemics, collapsing economies and crumbling empires: the turmoil that provides the occasion for the great 'prophetic' poems of the early 1920s, 'The Waste Land' itself and W. B. Yeats's 'The Second Coming' (1920). Eliot's point is that in a period when – in Yeats's phrase – things fall apart, the artist requires all the more urgently some means by which the world-anarchy may be brought under imaginative control and comprehension. The times themselves, then, called for literary reinterpretation in the light of the timelessness of myth.

In an aside from the passage quoted above, Eliot observes that the first modern writer to foresee this requirement for mythic illumination had been Yeats himself. Here Eliot may have had in mind Yeats's larger and long-established project of reviving Celtic myths in commenting upon contemporary Ireland; or possibly he was thinking of specific poems such as the recent 'The Second Coming' or the older 'No Second Troy' (1910), in which the living Irishwoman Maud Gonne – although unnamed in the poem – is with overt anachronism identified with Helen of Troy. Whatever the particular occasion for the remark, it was in important ways to be both confirmed and superseded in the 1920s, as the astonishing renewal of Yeats's poetic powers proved him to be not only a forerunner of the mythical method but in continuing creative practice its boldest modern practitioner.

Some of Yeats's greatest poems of this decade illustrate the imaginative force both of anachrony (that is, the 'flashback' of individual memory) and of historical anachronism proper, giving eloquent voice to that great hunger for the eternal that in this period noticeably marks some uses of anachronistic methods. To take one outstanding example, the sonnet 'Leda and the Swan' (1924) is an unusual case of 'silent' anachronism in that no mention of a historical present time appears there: the poem seems to confine its attention to a mythological event often represented in visual art: the rape of Leda by Zeus in the form of a swan. Its octave describes the violation itself, in disturbingly vivid terms; then the sestet brings us to its legendary consequences, from the births of Leda's daughters Helen and Clytemnestra to the Trojan war and the subsequent murder of its victor Agamemnon. The extraordinary feat of the poem is to foreshorten that epic sequence into two and a half lines that elide sexual and world-historic convulsions:

> A shudder in the loins engenders there
> The broken wall, the burning roof and tower
> And Agamemnon dead.
>
> (Yeats 1990: 260)

The sonnet closes by asking whether Leda was granted an annunciation of sorts, that is, a forewarning of the eventual results of her rape. All of this looks like an enquiry solely into the meaning of an ancient Greek tale, but there can be no doubt from its composition and publication in the early Twenties and from Yeats's reported remarks at the time (see Foster 2003: 243) that the true but unspoken subject of the poem is the catastrophic course of recent history in Yeats's and his readers' own time, from the Great War and Russian Revolution to the massacres in Armenia and the Irish Civil War. By adopting the mythical method, Yeats gives a shape and a significance to those events – are they, the sonnet expects us too to ask, afflictions visited upon humanity by brutally indifferent powers? – without even needing to name them.

The great Yeatsian exercise in anachrony is 'Among School Children' (1928), in which we follow the thoughts of a 60-year-old man, clearly Yeats as a senator visiting a girls' school as part of his public duties, as he recalls the again unnamed (and again mythically Greek, as a 'Ledaean body') Maud Gonne's tales of her own schooldays, wondering whether she had looked like the girls presently before him. In a startling momentary vision that suddenly abolishes those distinctions between past and present, she 'stands before me as a living child' (Yeats 1990: 262). His thoughts shuttle back to what is now the mature age of Maud and himself, then to the way in which every mother imagines a future for her child only to be mocked by it. These slippages that erase boundaries between one time and another prepare us for the great rhetorical conclusion of the poem, in which other fundamental distinctions – between spirit and matter, life and art – are dissolved into a sublime indifference.

When the speaker of 'Among School Children' summons to the classroom the vision of Maud Gonne as a young girl, Yeats is engaging in powerfully original artistic work; but the device of anachrony by which a remembered image or scene flashes before a lyric speaker is not in itself a revolutionary modern invention. It had been adumbrated in, to take only one famous example, William Wordsworth's poem known usually as 'Tintern Abbey' (properly, 'Lines Composed a Few Miles above Tintern Abbey, on Revisiting the Banks of the Wye during a Tour. July 13, 1798'). In that poem, Wordsworth had devised a double image of a particular scene, the one retained from memories of a visit to the same site five years earlier, and the other witnessed in the poem's present moment as the 'picture of the mind revives again' (Wordsworth 1984: 61). By superimposing the one image upon the other, the speaker is able to measure his own imaginative growth in the intervening period. Yeats's use of a similar device has its own unique features – it is certainly more dramatic and abrupt than Wordsworth's recollection in tranquillity – but is still a revisiting of traditional methods, here of Romantic self-communion. Our interest in the anachronic literary principle in the 1920s, then, is not a matter of claiming unprecedented technical breakthroughs but of understanding the specific compulsions that in this period return anachrony so significantly to the foreground of literature and its modern remaking.

It is once again Yeats who defines this important artistic trend of the times, with its horrified flight from an unbearable history into the stable order of myth. 'Sailing to Byzantium' (1928) is another resumption of the English Romantic tradition, specifically of the lyric in which the speaker identifies with the imagined utterance of a bird: Keats's Nightingale and Shelley's Skylark can be heard flapping their wings behind it. The poem is in its most credible sense an old man's farewell to youthful sensuality as he turns to a life of contemplation, figured as a voyage from one symbolic country to another. But as the destination, Byzantium, is (like Mylae in 'The Waste Land') the long-superseded name of an ancient city, this is seemingly also a voyage from the present to the past. It turns out to be more exactly a passage from the timebound realm of organic life with its 'dying generations', launching the wearied speaker 'out of nature', out of 'Whatever is begotten, born, and dies' and into the 'artifice of eternity': the atemporal and artificial sphere of art, where he will take on a new form as a golden bird singing, in a matching triple formulation,

> Of what is past, or passing, or to come
>
> (Yeats 1990: 239–40)

Distinctions of time appear to be retained in this concluding line, but are in the same breath cancelled from the perspective of the now inorganic bird (as figure of the immortalised singer, poet, or artist), under whose eternalising eye they are matters of indifference, past, present and future being simultaneously available as repertoire, no longer ordained as destined sequence. The conceit is of course a flagrant impossibility, tenable only within the highest rhetorical mode of Romantic rhapsody which Yeats adopts and even outbids here. That such a headlong lunge at transcendence should have been attempted at all, though, tells us something important about the lure of mythic timelessness for leading writers of the 1920s, for whom high art was called upon not only to make sense of a chaotic age but to serve as a sanctuary from historical time itself.

From Here to Simultaneity: Criticism against History

The manner in which a yearning for eternity is voiced in 'Sailing to Byzantium' is unique and inimitable; but in tamer, less rhetorical forms a similar impatience with process, sequence, chronology and history is to be found more widely in the decade. In certain major instances of Modernist creative innovation reviewed or mentioned above – in Proust, Joyce, Eliot, Ford and Woolf – we find a distinctive distrust of linear narrative sequence converted into highly original new techniques and forms. Further signs of an anti-temporal inclination are to be found in the critical writings of the period, both Modernist and non-Modernist. Eliot's despairing summary of contemporary history as an 'immense panorama of futility and anarchy', quoted above from his essay on Joyce, is one such symptom, and offers a likely motive for the new favouring of the mythic over the narrative and historical principle in literature. One major consequence in 1920s criticism is a distaste for evolutionary accounts of literature, and a corresponding insistence upon its atemporal status. Eliot's most influential essay, 'Tradition and the Individual Talent', offers the strongest version of this position, in its audaciously paradoxical appropriation of the term 'historical' on behalf of something more like its opposite: for Eliot, the historical sense grasps the presence of the past along with its pastness, being a sense 'of the timeless and of the temporal together'. In this light, Eliot suggests that the modern writer should write as if all of European literature since Homer 'composes a simultaneous order' (Eliot 1975: 38). The striking originality of Eliot's new model of living tradition lies in its direct repudiation of literary evolution as commonly understood in his time both in the Hegelian tradition (literature as a constantly unfolding expression of the world-spirit) and in the everyday academic practice of literary history (literature as the reflection of a given nation's history in its successive stages).

A similar repudiation of literary-historical temporality is to be heard in E. M. Forster's series of lectures published as *Aspects of the Novel* (1927). Where Eliot's conception of tradition outlines a considered principle of simultaneity, Forster expresses a more personal distaste for the academic study of novels in evolutionary terms as examples of successive movements, tendencies, or influences. His reaction, possibly inspired in part by Eliot, was to offer an account of the novel in which Time and History are to be regarded as irrelevances:

> Time, all the way through, is to be our enemy. We are to visualize the English novelists not as floating down that stream which bears all its sons away unless they are careful, but as seated together in a room, a circular room, a sort of British Museum reading room – all writing their novels simultaneously. (Forster 1962: 16)

The resulting model is another simultaneous order of writers, arranged significantly in a circle rather than as a linear sequence with one following another. Forster's impatience with 'that demon of chronology' and with 'the great tedious onrush known as history' is in evidence throughout *Aspects of the Novel* (Forster 1962: 21, 173). He finally justifies his atemporal approach to the study of novels with a blunt aphorism: 'History develops, art stands still' (Forster 1962: 171). Eliot, we may note, had made a similar but more judiciously qualified observation in his essay on Tradition, acknowledging that literary tradition shows change and development but advising that poets must be aware of 'the obvious fact that art never improves' (Eliot 1975: 39). For Eliot, the materials upon which art may work undergo change, but artistic development never supersedes the classics of tradition: Homer and Shakespeare never become outdated as a consequence. Virginia Woolf too opens her essay 'Modern Fiction' (1925) with a version of the same point.

There is more than one sense in which a literary work may be considered to be exempt from considerations of normal temporality. It enjoys, in common with non-literary writings, the written word's suspension from biological and historical time; hence the convention by which we summarise its events in the present tense. Furthermore – and here we come closer to the arguments of Forster and Eliot – as a work of art it is not susceptible to obsolescence in the light of subsequent discoveries, as a treatise on medicine or agriculture would eventually be: *Oedipus the King* is neither disproved nor displaced by *Hamlet*. Even a minor drama in outmoded fashion or a poem of negligible quality may suffer deserved neglect but still does not belong in the dustbin of history to which exploded prophecies and discredited medical theories are consigned. Such exemptions account for most claims for the 'timeless' quality of literary works, claims that assumed a special urgency in the 1920s. So far, we have sought to explain this decade's hankering for the atemporality of literature by reference to a flight from the horrors and confusions of recent history, from which aesthetic timelessness could appear as a refuge. A more nuanced answer, though, might lie in the suggestions found in Forster's and Eliot's critical propositions, also advanced by Woolf: that literary value is of a non-developmental kind, standing aside from any imagined march of Evolution or of Progress. In this lay its timeliest virtue for writers in the wake of the Great War, when the idea of Progress itself seemed, as we shall see in more detail in the next chapter, to have been exposed as a 'Victorian' illusion. If History develops into the Battle of the Somme, then Art, by standing still, vindicates itself as a superior undeluded mode of understanding.

Before we leave the critical arena, it will be worth insisting that distrust of clock-measured Time and by implication chronology and History along with it is by no means an attitude coterminous with the theory or practice of literary Modernism. The classic works of high Modernist writers – Joyce, Eliot, Woolf, Ford, Proust, Faulkner – indeed exhibit the artistic fruits of original anachronic and anachronistic techniques. Yet it would be misleading to identify time-scepticism, consciously Bergsonian or otherwise, exclusively with a Modernist 'camp' by contradistinction from non-Modernist literary currents. The major embarrassment to such a binary model is the case of Yeats, the great singer of timelessness, who was qualified for that role because he was a latterday Romantic rather than a Modernist in practice. Forster is another example of a distinctly non-Modernist writer who nonetheless participated, as we have seen, in the cultivation of anti-temporal perspectives in his critical lectures although not in his novelistic practice.

That positions taken on the question of temporality fail to distinguish Modernist from 'traditional' literary groupings can be demonstrated perhaps most clearly by reference to Wyndham Lewis and his polemical work *Time and Western Man* (1927). Lewis, formerly editor of the provocative avant-garde magazine *Blast* (1914–15), was without any doubt a Modernist in both literature and visual art, but in the 1920s he found himself completely at odds with contemporary trends in matters of time-awareness. 'The *fashionable* mind is par excellence the *time-denying* mind', he complained in his sustained assault on Bergsonism (Lewis 1993: 7). Lewis's lavishly paranoid view of contemporary culture imagined Bergsonites popping up everywhere: not only had Proust, Gertrude Stein, Joyce, Woolf, Ezra Pound and the German historian Oswald Spengler been enrolled, but Freud and Einstein were somehow implicated in this creeping menace, and even Charlie Chaplin was collaborating with them. For Lewis, the pretence that all ages are in some sense contemporaneous (as Spengler had indeed suggested, although Chaplin had not), or that archaism represents novelty, is only a pseudo-mystical evasion of the temporal facts of life and the distinctions that follow from them. The strange case of Wyndham Lewis shows Modernism to be too disparate and internally divided to be equated with Bergsonism or with any consistent time-doctrine.

Powys: *Mr Weston's Good Wine*

The one work of this decade that treats time and eternity most overtly and playfully comes from well outside the Modernist current: T. F. Powys's prose fable *Mr Weston's Good Wine* (1927). In its narrative form, the story is perfectly conventional, cast as an orderly omniscient third-person account of events in the autumn of 1923 in an English village, Folly Down, presumably in Dorset, where Powys lived as a recluse. The story concerns the arrival in the village of Mr Weston, an itinerant wine-merchant accompanied by his assistant Michael in a Ford car. The more we learn of Mr Weston as the tale proceeds, though, the clearer it becomes that he is in fact God Almighty travelling incognito for reasons best known to Himself and his archangelic deputy. Once we have been introduced to the numerous odd characters of the village, variously morose, mad, or oversexed, things take a curious turn in the nineteenth chapter, entitled 'Time Stops'. The clocks all suddenly stop one evening as the whole village enters into Eternity, although this condition looks remarkably like ordinary Time, with conversation in the Angel Inn carrying on much as before:

> No one in the room appeared to be the least surprised that, though the clock had ceased to tick and time was stopped, all should go on exactly as before: that Mr Kiddle should wish to deal, and that Mr Meek should wish, by a little cough, to bring the talk back again to women. Indeed, the word spoken by Mr Grunter had been but a word, and Eternity, for all the company knew to the contrary, might be as pleasant to live in as Time. (Powys 1937: 112)

At this point Mr Weston enters, affably advertising his wine, which is 'as strong as death and as sweet as love' (Powys 1937: 119). He then goes on to visit several of the characters to whom he sells his wine, meting out their deserts in the form of death or love. For example, the village rector, Mr Grobe, who has lost his faith, longs to be reunited with his deceased wife, and eventually has his wish; while his daughter, convinced that she will marry the angel represented on the sign of the local pub, is mated briefly with Michael. The sinister local procuress Mrs Vosper, however, is consigned to a terrifying end.

The basic design of the story is allegorical, but without ever becoming in the least didactic: Mr Weston's purposes in his rustic sojourn, which he pretends are merely commercial, remain teasingly obscure, largely on account of their remoteness from recognised versions of Christian doctrine. Mr Weston confesses he has never set foot in a church before this day, preferring to hawk his wares in prisons and brothels, and he seems uneasily evasive too at any mention of the Cross. His occasional references to his Creation hint that it was a whimsical error of a kind that still baffles and embarrasses him, while he often refers to himself as the sometime author of a prose poem that should not be taken too literally. As allegory, *Mr Weston's Good Wine* is not of the kind that can be decoded into a simpler message. Indeed it dissolves theology into a grotesque rustic comedy of angels and farm animals, human delusions, absurd lusts and transcendent intoxications.

Shaw: *Saint Joan*

An altogether different case of literary anachronism, in that its aims are overtly didactic, is Bernard Shaw's historical play about Joan of Arc,

Saint Joan (1924), a drama in six scenes representing the tragic events of 1431 followed by a comic Epilogue cast as a dream sequence about Joan's afterlife, culminating in her official canonisation in 1920. The most obviously unusual feature of the play, in the context of atemporality in 1920s writing, is this Epilogue, which propels us out of Joan's historical moment in fifteenth-century Rouen, and into a future in which Joan and her persecutors reappear to discuss her later rehabilitations. In this dramatic coda, a soldier appears from the eternal fires of Hell, and others pronounce lessons of a timeless application: 'The heretic is always better dead,' says one; 'it is always you good men that do the big mischiefs', says another (Shaw 1946: 149). From the reflective distance that the Epilogue permits, Shaw draws our attention both to change – the spectacular reversal of the Maid's posthumous reputation from heretic to saint – and simultaneously to what remains unchanging about the course of change: that its pioneers will always be persecuted as heretics by otherwise well-meaning people who cannot understand them.

It is not only in the Epilogue, however, that Shaw resorts to anachronism. The play's fourth scene, in which the Earl of Warwick, commander of the English forces, sounds out Cauchon, Bishop of Beauvais, about the prospect of Joan being tried for heresy, is a sustained exercise in anachronistic exposition. In the scene's opening dialogue between Warwick and his chaplain de Stogumber, it is made clear that for anyone to describe France or England as 'their country' is a newfangled and scarcely credible idea, since before the full emergence of nation-states one could be a Burgundian or a Picard but not in our modern sense a 'Frenchwoman' or 'Frenchman'. Yet having established that point, Shaw proceeds to present de Stogumber as a blinkered English patriot of the kind one might expect to encounter in one of his plays set in contemporary times. De Stogumber utters the modern slogan 'England for the English', and proclaims England's 'peculiar fitness to rule over less civilized races for their own good', just like a Jingoist of the 1890s (Shaw 1946: 99–100).

At this point in the play, Shaw's purpose is to instruct his audience in what he sees as Joan's own anachronistic status as a harbinger of ideas whose time is yet to come, namely Protestantism and Nationalism. Shaw's problem is that Joan's enemies would not at the time understand such modern notions any more than she herself would, the English words for these historic tendencies having first appeared in 1649 and 1844 respectively, the *OED* tells us. In fact their incomprehension is central to Shaw's efforts to treat Joan's story as true tragedy – involving the inevitable clash of irreconcilable principles – rather than as melodrama, in which we would have merely the tormenting of pure innocence by sheer villainy. Above all, Shaw needs us to recognise that the spiritual and temporal powers responsible for Joan's burning at the stake acted not from sadism but from sincere motives. The awkward result in this fourth scene is a dialogue in which the high representatives of Church and State sink their differences and agree in a sequence of parallel speeches that Joan's actions are equally subversive of feudal lordship and of the Church's authority, embodying as they do two similar ideas that are unacceptable and even unspeakable in that they have in 1431 no names. Thus Warwick is made to say 'It is the protest of the individual soul against the interference of priest or peer between the private man and his God. I should call it Protestantism if I had to find a name for it' (Shaw 1946: 98–9). Cauchon then neatly matches him by saying of Joan 'To her the French-speaking people are what the Holy Scriptures describe as a nation. Call this side of her heresy Nationalism if you will: I can find you no better name for it' (Shaw 1946: 99). In this most implausible fashion Joan's adversaries, speaking in the strange tongues of Shavian hindsight, identify her in Hegelian terms as the precocious mouthpiece of the world-spirit in its coming phase.

The contradiction that places such strains upon *Saint Joan* is between Shaw's tragic and his didactic ambitions. For the play to attain any tragic quality, its characters must be blind to the irresistible forces that compel them into deadly collision; but for the sake of Shaw's argument about the place of heresy and persecution in the course of human Evolution, these same characters must be so clear-sighted about their motives that they can speak of them in terms derived from Victorian history-books and nineteenth-century philosophy. In this same fourth scene, Cauchon announces his awareness 'that there is a Will to Power in the World' (Shaw 1946: 98), clearly invoking a concept derived from Friedrich Nietzsche's writings of the 1880s. Of course all historical dramatists, like historical novelists, must to some degree foist modern phrases, modern ways of thinking and modern interpretations upon events and human figures of ages past. Anachronism of some sort is necessary to those literary forms, which are always of course addressed to contemporary audiences, and which always invite some downplaying of important differences between historical periods. Our concern here is with the particular kind of anachronism that Shaw deploys in *Saint Joan*. Not surprisingly in the light of his lengthy previous career as a dramatist of discussion and debate, the anachronistic mode in which Shaw works here is primarily intellectual. Joan appears to us less as a creature of her own age than as a bearer of Ideas, even of 'Isms', that became clarified in later centuries.

If we turn to the Preface that Shaw attached to the published edition

(1924), we learn more about his purposes and his particular way of seeing fifteenth-century events in terms of twentieth-century problems. His opening tribute to Joan of Arc presents her as a herald of the future:

> she was in fact one of the first Protestant martyrs. She was also one of the first apostles of Nationalism, and the first French practitioner of Napoleonic realism in warfare, as distinguished from the sporting ransom-gambling chivalry of her time. She was the pioneer of rational dressing for women [. . .] She had an unbounded and quite unconcealed contempt for official opinion, judgment, and authority, and for War Office tactics and strategy. (Shaw 1946: 7)

The reference to the War Office, still blamed by many in 1924 for the wasteful slaughter of the Great War, is of course deliberately anachronistic, and intended to identify Joan with more recent rebels or malcontents. The argument of the Preface, as with all Shaw's Prefaces, lengthy and bristling with heterodox assertion, is that history moves forward through the agency of pioneer spirits who are 'ahead of their time', as Shaw certainly believed too confidently was his own case. When it comes to resistance against change, though, nothing much changes, the impulse to persecute these pioneers being as strong today as in the fifteenth century, despite burning at the stake having gone out of fashion as a punishment. On this point Shaw calls in evidence the treatment of the suffragettes: 'If Joan had to be dealt with by us in London she would be treated with no more toleration than Miss Sylvia Pankhurst' (Shaw 1946: 27). The lesson Shaw most wants the members of his audience to draw is that they too would in their own well-meaning and sincere way demand the punishment of Joan or her latest counterpart.

> If you confuse the Middle Ages with the Dark Ages [. . .] and are quite convinced that the world has progressed enormously, both morally and mechanically, since Joan's time, then you will never understand why Joan was burnt, much less feel that you might have voted for burning her yourself if you had been a member of the court that tried her; and until you feel that you know nothing essential about her. (Shaw 1946: 25)

That final pronoun 'her' is a curiosity in its context, because Shaw's most urgent demand is plainly that the audience learn something about *themselves* as members of a social order still armed against those it considers enemies within. The specific historical individuality of Joan is less important to him than the more 'essential' fact – underlined especially by his Epilogue – that she is always still with us.

Shaw's use of anachronism stands out in contrast to others we have considered in this chapter, most obviously on account of its clearly didactic motivation, but additionally in that *Saint Joan* is a 'chronicle play' (as the subtitle has it) based quite solidly on historical sources. Another unusual feature of Shaw's case is the apparent confusion in his Preface on the question of historical progress. On the one hand he tells us that History or human Evolution does advance through its forward-looking heretics, but on the other he scolds his readers for their conceit in imagining that they have really progressed much beyond the witch-hunting mentality of earlier centuries. The significance of this matter follows from our earlier suggestion of a link between the adoption of anachronic and anachronistic literary methods and a discrediting of 'Progress' in the wake of the Great War. In such cases as those of Eliot, Yeats and Ford, whose creative and critical works alike suggest a broadly 'declinist' or progress-denying distrust of modernity, that equation may be accepted relatively straightforwardly. The difficulty with Shaw is that he was regarded in the public mind as a champion of 'progressive' thought, and as we saw in the previous chapter he was committed as a matter of almost religious faith to a doctrine of 'Creative Evolution' in which progress is a law of Nature. The seeming contradiction may be resolved by discriminating between Shaw's general progressivism and the particular illusion of progress against which he warns his audience, the latter being a complacent English 'Whig' or Liberal trust in emancipation following automatically upon the establishment of given legal rights. Logically, it is possible to be an advocate of Progress and at the same time to argue that not enough progress has actually been achieved, and this appears to be Shaw's position. It ought to remind us that there is no simple division to be made when it comes to Progress between its devotees and its sceptics. Plenty of writers in the 1920s felt that a certain naïve confidence in historical Progress from lower to higher forms of civilisation no longer looked credible after the War. But in the very process of abandoning that 'Victorian' illusion, they can hardly have avoided feeling that they were themselves making some sort of progress. As we shall see in the next chapter, the 'disillusionment' of 1920s writing is marked by this very contradiction.

Some conclusions may be drawn from our survey of anachrony and anachronism in this decade's literature. First, that although some of the most sophisticated uses of these methods are found among works of Modernist writers, they are by no means an exclusive preserve of Modernism, as we have seen in their deployment by non-Modernist authors led by Yeats and including Forster, Powys and Shaw. Nor is time-shifting or time-scepticism an essential feature of Modernist theory or practice, as we saw in the antagonistic case of Wyndham Lewis. We may with certain qualifications and cautions associate the prominence of these methods with a new post-War scepticism about Progress, or even regard the one as prompted by the other. It does not follow, however, that a strongly nostalgic, Romantic or 'Tory' resistance to the idea of Progress is a necessary precondition for the creative exploitation of time-shifts and anachronistic devices in literature: Woolf did not belong in that tradition any more than Shaw did. As for any simple, still less wholesale, repudiation of Progress, we should not even expect to find it. Blendings of memory with desire and deliberate confusions of one historical time with another arose significantly in 1920s writing, on the basis of attitudes to historical progress that were inevitably mixed and contradictory. While the War could be lamented as a reversion to barbarity, other developments in medicine (which warfare often spurs to new discoveries), communications, education, transport and much else were commonly enough greeted as improvements; and there was good news for some even in the political realm: voting rights for women and the establishment of the Irish Free State, for instance. Like most other periods, the 1920s were the best of times as well as the worst of times. The timeliness of literary atemporalities in that decade, then, is no simple matter of any uniform revulsion from contemporary chaos, but rather a response to historical conditions in which starkly contradictory views about progression and retrogression demanded to be held, and held simultaneously.

Chapter Three

Never Such Innocence: Versions of Experience and Disillusionment

> We believed in highdays then,
> And could glimpse at night
>   On Christmas Eve
> Imminent oncomings of radiant revel –
>   Doings of delight: –
> Now we have no such sight.
>
> Thomas Hardy, 'Yuletide in a Younger World' (1928)

In Waugh's *Decline and Fall* (1928), we meet a teenage boy, Peter Beste-Chetwynde, whose favourite reading matter comprises two works: Kenneth Grahame's *The Wind in the Willows* (1908) and Havelock Ellis's seven-volume *Studies in the Psychology of Sex* (1897–1928). That conjunction encapsulates Waugh's own diagnosis of the disturbed youth of the Twenties, one that he would develop more fully in the dissection of the Bright Young People in his later novel *Vile Bodies* (1930). While still not emancipated imaginatively from the world of the nursery, these young people were precociously absorbing more knowledge than they could digest, meanwhile affecting a world-weariness beyond their years. Part of the paradoxical problem of over-ripened immaturity afflicting his own generation – those who had still been at school during the War – Waugh attributed to an unusual burden placed on them by their elders. In an article of 1932, he recalled that

> The Responsibility of Youth legend took a soberer form. I hardly remember a single speech or sermon made to us at school that did not touch upon this topic. 'You are the men of tomorrow,' they used to say to us. 'You are succeeding to the leadership of a broken and shaken world. The cure is in your hands,' etc. etc. (Waugh 1983: 126)

The reckless irresponsibility of the party-going youngsters of the 1920s was, Waugh guessed, a reaction against that curse, a perverse resolve on the part of the prematurely world-weary to remain childish.

D. H. Lawrence identified a similar paradox in his poem 'Old People' (1929):

> Nowadays everybody wants to be young,
> so much so, that even the young are old with the effort of being young
>
> (Lawrence 1971a: 502)

Writers of the 1920s commonly imagined that the customary rhythms of human maturation had recently been broken by contradictory pressures of retardation and untimely acceleration.

If Waugh's contemporaries felt that they were being hurried too soon into responsibility, then the slightly older War generation itself, now made up of premature 'veterans' and many still-youthful widows, had even greater reason to feel that it had grown old before its time, robbed of its proper youth. Even the non-combatants imagined themselves as decrepit: T. S. Eliot, the acknowledged leader of the decade's younger poets, opened his 1920 collection *Ara Vos Prec* significantly with the enigmatic poem 'Gerontion', spoken in the voice of a weary elder (the title means 'little old man'), although Eliot himself was thirty-two at the time. The verse epilogue to Richard Aldington's war novel *Death of a Hero* (1929) is spoken by survivors of the Trojan War, who nonetheless speak for the ex-servicemen of the 1920s in announcing themselves as

> We, the old men – some of us nearly forty –
>
> (Aldington 1984: 375)

Edmund Blunden's poetic reminiscences of his war service on the Western Front, published in several successive collections through the 1920s, capture some of that generational exhaustion, for example in the opening line of 'Festubert, 1916' (1922):

> Tired with dull grief, grown old before my day
>
> (Blunden 1982: 32)

Blunden was twenty-six years old when this was published.

Meanwhile the fiction and drama of the decade are populated by middle-aged characters who have refused to grow up: Florence Lancaster in Noël Coward's play *The Vortex* (1924) and Mrs Aldwinkle in Aldous Huxley's novel *Those Barren Leaves* (1925) are two examples among many. One aim of this chapter is to consider such curious inversions of Age and Youth found often in this decade; another is to investigate the larger importance of 'disillusionment' as a defining topic of 1920s literature, both in direct relation to the War and in other accounts of passages from innocence to experience.

Dividing Lines

Our starting point here is an observation made by Paul Fussell in the third chapter of his classic study of British writing about the trench warfare of the Western Front, *The Great War and Modern Memory* (1975), in which he notices how 'gross dichotomy' characterises both the wartime mentality and much of the Western imagination shaped by it thereafter (Fussell 1977: 79). Fussell finds in soldier-poetry and in War memoirs a recurrent resort to sharp and simple divisions between Us and Them, in various versions: Friend versus Foe, Combatant versus Non-Combatant, Young versus Old, among others (and we might well add Disillusioned versus Deluded), along with a similarly emphatic division between Time Before and Time After, in which the outbreak of the War, or some experience within it, is taken as a clear boundary between separate and indeed antithetical historical and personal ages. The analysis of such simplified antitheses was taken up later by Samuel Hynes in his book *A War Imagined* (1990), which offers in its later chapters many valuable insights into 1920s literature in particular. Hynes traces the development from 1914 and the eventual consolidation by the late 1920s of what he calls the Myth of the War, by which he means not an outright falsification but a set of selective simplifications, among which the most important is an imagined 'sense of radical discontinuity of present from past', in which the War represents a chasm or gulf in history between an idealistic age of generalised innocence and a new era of embittered experience (Hynes 1990: ix). The study of innocence and experience in 1920s writing that I offer here serves both to confirm the importance of that War Myth and to complicate it by distinguishing some of its versions.

The Before/After dichotomy noticed by both Fussell and by Hynes being a temporal construction, we are of course revisiting here the time-sense of 1920s literature, but not quite as we were doing in the previous chapter. There, we looked at ways in which certain writers of that decade collapsed or obliterated distinctions between historical periods by deliberate and imaginatively productive anachronism, or reshuffled the then/now distinctions of narrative chronology in anachronic presentation. Here, we will examine ways in which 1920s writers to the contrary highlight, insist upon and exaggerate distinctions between historical periods and phases of personal memory. We are not dealing here with two separate or competing tribes of anachronists on the one side pitted against chronometrists on the other: the writers who confound times and those who treat them as discontinuous will often be found to be the very same authors, writing in different modes or (a fact that literary history cannot anachronise) at different times. The works considered in this chapter differ from those treated in the last, not as productions of a rival camp but rather in literary mode. Considered rhetorically, anachronic and anachronistic works tend to rely upon the principle of *metaphor*, in which they identify – or as simile, liken – one time with another, whereas works in which orders of time are presented as radically distinct do so under the trope of *irony*, producing a discrepancy of awareness, typically between contrasted times of blindness and insight, naïvety and disillusionment, innocence and experience. The larger argument of Fussell's work, it should be remarked in this context, is that modern literature in the wake of the Great War comes to be governed by the master-trope of irony.

As for the division of writers into antagonistic camps according to such principles, two observations should be made here. First, the gross dichotomy between writers who belong to a blinded Before and those who belong to an insightful After is a powerful critical myth that we inherit from the 1920s, most influentially from Virginia Woolf's polemical essay 'Character in Fiction' (1924), in which she divides writers of her own generation – the War generation, in fact, although she calls them Georgians – from writers of the pre-War generation, who are pushed firmly into the past by being labelled Edwardians. That Woolf's dichotomous scheme is a version of the War Myth transposed into critical valuation should be clear from the fact that it activates the historical Before/After division as Edwardian/Georgian in the service of a generational antagonism between Us and Them: They are blinded by materialistic attention to superficial appearances of dress or habitation, while We attend insightfully to inner spiritual realities. As codified in an academic canonisation of Modernism, the dichotomy is still with us, reformulated as a contrast between kinds of reader: They naïvely ingest the ideological complacency of Realism (imagined presumptuously as the Before of Modernism), while We can respond to the radical challenges of Modernism itself. Any scrupulous literary history, especially in dealing with the 1920s, must be at least suspicious of such models, and at best vigilant in unpicking them.

In the second place, before we dismiss any connection between temporal dichotomies in literature and identifiable groups of writers, it should be conceded that some authors resort to those imaginary oppositions more than others. It is noticeable that the hardest dividing lines between Us and Them as between Before and After are drawn in this decade by writers who had experienced the worst of trench warfare, including gas attacks and shell-shock, notably Siegfried Sassoon, Osbert Sitwell and Richard Aldington. In Fussell's account, the first extended examples of dichotomous literary imagination are illustrated from the writings of Sassoon, in which Fussell sees the adversarial spirit as both a focusing strength and as a simplifying weakness. Sassoon's preferred mode both in wartime and in the 1920s was satire, most clearly in his *Satirical Poems* (1926); and the necessary simplifications and asperities of satire accommodate the Us/Them habit, as for example in Aldington's *Death of a Hero* and in D. H. Lawrence's satirical poems, more than other modes do. On a broader view, the dichotomous imagination is to be observed more commonly, although not exclusively, among writers of the war generation, including Lawrence and Woolf, than it is among their elders.

A distinction needs to be made here between literary representations of disillusionment that belong to the late wartime period of 1917–18 and those that develop in the 1920s. In Sassoon's wartime poems there is a simple contrast between the empty slogans of politicians, journalists and clergymen and the horrifying experience of combatants; and a similar structure is carried over into the posthumously published work of Wilfred Owen, most of which was unknown until the appearance of his *Poems* (1920), edited ostensibly by Sassoon but in fact by Edith Sitwell. Owen's now-famous poem 'Dulce et Decorum Est' (1920) relies upon a stark collision between the 'old lie' of military glory and the new experience of trench horror. The 16-line poem that we now read under the title 'The Parable of the Old Man and the Young' presents an accusatory dichotomy in which the young appear as sacrificial victims to the blasphemous blood-lust of the Old. A mistranscription on Sitwell's part in the 1920 *Poems* led to this poem being read in the 1920s and long after in an incomplete 15-line form under the generationally provocative title 'The Parable of the Old *Men* and the Young'. The literature of disillusionment in the 1920s, however, although it re-echoes with hostility towards the Old, hardly ever adopts the simple glory/reality antithesis.

Novels of this decade not only qualify and complicate that aspect of the Myth but in some cases overtly challenge it as presumptuous. Rose Macaulay in her chronicle-novel *Told by an Idiot* (1923) stages an argument between one of her characters, Amy Garden, and her son Roger, who has served in the War and written a number of trench poems which she dislikes as being 'too beastly and nasty and corpsey'.

> 'Unfortunately, mother,' Roger explained, kindly, 'war *is* rather beastly and nasty, you know. And a bit corpsey, too.'
> 'My dear boy, I know that; I'm not an idiot. Don't, for goodness' sake, talk to me in that superior way, it reminds me of your father. All I say is, why *write* about the corpses? There've always been plenty of them, people who've died in their beds of diseases. You never used to write about *them*.'

'I suppose one's object is to destroy the false glamour of war. There's no glamour about disease.'

'Glamour indeed! There you go again with that terrible nonsense. I don't meet any of these people you talk about who think there's glamour in war. I'm sure *I* never saw any glamour in it, with all you boys in the trenches and all of us at home slaving ourselves to death and starving on a slice of bread and margarine a day. Glamour indeed. I'll tell you what it is, a set of you young men have invented that glamour theory, just so as to have an excuse for what you call destroying it, with your nasty talk. Like you've invented those awful Old Men you go on about, who like the war. I'm sick of your Old Men and your corpses.' (Macaulay 1983: 293)

In her refusal to be talked down to as naïve, and in rejecting the caricature of war-glorifying Old Men as an invention contrary to her own experience, Amy Garden here highlights one of those inverted attributions of Innocence to the older generation and of Experience to the younger, by which 1920s writing is so often troubled.

Cracks across History

A preliminary complication of the Before/After myth is required before we consider its manifestations in literary practice. In its simplest and thus most powerful version, the myth must favour a binary form, for instance as pre-War versus post-War. But in that case the War itself becomes reduced to a transformative instant, in contradiction to the most glaring and appalling historical reality, which was that the War had been prolonged well beyond some initial expectations of its being over by Christmas 1914 and into more than four years of suffering, of anxiety and – in the luckiest cases – of tedium. In the War's later stages, some people had even speculated that it might simply go on for ever. In the face of that contradiction, the myth can retain its binary form most securely by finding some watershed date at which the world lost its innocence.

In a few literary works of the 1920s, we find authors adopting different dates, or undated moments of initiatory insight, according to their own circumstances or those of their fictional characters, or their peculiar interpretations of wartime history. As we shall see later, D. H. Lawrence's novel *Kangaroo* (1923) proposes the fall of Asquith's government in December 1916 and its replacement by the Lloyd George coalition as the moment when civilisation collapsed into barbarism. We have noticed also in Chapter 2 that Ford Madox Ford's *Some Do Not...* (1924) draws attention to the eve (3 August 1914) of the War by setting certain important events on that date. Ford continues in that habit in the third volume of his sequence, *A Man Could Stand Up—* (1926), setting the first and last of its three parts on Armistice Day itself. In its opening episode, the heroine, Valentine Wannop, is charged with ensuring that her pupils in a girls' school do not run amok at the announcement of the War's end. Valentine reflects upon the senior teachers' fear of disorder:

> A quite definite fear. If, at this parting of the ways, at this crack across the table of History, the School – the World, the future mothers of Europe – got out of hand, would they ever come back? The Authorities – Authority all over the world – was afraid of that; more afraid of that than of any other thing. Wasn't it a possibility that there was to be no more Respect? None for constituted Authority and consecrated Experience? (Ford 2011: 17–18)

As the caricaturing capitalised terms suggest, Valentine's train of thought fancifully parodies accepted simplifications, including the notion of a clear epoch marked by the date's 'crack'. In this novel, Ford indeed presents Armistice Day as a chaotic muddle rather than as a clear dawn of any new age, its confusions, within his larger design of the novel-sequence, representing kinds of moral and social disintegration that originate long before the War itself.

The various alternative turning-points tend to indicate a variety of different disillusionments, which it would be well to discriminate. The widely adopted date of 4 August 1914, which had been recognised by many at the time as a watershed, cannot of course signify any revelatory encounter with the horrors of industrialised warfare, because those came later. What it indicates rather is the suddenly discredited assumption that European civilisation had arrived at an irreversible condition of pacific Progress. That is why non-combatants and men who had yet to experience military action could regard themselves as, in this sense, disillusioned at such an early stage by the very fact of the War's outbreak, irrespective of its specific ensuing horrors or confusions. The second available watershed is a moveable one: historians often prefer the opening day (1 July 1916) of the Battle of the Somme, for its unprecedented casualties, but authors of War memoirs and War novels could of course use a different battle in which their protagonist endures a baptism of fire. The use of such a moment is suitable to dispelling naïve illusions of old-fashioned glory, but we rarely find such a simple pattern in 1920s narratives. A third possible watershed date – used semi-ironically by Ford, as we have seen – is that of the 11 November 1918 Armistice, which in turn signifies another kind of disillusionment: the point at which hopes for an end to the conflict turn to recognition that it had wrecked rather than salvaged the world. Post-War disillusionment in 1920s writing can refer back to any or all of those moments,

each with their rather different significance. On the other hand, it may
– and more often in practice does – recollect a more gradual, grinding
demoralisation brought on less by an identifiable turning-point than by
a prolonged 'education' in the ways of the modern industrial-military-
bureaucratic world, one in which the assumptions of pre-War existence
are overturned.

Blunden's cycle of War-retrospect poems includes the sardonic
'Report on Experience' (1929), in four stanzas of which the first follows
Owen's example in his 'Parable' by inverting the message of a well-
known Biblical verse, in this case Psalms 37:25:

> I have been young, and now am not too old;
> And I have seen the righteous forsaken,
> His health, his honour and his quality taken.
>   This is not what we were formerly told.
>
>   (Blunden 1982: 67)

Blunden's ironic testimony to his generation's experience presents it,
without having to refer directly to the War, as a kind of re-education
that is not momentary but an accumulation of what are called later in
the same poem 'these disillusions'.

Triptychal Permutations of War Literature

With the exception of Lawrence, the most significant tendency among
writers of this decade who recollect or span the War period in their fictions or memoirs is that they do not make their accounts hinge upon
a revelatory crisis. There are very few stories either that involve any
single rude awakening from dreams of innocence to realities of war.
Moreover, all writers and readers in the 1920s remembered well enough
that they had lived through three times, not just two; which meant that
any Before/After antithesis had in narrative practice to accommodate
itself to a commonly shared triple or triptychal model of recent history
as Before-*During*-After. The narrator of Aldington's *Death of a Hero*
puts it clearly: 'Adult lives were cut sharply into three sections – pre-war,
war, and post-war' (Aldington 1984: 199). This three-phase memory
did not at all debar the use of binary antithetical patterns, but it did
multiply the available permutations of time-scheme within which they
could be imposed upon historical time.

Writers who addressed the War period were of course under no obligation to 'cover' all three phases in their narratives, although several
chose to do so. The range of time-schemes in 1920s War-fictions and

reminiscences shows other permutations of the Before-During-After succession, some treating only one of those phases, others exploring only two of them. The following schematic survey of the varieties divides them into Single-Phase, Double-Phase and Triple-Phase narratives.

Single-Phase Narratives

Most single-phase narratives recount events that take place during the War itself, with little or no direct attention to times before or after. The major examples are Edmund Blunden's memoir *Undertones of War* (1928) and the second of Ford's Tietjens novels, *No More Parades* (1925). Another case is Arnold Bennett's novel of wartime political intrigue, *Lord Raingo* (1926), while Agatha Christie's debut novel *The Mysterious Affair at Styles* (1920) and some of the short stories in C. E. Montague's *Fiery Particles* (1923) are of this kind, too. In a distinct sub-class we find a good number of relatively pure aftermath narratives, set in the post-War period and following characters who have been variously damaged or exhausted by the War years: Lawrence's *Aaron's Rod* (1922) and *Lady Chatterley's Lover*, and Ford's final Tietjens volume, *Last Post* (1928), are examples, as is Mary Butts's remarkable tale of shell-shock, 'Speed the Plough' (1922). In the same category belong Enid Bagnold's novel set in France just after the Armistice, *The Happy Foreigner* (1920), Katherine Mansfield's story 'The Fly' (1922) and Dorothy L. Sayers's detective novel set among veterans commemorating the anniversary of the Armistice, *The Unpleasantness at the Bellona Club* (1928). A much rarer species is the anterior narrative, set in the pre-War years but inviting us to read the events with the hindsight afforded by awareness of the impending War. As its title suggests, Osbert Sitwell's novel *Before the Bombardment* (1926) is of this type, its story set in 1907–8 but reinterpreted in an Epilogue that briefly follows the characters' fates and legacies through to the post-War period.

Double-Phase Narratives

Double-phase narratives, intrinsically more suited to the articulation of the Before/After myth and its ironies of disillusionment, come in several kinds. Some adopt the Before/During design, tracing the fortunes of their protagonists from the pre-War world into the midst of the War: Sassoon's fictionalised *Memoirs of a Fox-Hunting Man* (1928) is a notable example, along with Ford's *Some Do Not . . .* (1924), Virginia Woolf's *Jacob's Room* (1922) and Lawrence's story 'England, My England' (1922). Less commonly offered is the During/After sequence;

however, all three of the novels making up R. H. Mottram's *The Spanish Farm Trilogy 1914–1918* (1927) have, despite the subtitle, a time-scheme that runs from the War's second year until the demobilisations of early 1919. A number of narratives focusing upon traumatic experiences in wartime adopt rather the After/During/After plan, in which the story is interrupted by a flashback or embedded recollection. In such cases, we have two periods, but presented in a three-part structure. The major examples of this are Ford's *A Man Could Stand Up—*, in which the Armistice Day episodes frame an account of Tietjens's war experiences, culminating in a scene in which he is buried in mud; and Lawrence's *Kangaroo*, which in one chapter cuts back from 1922 to 1916 in recounting the protagonist's persecution and humiliation by wartime officialdom. A further example is Kipling's story about a disturbed War veteran, 'A Madonna of the Trenches' (1926). The final permutation in this class is the simple Before/After design in which there is no 'During' because the War years have been skipped over, as in John Galsworthy's *The Forsyte Saga* (1922), where the action of the first two parts concludes in 1901, with the third volume, *To Let* (1921), picking up the story again in 1920.

Triple-Phase Narratives

Virginia Woolf's *To the Lighthouse* (1927) comes very close to repeating Galsworthy's feat of overleaping the War. Although written in a strikingly different manner, it is another family novel in three parts that follows the passing of the generations. The first part introduces us to an English family group at their Scottish holiday home at some time before the War; the last part shows several members of the same group regathered at the same place ten years later; while the short middle section, 'Time Passes', describes the vacated house in the intervening period, with only the briefest parenthetical reference to three characters who die over the course of that decade, one of them killed by a shell-blast in the War itself. Another family novel that hurries through the War period almost as briskly is Rose Macaulay's *Told by an Idiot*, a saga that covers the political events and social fads of the years 1879–1920 in light-hearted summary while following the fortunes of the Garden family over that time. The chapter devoted to the War runs to only nine pages, before we are led on to a round-up of the surviving characters in the post-War years. Rudyard Kipling's short story 'The Gardener' (1926), which concludes amid the vast War cemeteries of Flanders, also spans the three periods with the briefest summary of wartime events.

By contrast, the novels and autobiographical works in this category written by former combatants devote considerable space to their protagonists' war service, usually including training and home leave as well as action at the Front. Ford's *Parade's End* tetralogy taken as a whole does this most substantially in its middle two volumes, sandwiched between pre-War and post-War episodes. Robert Graves's unreliable autobiography *Good-bye to All That* (1929) has a similar although simpler and more continuous three-phase construction, beginning with his earliest memories in 1897 (set in Queen Victoria's Diamond Jubilee celebrations) and taking us through the War period to the late 1920s. Aldington's *Death of a Hero* begins with the death of George Winterbourne in battle, a week prior to the Armistice, then goes back to the circumstances of his parents' marriage in the 1890s and George's early life before devoting its third part to his War experiences; the post-War world is brought in by the narrator's repeated lamentations.

From this survey of the highly varied temporal designs of 1920s War literature we may conclude that the Before/After myth of idealism followed by disenchantment very rarely coincides with the complex patterns and idiosyncratic emphases of narrative development in practice. In the family novels, moreover, contrasts between pre-War and post-War phases of the action usually have less to do with the War itself than with adjustments to personal loss and growth, as parents die and children assert new values: in *To the Lighthouse*, the death of Mrs Ramsay creates a more important absence than that of her son Andrew in the War, while in *The Forsyte Saga* none of the principal characters is directly affected by the conflict. Among the works more properly described as war-novels and war-memoirs it is rare to find any protagonist who enlists in the hope of finding glory in battle, only to be disabused by the horrors of trench warfare. Even in the notably embittered *Death of a Hero*, in which Aldington's narrator rails against the crime of the Old Men in sending the young out to die, we do not find that development. George Winterbourne goes to war not in a spirit of patriotic delusion – he already regards that as humbug – but as an escape from his tangled private life, and indeed the surprise that awaits him at the Front is that he likes and respects his comrades, who are as cynical as he is, only more cheerfully so. His death comes not as a martyrdom to the bloodthirsty old colonels but as a reckless suicide. In these and other respects the 1920s narrative of passage from pre-War to wartime and then post-War awareness does not serve so much to exemplify the simple binary oppositions of the War Myth as to dissipate them in new complexities.

Versions of Experience and Disillusionment 111

Ironies of Trench Education: Blunden, Sassoon, Graves

Among the major prose 'war books' of 1928–9 we find varying chronological frames, and differing kinds and degrees of fictionalisation at work, too. Edmund Blunden's *Undertones of War* is a single-phase 'During' narrative, and of a very selective and almost anonymous kind, staying close to the Front in the 1916–18 period, omitting anything of the narrator's periods of home leave, let alone his life before or after military service. Siegfried Sassoon's *Memoirs of a Fox-Hunting Man* has a Before/During design heavily weighted to the Before period: it is very largely an account of the pre-War life of a semi-fictional 'George Sherston', who is not shown actually approaching and finally arriving at the Front until the final chapter. Such a leisurely pace – and leisure is very much a theme of the book – makes sense only because this was the first volume of a war trilogy, the substantial military experience being withheld for the sequels, *Memoirs of an Infantry Officer* (1930) and *Sherston's Progress* (1936). As we shall see, the invention of the 'Sherston' narrator as a radically simplified version of Sassoon himself is, in the *Memoirs of a Fox-Hunting Man*, crucial to the representation of pre-War innocence. Robert Graves's *Good-bye to All That* differs from both its immediate predecessors not only in its broader Before-During-After triple structure of coverage but also in its undisguised autobiographical status. Graves's autobiography, written very hastily in order to pay off financial debts, is sometimes scandalously indiscreet, and gives the duplicitous impression of offering the unvarnished truth partly withheld by his ex-comrades. Blunden and Sassoon, though, having known and served with Graves, were in a position to point out that several of his anecdotes of life in the Royal Welch Fusiliers were exaggerations, distortions, sheer inventions, or tales picked up at second hand and passed off as his own experience.[1] All three books in their different ways present us with masked narratorial identities and with carefully selective memories of war experience.

Blunden's *Undertones of War* does not offer any picture of pre-War life in Britain, but instead builds its ironic contrasts by constant invocation of a pastoral poetic tradition, mostly of the eighteenth century. At one point he records that when stationed in a pillbox under repeated fire he read and reread Edward Young's *Night Thoughts* (1742–5), finding some of its lines strangely applicable to his own condition, and thus staved off despair (Blunden 1937: 217). One of the poems published in the book's verse appendix, 'The Prophet', follows the same pattern by giving an ironic commentary on an eighteenth-century English guidebook on Belgium that mentions some of the towns and villages that

Blunden had seen smashed up in the War. *Undertones* concerns itself simultaneously with two kinds of innocence being violated: that of the young Blunden, only 19 years of age when sent to the Front, and that of the landscapes, riverbanks and flora around Festubert, Thiepval and Ypres, where he had seen action. The book is unusual in its focus upon the land and its fate, a focus that seems to work as a displacement or metonym for the damage done to Blunden himself and to his comrades. Blunden's version of the Before/After myth is, as Fussell emphasises, a bucolic and highly literary antithesis in which what was once the calm of Nature (and humanly of Agriculture) has been despoiled by the noise and inexplicable violence of an industrialised war. What the War Myth might encourage us to expect in Blunden's memoir is a story in which dreams of glory are shattered by experiences of horror; but the very first sentence of *Undertones* – 'I was not anxious to go' – denies us the preliminary illusion, while Blunden's reticence about his own suffering (he fails to mention that he was gassed three times) tends to remove the subsequent disenchantment too. The kind of story Blunden is in fact telling is indicated in some of his chapter headings: 'Trench Education', 'Coming of Age' and, with his usual fondness for literary allusion, 'School, not at Wittenberg'. The book is not about any puncturing of illusions, but tells us how Blunden learned in the trenches the ways of a suddenly disordered world, at an age when he had expected to be studying peacefully (like his friend Graves, Blunden had had to postpone his studies at Oxford until peacetime). *Undertones of War* knows itself to be, perforce, a substitute for the autobiographical *Bildungsroman* or education-novel about coming of age; and the chapter title mentioning Wittenberg reminds us that Blunden's education had turned out to be quite unlike that provided at the university of Martin Luther and of Shakespeare's Hamlet.

Sassoon's and Graves's accounts differ from Blunden's in offering selective descriptions of the pre-War years. In Sassoon's case, most of the *Memoirs of a Fox-Hunting Man* are taken up with reconstructing that period as a personal idyll of blissful ignorance. The innocence of 'George Sherston' is contrived by radical excisions from Sassoon's own life: Sherston has no parents or siblings (Sassoon spent his real boyhood with his mother and brothers), no interest in literature, no sexuality and perhaps most significantly no education, his schooling and his time at Cambridge taking place only 'offstage'. The removal of formal education from Sherston's early life has two principal consequences: he appears all the more innocent for it, and the 'trench education' that is to come in the second volume can thus be taken as his true initiation into knowledge. Sherston's pre-War education is almost entirely a matter of outdoor sports, chiefly horse-riding but with some episodes of cricket and golf. This outdoor world of manly exertion to some extent prepares us for the later terrain of the trenches, and provides some carefully planted premonitions of it, as when Sherston learns that barbed wire is the most feared enemy of the modern horseman. For the most part, though, it appears as a paradise of purely physical culture enjoyed unthinkingly: the emphasis throughout is on Sherston's callow inexperience of the world, as when he awakens to birdsong and river-mist on the sunny morning of an impending cricket-match, at which point his older and wiser narrative voice intervenes: 'How little I knew of the enormous world beyond that valley and those low green hills' (Sassoon 1960: 53). Even when Sherston has enlisted he finds that 'there was something almost idyllic about those early weeks of the War' (Sassoon 1960: 245); and when he reaches his training camp, the stress is still on his ignorance: 'I was totally ignorant of all that I had to learn before I was fit to go to the Front' (Sassoon 1960: 262). It almost goes without saying that Sherston had confidently predicted that there would be no war with Germany, and that when he is in training, he believes the conflict will be over by Christmas – these being already established as the stock ironies of 1920s hindsight. *Memoirs of a Fox-Hunting Man* contributes consistently to that aspect of the War Myth that imagines the pre-War world as essentially untroubled.

Graves's *Good-bye to All That* offers an altogether livelier and more complicated picture both of the pre-War world than Sassoon provides and of war experience than Blunden gives us. Possibly from competitive motives, Graves decided to pack into it all that his former comrades had left out: family, schooling, erotic attachment (he falls in love platonically with a younger boy at Charterhouse) and literary life, especially encounters with poets. Unlike the ostensibly unlettered 'George Sherston', the young Graves is shown as being born into literature, his father being a poet whose wife takes part in his Shakespeare reading circle. Part of the book's distinction is that it portrays the young Graves as knowing rather than innocent, and as already embattled and embittered before he sees action at the Front. Indeed Graves takes this premature knowingness to improbable lengths, claiming in the opening pages that at a very early age 'I had no illusions about Algernon Charles Swinburne,' (Graves 1929: 15) the poet being a neighbour who would pat and kiss the infant Graves in his pram. Such a far-fetched claim to having been already disillusioned in infancy forewarns us that we should not expect this story to be one of innocence shattered by war; rather, we find a continuous running battle between the young Graves's combative scepticism and the absurdities of successive institutions – family, school, army – which resemble one another in their arcane codes of honour, conduct, jargon and internal rivalry. These continuities, underscored by the fact of Graves's almost direct passage from public school to Army, are significant in the book's satirical analysis of 'All That', in other words of British social institutions, and they are matched by continuity in the young Graves's own attitudes towards them, which combine mocking disdain with a certain loyal pride.

The figure of Graves as a boy offered by *Good-bye to All That* is by no means that of a harmless dreamer. At school he is already a fighter, having taken up boxing as a way of protecting himself from the domineering elite of cricketers; and he attends an Officer Training Corps camp to be shown modern machine guns and artillery. He knows something of modern warfare from his elderly relatives' reminiscences of the Crimean and Franco-Prussian wars. The schoolboy Graves does have an innocent side to him, being shocked by sex-talk and irreligion among his peers, but this is only one aspect of what we recognise as a character of novelistic complexity, in a story that reads at times more as education-novel than as credible autobiography. By the same token, the pre-War world it recalls, although comfortable for the prosperous Graves family, is no harmonious idyll either. It is shown from the perspective of the late 1920s to be a world of strict caste distinctions, patriarchal family relations and narrow chauvinism (he is ostracised at school, for having a German middle name, von Ranke, from his mother's German family), in which codes of schoolboy honour allow bullying to go unchallenged. As Graves departs from Charterhouse, he agrees with a schoolfellow that the only cure for the fundamental evil of the public schools is to raze them to the ground. In the same conversation, both boys expect to be still at Oxford in 1917, which we know will not happen.

The pre-War chapters of *Good-bye* are seeded with such ironic moments. When discussing one or other of his schoolfellows, Graves will by sudden prolepsis disclose what later happened to him in the War. That kind of proleptic illumination, though, has already begun in the fourth chapter, which is devoted to the happiest times of his childhood, the summer holidays spent with his German relatives outside Munich and in the Bavarian Alps. His uncle Siegfried, heir to a medieval castle, shows young Robert the family burial vault in the chapel, saying he himself will go there one day: a prediction immediately contradicted by Graves the narrator, who tells us that Siegfried was killed in the War, his body not even being found. Another such jolt comes cunningly wrapped within a nostalgic sentence about a granary at his grandfather's manor house: 'It was up here that my cousin Wilhelm, who was killed in an air-fight during the war, used to lie for hours shooting mice with an air-gun' (Graves 1929: 47). Graves's pre-War world, it may be noticed here in contrast with Sassoon's, is one that includes death and weaponry.

In due course, the enlisted and trained Captain Graves undergoes his own trench-education, beginning in the twelfth chapter. Again, this part of the story is by no means a tale of idealistic dreams dispelled by gory realities. It does involve a series of expectations that are surprisingly overturned, but often enough with the reverse tendency. Arriving at his battalion headquarters, he expects to find soldiers standing waist-deep in mud under shellfire and living only on biscuits. What he finds instead is good food eaten with polished silverware, pictures on the walls, a gramophone and proper sprung mattresses. A grimmer episode unfolds on Graves's first night-watch along the front line, when he comes across a soldier lying face-down and barefoot in a machine-gun shelter, and orders him to stand-to, only to be told by his comrade that the man has committed suicide. Two officers arrive, one reminding the other to write to the man's family saying he had died a soldier's death. Later in the same chapter, breakfast at company HQ is interrupted by a panicked soldier announcing a gas attack, at which the company commander calmly asks for his respirator and another jar of marmalade. The supposed gas turns out to be smoke drifting over from the cooked breakfasts the Germans are preparing in the trenches opposite. At this point Graves observes of the respirators issued for real gas attacks that nobody at the Front believed in their efficacy, as successive instructions from higher authority about their correct use (all on pink forms marked 'Urgent') were entirely contradictory.

These opening episodes set a pattern for what will follow through the central wartime chapters of the book. The principal lesson learned by our inexperienced officer is not that modern war is gruesome (he had guessed that already), but that it is a world of incompetence, absurd muddle and blundering confusion, in which official versions of events hardly ever tally with the events witnessed – as when Graves's own death is mistakenly reported in the newspapers while he convalesces from wounds sustained in battle. He also learns that the soldiers cope with the alarming contradictions of the trench-world by developing a unique form of *sang-froid* compounded of weary cynicism, superstition and ironic gallows humour. The strong current of grimly farcical humour that runs through *Good-bye to All That* is a kind of memorial tribute to that wartime spirit. In other ways, though, Graves's autobiography shows how strongly that spirit persisted into the late 1920s, as a habit of mind that took life to be mostly a bitter farce in which the pretensions of institutional authority exposed themselves as especially risible. It is the same spirit that animates such contemporary novels as *Death of a Hero* and Waugh's *Decline and Fall*.

The three war-books that we have examined here illustrate in special form some of the generic distortions which, as we noted in the Introduction, are among the peculiarities of this decade's literature. In the first place, they appear as substitute versions of the semi-autobiographical 'first novel' subgenre, retaining its emphasis on initiation and learning. Indeed Graves admits at the start of his twelfth chapter that this part of his account has been derived from a novel that he had earlier abandoned; and, as we have seen, Sassoon's protagonist-narrator 'Sherston' is a clearly fictional device. Secondly, these books, particularly Graves's, strangely combine that youthful genre with another formerly reserved for the elderly: the memoir devoted to famous battles, celebrated persons and the commemoration of deceased friends. Sassoon was forty-two years old when his *Memoirs of a Fox-Hunting Man* were published, while Blunden and Graves were both still in their mid-thirties at the time their equivalent works appeared. The justification for such unwontedly premature memoirism was of course that the War had provided each with at least a volume's-worth of remarkable experience while still young. Considered simply from this generic angle, all three books are distinctive 1920s productions marked by that confounding of life-stages typical of the young-veteran generation.

War-experience in the Novel: *The Spanish Farm Trilogy* and *Kangaroo*

The war memoirs of the late Twenties had been preceded by various openly fictional accounts of war experiences presented in novels. By far the greatest artistic achievement among those works is that of Ford Madox Ford in his first three Tietjens novels (1924–6) of the *Parade's End* sequence. Some aspects of Ford's remarkable time-shifting narrative have been discussed in the previous chapter. Here we will look instead at two lesser works that focus upon the War in a way that Ford tends not to pursue: as a crisis that tests and transforms the fictional hero.

R. H. Mottram's *The Spanish Farm Trilogy* is a 'conventional' fiction in that it springs on the reader none of the narrative disorientations or stylistic bewilderments that characterise Ford's works and those of the larger Modernist current in fiction. Published at first as three independent novels, it became an expanded trilogy with the addition of interlinking short stories – much as John Galsworthy had tied together *The Forsyte Saga* (1922), although Mottram's structural design diverges from Galsworthy's in that its second and third novels take us back over events of the 1915–19 period, each time through the eyes of a different central character. The first novel, *The Spanish Farm* (1924), follows the fortunes of Madeleine Vanderlynden, a young Frenchwoman whose father owns the titular farm, 'L'Espagnole', used as a billet by a British battalion behind the lines of the nearby Front in French Flanders. Madeleine is separated by the War from her young aristocratic lover, Georges d'Archeville, who eventually dies at the Front in 1917; meanwhile the hitherto small world of this farmer's daughter expands as she takes up clerical work for government offices in Amiens and then Paris, while also engaging in an affair with an English officer in his early thirties, Lieutenant Geoffrey Skene. ('Hardly a breath of disillusionment spoiled their few hours together,' the narrator tells us, using significant Twenties diction to describe their first night as lovers (Mottram 1979: 88).) The second novel, *Sixty-Four, Ninety-Four!* (1925) follows the course of Skene's war. An architect in civilian life, he has volunteered, not in the hope of achieving some imagined glory but merely from a determination to play his proper part in the rescue of Belgium. At the novel's end he reflects that through his war service he has 'fulfilled a need, worked out a destiny', and earned a kind of self-esteem just by having taken part (Mottram 1979: 379).

The concluding novel, *The Crime at Vanderlynden's* (1926), tells the story of another British officer, the unimaginative former bank clerk Captain Stephen Dormer, a temporary staff officer at Divisional Headquarters. He too has 'never been taken up with the honour and glory of war', but sees his service just as a job that must be done (Mottram 1979: 454). Dormer is assigned the duty of investigating and arranging reparation for an act of vandalism at the Spanish Farm in which an unidentified British soldier has smashed up a roadside religious shrine in order to shelter his mules. When local French politicians demand that the culprit be arrested, the story is then structured as a detective quest that turns out to be a fruitless fool's errand, left unresolved as Dormer is taken off duty on grounds of ill-health and the War comes to an end. Dormer's role in negotiating with French authorities over compensation for damage done by British forces to local property is, incidentally, one that matches Mottram's own part in the War.

In the context of war fiction, Mottram's trilogy has two salient peculiarities: first, that its focus is more on the logistics of modern war than on combat or trench-life. The plots of all three novels concern various consequences of billeting British soldiers on French properties, while *The Spanish Farm* also explores the employment of women to carry out the paperwork of the war-machine. *The Crime at Vanderlynden's* in particular continuously follows the bureaucratic processes of local Franco-British diplomacy, of troop transportation and supply, and of military policing. In the second place, Mottram's pictures of human suffering and frailty have far more to do with illness (including the huge influenza pandemic at the War's end) than with shrapnel wounds or poison-gassing. Madeleine's lover d'Archeville in *The Spanish Farm* dies on the field of battle, but not from enemy fire; rather it is from tuberculosis, having prematurely discharged himself from hospital in impetuous eagerness to join the battle. In the later novels, both Skene and Dormer find themselves sent away from the war-zone when their health collapses.

Of the three Spanish-Farm novels, it is the centrally-placed *Sixty-Four, Ninety-Four!* that most clearly pursues a narrative of initiation and education in the ways of modern war, in which the novice hero is shown becoming martially experienced. It is the only one, moreover, in which episodes of combat put the protagonist through a baptism of fire. Before we come to that, though, we are conducted through Skene's first and most enduring lesson, which is that modern warfare for the most part involves crowds of men waiting around becoming increasingly ill. Skene is indeed described on his first day at the base camp as being 'struck with horror' by a large sick-parade of unhealthy soldiers: 'It was a shock to find that the fighting depended on a large stationary military population, as vulnerable to illness or accident as the population of London' (Mottram 1979: 187). For Skene, the 'waste' of this war is not in the first place a matter of its casualties but of its constant squandering of human and material resources, its inefficiencies and muddles. It is within that context that his brief and confused taste of combat itself, during the Battle of the Somme, is framed in the twelfth chapter.

Two weeks prior to the battle, Skene experiences a mood of elated expectation, feeling 'like a happy schoolboy, after the Easter holidays going back, not so much to school, as to cricket', and rediscovering the 'heroical' vision of 1914 (Mottram 1979: 261). On the night that he leads his platoon into action, he suddenly finds himself flat on his back, fainting, to awaken two days later, vomiting on a stretcher inside a cattle-truck, and to be told that he is one of the few survivors from his unit. Patched up and recuperated, Skene rejoins what is left of his company several days later, and at last takes part in a sustained and successful attack; he shoots one German soldier in a rather apologetic fashion, then passes out again from illness. This brief but climactic episode of action on the Somme is the only part of the entire trilogy that follows the revelatory pattern of the punctured dream that we expect from the War Myth; and even then, the dispelling of illusion takes the form of bewildered collapse rather than of gory horror. This emphasis on the confusion and sheer opacity of war experience rather than on any claimed illumination of the 'truth of war' is consistent with Mottram's unspectacular achievement in the *Spanish Farm Trilogy* as a whole, a work that renders convincingly a war experienced mostly as inconclusive movement and unanswered questions amid endless waiting.

Mottram's trilogy shows little interest in presenting war-experience according to any dominant pattern of disillusionment, tending rather to dissolve the strong Before/After and Us/Them binaries of the War Myth in favour of narrative designs that foreground endurance and personal growth. D. H. Lawrence's *Kangaroo*, on the other hand, voices a desperately intense investment in those same binary oppositions, without even being a war-novel in most accepted senses. Its story is set on the other side of the world (in and around Sydney, Australia) nearly four years after the Armistice, and describes the thoughts and experiences of an English poet and essayist, Richard Lovatt Somers, who has arrived in Australia with his wife Harriett for no apparent reason other than whim. Somers is far more transparently than his fictional counterparts in *Women in Love* and *Aaron's Rod* (Rupert Birkin and Rawdon Lilly, respectively) a portrait of Lawrence himself in the process of dramatised self-analysis; indeed, the mask of fiction at times slips away as the narrator addresses us directly as an essayist, the Somers figure being cast off in temporary forgetfulness or impatience. The agenda of *Kangaroo* recapitulates the preoccupations of those earlier novels with the problem of love between men and women (its insufficiency for the Lawrentian male, its fearsomely engulfing possessiveness) and with the fantasy of a counterbalancing blood-brotherhood to be established with another man.

Somers struggles with Harriett for mastery in their marriage, insisting that he needs to go out into the world to do things with other men. As it so happens, certain other men, Australians who have served in the War and have learned to value discipline and obedience, are interested in recruiting Somers to their fascist conspiracy. His neighbour Jack Callcott claims Somers as a trusted 'mate', and introduces him to the charismatic leader of the conspirators, Ben Cooley, nicknamed Kangaroo. Cooley, a wealthy Jewish lawyer, has already studied and become an admirer of Somers's writings (especially those repudiating democracy) and so he and Callcott regard Somers's arrival as a fated opportunity to pair his talents with Kangaroo's in the project of rescuing Australia from the chaos of democracy and from the blind materialism of the unionised working man. Today Australia, tomorrow perhaps the world: if he accepts the conspirators' invitation, it looks as though this stray English intellectual with no political experience may be on the brink of world domination and the establishment of a new Lawrentian dispensation not unlike the dawning of the Christian era. At a later point, Kangaroo's arch-enemy, the socialist leader Struthers, invites Somers to edit a new magazine promoting brotherhood as a new religion. The plot of *Kangaroo* beckons Somers towards the most unlikely megalomanic destinies which, for reasons that are obscure even to himself, he nonetheless declines. As a plot, it expires inconclusively: Kangaroo is shot in the stomach during a street-battle with socialists and dies later, while Somers and Harriett prepare to quit Australia.

Lawrence dashed off this novel in six weeks while still in Australia, and a good deal of it reads like hastily drafted padding: inconsequential descriptions of touristic outings, luncheon menus, or household chores, with snippets from a local newspaper and irrelevant summaries of gossip mailed from friends in Europe are mixed in with disconnected scenes of walks in the bush and with lyrically invoked seascapes. And yet the novel includes two chapters that stand out as being written with an altogether more gripping conviction. The seventh chapter, 'The Battle of Tongues', presents a crisis in the main action, as Somers rejects the doctrine of love on which Kangaroo's political project is founded, in the name of a holy separateness urged by the Dark Gods of the lower body. He then rejects a direct sexual appeal to his lower body offered by Callcott's wife Victoria, discovering that in his heart of hearts he is in fact 'stubbornly puritanical' for all his talk of pagan spontaneity (Lawrence 1997: 143). His imagination is in retreat from the warm-heartedness of Harriett, Kangaroo and Victoria, pulling away into fantasies of clear, cold isolation, like that of a fish or of a diving gannet. Toward the chapter's end, Somers impulsively runs naked into the sea, as if to cleanse himself of all human attachments (as always for Lawrence, baptism is the prime sacrament and must precede marriage), before reclaiming his wife sexually. Harriett congratulates him on the fine style in which he has done this: '"Straight from the sea, like another creature"' (Lawrence 1997: 147). It is important to Lawrence that Somers be seen here not as an ordinary domesticated husband driven by tamely uxurious desire, but as another creature that is fearsomely non-human: a divinity, a totemic animal or bird (apart from the fish and gannet, Somers is identified at various points with the tiger, the scorpion and the kestrel), even a kind of conquering hero. The chapter seems designed like a miniature *Odyssey* in which the hero evades monsters of different kinds and returns from the sea-world to establish command over his kingdom.

More extraordinary still is the twelfth chapter, 'The Nightmare', in which Somers's irritable mood, his perverse refusals of all that he has previously thought he had wanted, and even his hitherto unmotivated exile in Australia are at last given an explanation, in the form of a long-repressed memory. It is here that the novel takes us back unexpectedly to the War period, of which Somers's own experience has curiously gone unmentioned in his conversations with Australian war-veterans. Now, though, it all comes back to Somers in a rush, 'like a volcanic eruption in his consciousness' (Lawrence 1997: 259). The experience Somers recalls is not of military service but of non-combatant life in Cornwall and London. It is also virtually identical to the story of Lawrence's own wartime misadventures, in which he and his German wife Frieda had come under harassment as alleged spies, having their cottage ransacked, their shopping bags searched and being required to leave Cornwall and report regularly to police stations. Meanwhile Lawrence had rejected both the War and the pacifists, in turn being thrice rejected himself by the medical boards as – to his mixed relief and indignation – unfit for military service. The chapter is an exercise in autobiographical exorcism disguised, some years before Siegfried Sassoon adopted this method, as a fiction.

In 'The Nightmare', Lawrence provides, sometimes in the tones of Biblical prophecy, his most apocalyptic endorsement of the War Myth. 'It was in 1915 the old world ended,' he tells us (Lawrence 1997: 216); although the historic collapse did not work its way through to the political leadership until late 1916:

> From 1916 to 1919 a wave of criminal lust rose and possessed England, there was a reign of Terror, under a set of indecent bullies like Bottomley of *John Bull* and other bottom-dog members of the House of Commons [...] The torture was steadily applied, during those years after Asquith fell, to break the independent soul in any man who would not hunt with the criminal mob. (Lawrence 1997: 212)

Lawrence pinpoints the turning point from civilisation to barbarism as the replacement in December 1916 of H. H. Asquith's Liberal-led coalition government by a new coalition headed by David Lloyd George. The years following that were, in Lawrence's account, the 'years when the world lost its real manhood', swept up by the mob-spirit of democracy (Lawrence 1997: 213). As Lawrence presents it, the War may have been officially won at the Front but it was lost at home, as the once proud human spirit collapsed into ignominy, and London, once the true heart of the world, became a vortex of lusts, fears and horrors. 'The English soul went under, in the war,' Lawrence tells us (Lawrence 1997: 222), in part because it had, democratically, let itself be led by a Welshman: Somers comes to believe that 'all Jews, and all Celts' are secretly working to bring about the final betrayal and humiliation of England (Lawrence 1997: 226). The English people themselves, however, have willingly sold their souls to the war-machine and turned into a pack of baying jackals, or a *canaille* (rabble) of sub-humans who have in Somers's eyes proved their unfitness to govern themselves.

The climax of 'The Nightmare' comes in 1918 with Somers's third summons to medical examination for military fitness. The first two such procedures had been conducted in Bodmin in 1916 and 1917 by gentlemen-doctors who had respected the sanctity of a man's body. But this time at Derby – associated by Lawrence with the life-denying industrial world of the Midlands – Somers is led undressed into a room with other naked men, told to cough while an orderly cups his testicles, and then required to bend and part his legs for his anus to be inspected. Although thousands of other men (as Somers himself later concedes) must have gone through the same indignities, Somers – and we are entitled to assume Lawrence too – takes them personally, in a spirit of persecution mania, as the ultimate violation of his manhood, calling down in response a biblical curse:

> Never would he be touched again.– And because they had handled his private parts, and looked into them, their eyes should burst and their hands should wither and their hearts should rot. So he cursed them in his blood, with an unremitting curse, as he waited. (Lawrence 1997: 255)

Even before coming to this examination, Somers has decided that the policemen who question him politely, along with the population they represent, are

> *canaille*, carrion-eating, filthy-mouthed *canaille*, like dead-men-devouring jackals. I wish to God I could kill them. I wish I had power to blight them, to slay them with a blight, slay them in thousands and thousands. I wish to God I could kill them off, the masses of *canaille*. (Lawrence 1997: 250)

Somers's disillusionment is comprehensive. Before his violation, he had 'believed in the constitutional liberty of an Englishman' (Lawrence 1997: 217), and to an extent in some kind of democracy, but after the unleashing of the mob-spirit in the War things look very different. 'No man who has really consciously lived through this can believe again absolutely in democracy' (Lawrence 1997: 216). Not only democracy, though, stands discredited; its post-War competitors, the socialism of Struthers and the fascism of Kangaroo, Somers concludes, are just the latest expressions of the mob-spirit, both founded on the ideals of Love and Humanity that for Somers have been exposed as putrefied. There is nothing to do but cut loose from human beings and to cling to the Dark Gods.

Other Disenchantments and Awakenings: Mansfield

Having dwelt at some length on 'disillusioned' writing in the contexts of the War and of the War Myth, it is time to put that in a larger context, in the first place by reminding ourselves that disillusionment was not invented in 1920 or even in 1914, any more than sex was invented in the 1960s. Writers and readers in the Twenties may have persuaded themselves that the wool had been pulled from their eyes by unprecedented historical shocks, but then some of them were well placed to remember that disillusionment is itself a literary myth or essential narrative design of some antiquity. The story of a naïve idealist colliding with the disappointments and complexities of real life had been told many times before, and most often in the literary tradition that we call Realism. Especially since the mid-nineteenth century, under the literary influences of Gustave Flaubert, George Eliot and Henrik Ibsen, and sometimes inspired by the philosophical anti-idealism of Friedrich Nietzsche too, writers had played numerous variations upon the same theme. The realism that we find in war poetry of the 1917–18 vintage forms only one branch of a larger tradition that persists into the 1920s, often in forms that seem unrelated to any specifically post-War mood of bitterness.

A significant case is that of Katherine Mansfield's short stories. Mansfield had been publishing her fiction since 1911, and had often favoured daydreaming fantasists for whom life has nasty surprises in store – in 'The Little Governess' (1915) or 'Pictures' and 'Bliss' (both 1918), for instance. In her all-too-brief Twenties phase, before her death in January 1923, she carried on as before, showing a continuing interest in moments of initiation when a naïve protagonist runs up against unexpected jolts and disappointments, as the title of the story 'Her First Ball' (1921) suggests. One such tale, 'A Cup of Tea' (1922), concerns a wealthy and pampered young married woman, Rosemary, who while out shopping is approached by another young woman who is reduced to begging in the streets. Rather than give her the money she needs, Rosemary decides to invite her home to her own luxurious apartment, simply because it would provide a little adventure of the kind she has read about in novels. When Rosemary's husband comes home, she struggles to introduce her increasingly uncomfortable guest, not having even bothered to ask her name. Rosemary's dream of philanthropic sisterhood suddenly sours when it becomes apparent that her husband finds the object of her charity strikingly attractive.

The most celebrated of Mansfield's stories of disabused innocence is the title story of *The Garden Party and Other Stories* (1922). It is one of several set in Edwardian New Zealand, and it concerns a prosperous family with extensive grounds around their house. The action is viewed from the perspective of one of the daughters of the house, Laura Sheridan, whose age is never specified, although we guess her to be in her mid-teens. Laura's mother, assisted by her numerous children and servants, is preparing to host a lavish garden party with a band, a marquee and hired waiters when news arrives that an impoverished neighbour in a nearby cottage has been thrown from his horse and killed, leaving a widow and five children. Laura's first thought is that the party must be called off, as she dreads to think of the cottagers' mourning invaded by sounds of merriment; but her mother tells her not to be absurd, and so Laura postpones her concern for the bereaved until after the festivities. The party itself is skimmed over in less than a page, and then Laura is dispatched by her mother with a basket of leftover sandwiches and cakes to deliver to the widowed neighbour. Feeling self-conscious about her fancy party-hat, Laura ventures down the lane of shabby cottages which as a child she had been forbidden to enter for fear of disease and foul language, and expects to drop the basket off at the door. She is alarmed, however, to find herself ushered inside by the widow's sister and taken to view the body, which surprises her by its calm beauty. Emerging shaken and tearful, she is led home by her brother.

Mansfield closes 'The Garden Party' with no stated moral, and without identifying any lesson that Laura has learned. We do not know, for instance, whether this is Laura's first encounter with death, although it seems clear that she has not until now been inside a working-class home. The story nonetheless leaves us with a strong sense that Laura's world has suddenly become deeper and darker, against a background formed by the expensive flowers and pastries of the party. Earlier in the action, she has reflected on the pleasant manner of the workmen who erect the marquee, and told herself that she would prefer to have workmen rather than middle-class boys as friends, because she has no attachment to 'stupid conventions' or to 'these absurd class distinctions' (Mansfield 2002: 338). Her later nervous foray into the lane of washerwomen's cottages surely impresses on her that the gulf between leisure and poverty cannot be so casually brushed away; and she may have noticed too that her family's sympathy for the poor neighbours has been grudging at best (her mother has refused to send any of her large stock of lilies, in case they stain Laura's dress). Whether this is an experience from which she is capable of learning something remains an open question.

The Painted Veil and Mr Fortune's Maggot

Given the decline of the education-novel in the 1920s, and its partial replacement by the war-narrative, stories in which the innocent protagonist develops through peacetime experience are rarer, and the catalyst for maturation tends to become travel to some faraway place whose strangeness beckons the character out of the constraints of her or his upbringing. A clear case of this pattern is W. Somerset Maugham's novel *The Painted Veil* (1925), which takes a conspicuously shallow and unreflective young woman from Kensington and leads her to hell and back, or more exactly to a Chinese city ravaged by an outbreak of cholera. Kitty Garstin has been brought up by her snobbish and materialistic mother to make a 'good match' with a wealthy husband on the basis of her good looks, but by her mid-twenties has failed to find one. When her younger and plainer sister becomes engaged, Kitty unthinkingly accepts the first suitor who comes her way, an intelligent but shy bacteriologist, Walter Fane, who works for the colonial government of Hong Kong, where he takes her once they are married. Walter adores Kitty despite being aware of her shallowness, but Kitty feels nothing but bored irritation with her husband, and soon takes the senior colonial official Charles Townsend as her lover. When Walter discovers the affair, Kitty is relieved, because she is sure that the crisis will result in Walter allowing her to divorce him while Townsend will be similarly released by his own wife, and the lovers will end up married – or so she daydreams. Her husband, knowing Townsend better, tells her he will grant her a divorce only if Townsend's wife indicates that she will divorce him, and if Townsend himself signs a letter committing himself to marry Kitty. Failing those conditions, she must accompany him on what looks like a suicidal mission to take charge of the epidemic in the remote city. Trusting to the strength of the secret romance, Kitty puts this to her lover, and is abruptly disabused, just as Walter knew she would be: the careerist Townsend has no intention of wrecking his marriage or career for the sake of Kitty, even in the knowledge that his refusal will propel her into great danger. As she denounces her lover's cowardice, Kitty recognises that Walter has foreseen it all. 'It's strange that he should have judged you so accurately,' she tells him. 'It was just like him to expose me to such a cruel disillusion' (Maugham 1952: 82).

Walter has indeed engineered a sudden disillusionment, and it turns out to be a transformative one for Kitty. Not only does she turn from frivolous socialite to something resembling (to all eyes except hers and her husband's) a selfless heroine by travelling to the cholera-stricken city and doing menial work in a convent of French nuns who care for the dying. She also learns, after the shock of being let down by Townsend, to assess herself and others more coolly, having discovered from another colonial official, the sharp-witted Mr Waddington, that Townsend is a notorious philanderer and a man of no special qualities. She grows out of her initial hatred for her husband, coming to respect him for his dedicated life-saving work while pitying him for the secret self-loathing in which he has imprisoned himself. In part this change is brought about under the influence of encounters with two foreign women very different from her social-climbing mother, each of whom has left behind a life of privilege to pursue a more selfless existence: one is a Manchu woman who has become Waddington's devoted mistress; the other and more important is the Mother Superior of the convent, an aristocrat who has renounced an easy life for one of poverty and religious discipline. Kitty knows that she cannot become like these feminine marvels, but nor can she rest easy within her old identity, vaguely aware as she now is that her life ought to have some purpose beyond herself.

The plot of *The Painted Veil* brings us some of Maugham's usual well-crafted twists: just as Kitty has put the memory of Townsend behind her, she finds that she is pregnant, almost certainly by her ex-lover. Then as the epidemic abates, Walter suddenly dies, apparently from conducting bacteriological experiments upon himself. Kitty resolves to return to London, but must first dispose of her house in Hong Kong, where further surprises are sprung: first, Townsend's wife, who regards Kitty as some sort of saint, insists on her staying at her home, which brings her into daily contact with the very man she had hoped never to see again. Then, when Townsend finds her alone and kisses her, she is overwhelmed by her need for him – exactly what she thought her earlier disenchantment had extinguished for good – and takes him to her bed. Cursing herself afterwards as a slut, Kitty discovers that being disillusioned does not eradicate the cravings and fantasies that have given rise to illusion in the first place. She takes the next boat home, receives news of her mother's death and decides to make amends to her father, whom she has until now always treated selfishly as a mere provider. He has just accepted a position in the Bahamas, where Kitty will accompany him, hoping to bring up her child under unclouded skies. Assuming the child will be a girl, she determines to bring her up as a free self-possessed person, not – as Kitty herself had been – as a dependent husband-hunter. Travel beyond the small world in which she grew up has given Kitty a taste for further exploration as well as a fresh view of her responsibilities.

In a more fanciful and light-hearted mode, Sylvia Townsend Warner's prose romance *Mr Fortune's Maggot* (1927) takes its protagonist through a not dissimilar course of healthy disillusionment and self-transformation through immersion in the exotic. The title character is a middle-aged and easily good-natured Anglican missionary who decides (this being his 'maggot' or odd whim) to convert the population of a remote volcanic island in the Pacific. Before he arrives, he imagines that he will be able 'to live among them and gather their souls as a child gathers daisies in a field' (Warner 1978: 5). After three years spent evading the flirtatious curiosity of the native women, the Revd Timothy Fortune has made only a single convert: a beautiful adolescent boy named Lueli, whom he comes to love. The rest of the islanders pay not the slightest heed to his strange gospel, and merrily carry on worshipping graven images and dancing provocatively in a state of unashamed semi-nakedness. When at last he discovers that Lueli too has secretly carried on the cult of his private idol alongside the rote-learning of Christian doctrine, Fortune concludes that his mission has been not only futile but an unforgivable intrusion upon an essentially happy people. Shortly after this, the earth moves: an earthquake shakes the island, and is followed by an eruption of its dormant volcano, which destroys Fortune's house and Lueli's fetish. At this point Fortune's pocket-watch stops, and he loses his faith in God with no noticeable crisis of conscience, almost as if his belief had simply wound down like the spring of the watch. Eventually he decides to leave for home, but not before carving, by way of atonement, a new wooden fetish for Lueli to worship. On the boat to the nearest white settlement, he hears for the first time news of the outbreak of the Great War in Europe. We have been, without knowing it until this point, reading a 'Before' narrative that culminates with the exposure of European moral authority as hollow. Mr Fortune's personal disenchantment and his indulgence of innocent paganism have, it seems, foreshadowed the crumbling of the idols back home.

Learning from Experience: Huxley

We have seen that the protagonists of Maugham's and Warner's fictions learn from their experience of travel among people different from themselves, and that among the things they learn is that they must unlearn the certainties they have acquired from a more limited prior experience of life at home. This accords with Aldous Huxley's reflections on the value of travelling, as he sums up the impact upon him of the world tour recounted in *Jesting Pilate* (1926). Back in London after circumnavigating the globe, he describes himself as 'richer by much experience and poorer by many exploded convictions, many perished certainties' (Huxley 1994d: 200). He had set out thinking he knew how human beings ought to live, how they should educate their children and how organise their societies; he has returned with all those convictions overthrown ('Of knowledge and experience the fruit is generally doubt' (Huxley 1994d: 200)) in favour of a new conviction of the unity-in-diversity of humanity. Strongly-held opinions, as distinct from values, now seem to him to be somehow less than human: 'A dog is as full of certainty as the Veteran Liberal who has held the same opinions for forty years' (Huxley 1994d: 200). To many of Huxley's generation, an entrenched conviction about anything was to be seen as belonging with the falsehoods of war-propaganda or with the exploded creeds of the Victorians. Experience acquired through Travel or through war (itself a form of travel under compulsion) seemed in the 1920s to endorse a flexible scepticism.

Some kinds of disillusionment could be held, in these terms, to be valuably formative and even liberating to the modern spirit. That standpoint, though, could never entirely shake off a nagging doubt about whether people really do learn from experience. Travel, for example, might broaden the mind, but only for those with minds elastic enough to be broadened. Huxley's essay 'Why Not Stay at Home?', in his earlier travel-book *Along the Road* (1925), considers that problem and answers it with a distinction between the tourist and the genuine traveller. The tourist engages in travel not, as the true traveller does, from motives of curiosity about the wider world but in order to acquire conventional social esteem and topics of conversation. Instead of going to explore the real city of Paris, for instance, he will embark for a legendary place called Gay Paree and of course fail to find it, dutifully carrying on a pretence of enjoyment to cover his boredom and frustration. Huxley presents the general fate of tourists thus:

> They set out, nourished on fables and fantastical hopes, to return, whether they avow it or not, disappointed. Their interest in the real and actual being insufficiently lively, they hanker after mythology, and the facts, however curious, beautiful and varied, are a disillusionment. (Huxley 1994a: 6)

This kind of disillusionment, or so Huxley presumes, is unimproving, merely a dead-end of false hopes deflated.

The question whether experience really teaches anything was of pressing importance in the 1920s, because if nothing had been learned from the War, it seemed likely that its horrors would soon be repeated. R. H. Mottram introduced *Sixty-Four, Ninety-Four!* with a preface justifying its appearance on the grounds that the War 'is only tolerable, as a memory, when one can feel that some one learned something from it. Otherwise it becomes a mere nightmare of Waste' (Mottram 1979: 177).

The novel itself, though, provides several suggestions that wartime experience is not digestible into productive lessons, even in practical military matters. At one point its protagonist, Skene, when told that a group of fresh recruits at the Front simply needs a bit more experience, reflects that 'in this War, contrary to all others, experience rendered one less, and not more, fit to carry out one's duties', this reflection itself being of course the fruit of his own, mostly bewildering, experience (Mottram 1979: 268). It is Huxley again who pushes that kind of doubt to its larger conclusions. In *Antic Hay*, he has the protagonist's father, the architect Gumbril Senior, reflect on the general inability of humankind to draw lessons from its most glaring errors, denying the applicability of the Latin tag *Experientia docet* ('Experience teaches'): 'Several million people were killed in a recent war and half the world ruined; but we all busily go on in courses that make another event of the same sort inevitable. *Experientia docet? Experientia* doesn't' (Huxley 1994b: 129).

Although Huxley himself allows for the existence of older people who have learned something from life (Gumbril Senior is one, the sexagenarian Mr Cardan in *Those Barren Leaves* is another), the satirical writing of the 1920s more often assumes that the people most stubbornly self-blinded to the lessons of experience are the Old. Richard Aldington's *Death of a Hero* opens with an epigraph from the eighteenth-century writer Horace Walpole in which he observes of England that 'there is not a country upon earth where there are so many old fools and so few young ones' (Aldington 1984: 5); and the remark can only be meant to be taken as applicable to the England of Aldington's own time. The novel's narrator declares later, for example, that 'A nation which relies on the alleged wisdom of sexagenarians is irrevocably degenerate' (Aldington 1984: 142). Other young writers of the time indulged similar prejudices: Christopher Isherwood's debut novel *All the Conspirators* (1928) gives us a one-sided view of a 'domestic guerilla warfare' between a mother and her son, an account that Isherwood much later admitted was marred by youthful 'chauvinism' against the over-forties (Isherwood 1967: 73, 7). Against the background of such devaluations of experience and widespread derision of Old Fools, it becomes all the more instructive to listen to a few elderly voices of the decade.

The Elder Ironists and the End of Innocence

The elder writers of the 1920s were no longer the 'Edwardians' of Woolf's dismissive category but now senior Georgians or Moderns who had come through the War years with their own scars of anxiety and bereavement. They enjoyed certain advantages of perspective, including a stronger sense of historical continuity, an inoculation from their various prior disappointments against disillusioning shocks, and an acquired scepticism about simplified oppositions. In the context of Us/Them thinking and prejudice, Rudyard Kipling's late ditty 'We and They' (1926) mocks the childish binarism of cultural and racial antagonism from a seasoned multiculturalist standpoint that may still surprise readers who in like fashion regard Kipling as 'not one of Us': 'But – would you believe it? – They look upon We / As only a sort of They!' (Kipling 1999: 502). Meanwhile Arnold Bennett, in his capacity as chief book reviewer of the London *Evening Standard*, had occasion to deliver some choice rebukes to the arrogance of his literary juniors. Reviewing *Death of a Hero* in otherwise largely positive terms, he wrote:

> I think that the chief trouble with Mr Aldington as a writer is spiritual pride. He writes: 'I disbelieve in bunk.' Which somehow reminds me of the women who say: 'I loathe cruelty to animals.' As though nobody else did! As though they were in a tiny superior class apart! (Bennett 1974: 306)

As for disillusionment and irony, some of the elder poets had been experts in them before Sassoon and his contemporaries had even been born, and for them nothing much had changed in that respect or any other. The octogenarian Thomas Hardy's verse collections of the decade – *Late Lyrics and Earlier* (1922), *Human Shows* (1925) and the posthumous *Winter Words* (1928) – all exhibit his habitually ironic 'long view' of human hopes and disenchantments, as in the brief poem 'Just the Same' (1922):

> I sat. It all was past;
> Hope never would hail again;
> Fair days had ceased at a blast,
> The world was a darkened den.
>
> The beauty and dream were gone,
> And the halo in which I had hied
> So gaily gallantly on
> Had suffered blot and died!
>
> I went forth, heedless whither,
> In a cloud too black for name:
> – People frisked hither and thither;
> The world was just the same.
>
> (Hardy 1994: 166–7)

Here it is clear that the speaker has not attained through disappointment an awareness superior to his earlier hope, at least not until the final line. Both the halo of original innocence and the cloud of embittered experience serve to obscure from him the healthy equanimity of other people's indifference, which embodies the cyclical sameness of human life.

A similar perspective, as in Hardy's case informed by the study of ancient literatures, appears in the later work of A. E. Housman, the grave-haunting gloom of whose *A Shropshire Lad* (1896) was by now recognised as that of a modern classic. Even the title of his long-delayed second collection, *Last Poems* (1922), suggests that he was already dead, when in fact he was a reasonably healthy sexagenarian and just indulging in typically precipitate fatalism. In Housman's poetic world, the snatching by Death of young men and women, in war or private tragedy, is not only predictable but almost obligatory. Equally inescapable is the discrepancy between human expectations and the mathematically certain laws of existence, as lyric xxxv of the *Last Poems* suggests in its final stanza:

> – To think that two and two are four
>   And neither five nor three
> The heart of man has long been sore
>   And long 'tis like to be.
>
> (Housman 1989: 136)

Long inured to change and to loss, writers of Housman's or of Hardy's generations were less likely to adopt any modern myth according to which the world had changed utterly at some recent date. It was not that they were personally indifferent to the catastrophe of the War, or even ignorant of its unprecedented features, but that their literary voices had been attuned already to an ironic disillusionment with which their more readily-scandalised juniors were now catching up.

Younger writers who prided themselves on being wiser than their seniors were not always as free from illusion as they believed. Some spoke with the authority of military experience, but they could still be quite innocent about Innocence. An extreme case is Wilfred Owen's posthumously published poem 'Arms and the Boy' (1920):

> Let the boy try along this bayonet-blade
> How cold steel is, and keen with hunger of blood;
> Blue with all malice, like a madman's flash;
> And thinly drawn with famishing for flesh.
>
> Lend him to stroke these blind, blunt bullet-leads,
> Which long to nuzzle in the hearts of lads,
> Or give him cartridges whose fine zinc teeth
> Are sharp with sharpness of grief and death.
>
> For his teeth seem for laughing round an apple.
> There lurk no claws behind his fingers supple;

> And God will grow no talons at his heels,
> Nor antlers through the thickness of his curls.
>
> (Owen 1985: 131)

The fantasy into which this poem invites us is one of absolute boyish innocence: the curly-haired lad of the poem is presented not only as innocuous but – by his Creator's design, no less – as constitutionally incapable of any malevolence, 'all malice' being attributed exclusively to the weaponry that he strokes but will not, we are to imagine, actually wield. Among critically respected and regularly anthologised poems of the early twentieth century, this is the nearest thing we have to outright kitsch.

'Arms and the Boy' is of course a 1920s poem by date of delayed publication only. Its date of composition was most probably the early summer of 1918, not long after Owen's twenty-fifth birthday, so it is not only a young man's poem but a composition strongly influenced by Sassoon's extreme war-mythicising simplifications. Had Owen survived into the 1920s, it is hard to imagine him persisting in this vein amid a culture that was becoming notably inhospitable to the idea of childish innocence. One factor in the increasing dismissal of that ideal as 'Victorian' was the rise of Freudian thought, in which every little boy is a parricidal Oedipus. From another quarter entirely came the followers of the French right-wing polemicist Charles Maurras, proclaiming a new 'classicism' in which there was no more room for innate human innocence than there was in the Freudian world-view. The most important figure in this group was T. S. Eliot, although the clearest restatements of its position appeared in T. E. Hulme's essays, published posthumously (he had been killed in battle, more than a year before Owen) as *Speculations* (1924). For the Maurrasian classicists, the great error of post-Renaissance culture, whether in Romantic literature or in liberal-humanist politics and ethics, lay in its denial of Original Sin, from which had ensued the heresies of Progress, Perfectibility and Personality. The classicist in Hulme's scheme regards the human individual as not just imperfect or radically flawed but as 'essentially bad' and in need of external disciplinary restraint (Hulme 1924: 47). Hulme's selective adoption of one element of Christian dogma (while heretically disregarding the gospel of Redemption) for essentially cultural-political purposes opened up a second, non-Freudian front against the myth of essential human innocence upon which Owen relies.

It is worth remembering that both the Freudian and the Hulmean 'tragic' conceptions of humanity as radically flawed or imperfect are of pre-War vintage in their formulation, although we may count the respectful hearing granted to them in the 1920s among the cultural consequences of the War. The same applies to an older version of tragic pessimism that was affiliated neither to Freudianism nor to Christian doctrine: that of Thomas Hardy, the most famous literary unbeliever of his age. The way in which Hardy scrutinises the face of seeming innocence in his poem 'On the Portrait of a Woman about to be Hanged' (1923) offers an instructive contrast to Owen's 'Arms and the Boy':

> Comely and capable one of our race,
> Posing there in your gown of grace,
>   Plain, yet becoming;
>   Could subtlest breast
>   Ever have guessed
> What was behind that innocent face,
>   Drumming, drumming!
>
> Would that your Causer, ere knoll your knell
> For this riot of passion, might deign to tell
>   Why, since It made you
>   Sound in the germ,
>   It sent a worm
> To madden Its handiwork, when It might well
>   Not have assayed you,
>
> Not have implanted, to your deep rue,
> The Clytaemnestra spirit in you,
>   And with purblind vision
>   Sowed a tare
>   In a field so fair,
> And a thing of symmetry, seemly to view,
>   Brought to derision!
>
> (Hardy 1994: 192)

The specific occasion for this poem was the execution in January 1923 of the 28-year-old shop manageress Edith Thompson for the murder of her husband Percy in October 1922, after a famous trial known as the 'Thompson–Bywaters' case. Edith Thompson had taken a younger man, her former lodger Frederick Bywaters, as her lover, and written him what turned out to be fatally compromising letters mentioning her plans to poison her husband. In fact Percy Thompson was stabbed by Bywaters, as he and Edith returned to their Ilford home after a night of theatre-going in the West End (they had been to see Ben Travers's first farce, *The Dippers* (1922)), and there was no hard evidence implicating Edith Thompson as a direct accomplice to that act. Her conviction and the rejection of her appeal may well have been for that reason a miscarriage of justice, as some subsequent commentators on the case have suggested. Hardy and millions of other British newspaper-readers, though, had been reading transcripts of her letters, in which they had seen the 'tare' of murderous intention. Even if legally not guilty, she could not in their eyes be seen as innocent either. In the 1920s, no presumption of innocence applied to the larger understanding of human motives, as we shall see in the next chapter's account of crime-writing.

Disillusionment and All That

There is no doubt that 'disillusionment' and its cognates are especially important period terms by which writers and readers in the Twenties repeatedly attempted to define the moral or psychological condition in which they found themselves. We hear these terms all the way through the decade, from the 'disillusions as never told in the old days' in Ezra Pound's verse sequence *Hugh Selwyn Mauberley* (1920) (Pound 2003: 552) to 'these disillusions' in Edmund Blunden's 'Report on Experience' in 1929. In between we may find, among many scattered instances, Huxley's typically disillusioned tourists in the passage from *Along the Road* quoted above; the novice philanderer Humphrey Gresham in Rose Macaulay's comic novel *Crewe Train* (1926), whose erotic exploits always leave him a 'Disillusioned young man' (Macaulay 1983: 51); and the characterisation of Michaelis the Irish playwright in Lawrence's *Lady Chatterley's Lover*, which repeatedly refers to the disillusion visible in his eyes, obscurely deemed an inheritance of his 'race' (Lawrence 1990: 25, 31, 55). The very ubiquity of such terms, though, tends to drain from them any settled significance. Somewhere between specific disappointments with love-affairs or holiday destinations and a loss of belief in some always unspecific creed or ideal, disillusionment is like an elusive phantom that haunts the decade's writing, much spoken of but never seen in clear outline.

Uses of the term gathered especially around the figure of T. S. Eliot, and most often around his poem 'The Waste Land', although curiously the first such application is negative: Gilbert Seldes's review of the poem for the *Nation* in December 1922 tells us that 'the theme is not a distaste for life, nor is it a disillusion, a romantic pessimism of any kind' (Eliot 2001: 138–9). Then in the anonymous and far-from-glowing review of the poem in the *Times Literary Supplement* in September 1923, subsequently revealed to have been written by Edgell Rickword, mention is made of Eliot's habitual 'disillusioned smile' (Eliot 2001: 155). Rickword under his own name followed that up in an article in his journal *The Calendar of Modern Letters*, 'The Returning Hero' (1925), which suggests that if a new kind of hero is to emerge in modern literature, it must be 'an exhaustively disillusioned Hero', coming in the wake of recent literary depressions:

> The literature of disillusionment is reaching its last stage; it is becoming popular with the reading public. Mr Strachey and Mr Huxley have replaced Ruskin and Carlyle. No doubt, too, all young men of poetic ambition have their version of *The Waste Land* in their wash-stand drawer. (Rickword 1974: 179)

Then in 1926 the Cambridge critic I. A. Richards added a special appendix on Eliot to the second edition of his book *Principles of Literary Criticism*, in which, without actually employing the D-word, he praises Eliot's work for clearly realising 'the plight of a whole generation' (Eliot 2001: 173). That phrase is perhaps an echo of yet another Rickword article, his 1925 *Calendar* review of Eliot's *Poems, 1909–1925*, in which Rickword had commended Eliot's ability 'to explore and make palpable the more intimate distresses of a generation for whom all the romantic escapes had been blocked' (Rickword 1974: 180).

Eliot himself soon came to look back upon all this with some puzzlement. In his 1929 lecture to the City Literary Institute, he began to cast doubt upon the notion of the 1920s as a 'disillusioned' age: it was, he thought, just as deluded as any other age. Then in his 1931 essay 'Thoughts after Lambeth', he inaccurately – by synthetic misquotation – but tellingly recalled:

> when I wrote a poem called *The Waste Land* some of the more approving critics said that I had expressed the 'disillusionment of a generation', which is nonsense. I may have expressed for them their own illusion of being disillusioned, but that did not form part of my intention. (Eliot 2001: 112)

Uncomfortable at being associated with such an apparently secularising term, Eliot was calling a halt to the disillusion-speak of the 1920s, by querying the word's insecure prefix and thereby standing the idea on its head. Surely, he implies, to imagine ourselves emancipated from illusion as such is the most presumptuous illusion of them all? Coming from such a source, that forthright disavowal commands thoughtful attention. If we put the idea of disillusionment under any pressure of scrutiny, as Eliot invites us to do, we find it harder and harder to distinguish from re-illusionment, of a temptingly self-flattering kind. We are left with the conclusion that disillusionment was not in any secure sense a psychological fact of Twenties life, but rather an echo of the War Myth, a conventional catchphrase of the times, a sort of literary conceit.

Note

1. Richard Perceval Graves's 1995 edition of his uncle's autobiography reproduces among its own annotations the marginal objections and corrections made by Blunden and Sassoon (see Graves 1995: 327–80).

Chapter Four

Impunities: Crime, Comedy and Camp

'Oh yes,' said Lord Peter, 'but most of us have such dozens of motives for murderin' all sorts of inoffensive people. There's lots of people I'd like to murder, wouldn't you?'
'Heaps,' said Lady Swaffham.

Dorothy L. Sayers, *Whose Body?* (1923)

In the later chapters of Evelyn Waugh's *Decline and Fall*, we are introduced to Egdon Heath Penal Settlement, a fictional prison based on the real one at Dartmoor but renamed after the setting of a Thomas Hardy novel. The roads around this prison are sometimes frequented by motorists who stop and look around in the hope of seeing chained convicts being led out on stone-breaking expeditions. Whether they catch sight of any convicts or not, the forbidding appearance of the prison tends

> to send the trippers off to their teas with their consciences agreeably unquiet at the memory of small dishonesties in railway trains, inaccurate income-tax returns, and the hundred and one minor infractions of law that are inevitable in civilized life. (Waugh 2001: 172)

The state of civilised life in the 1920s was such that anybody wealthy enough to incur income tax or to drive a motor vehicle was at the very least strongly tempted to break the law, and many certainly did so. Waugh himself, who had been arrested in 1925 on a drunk-and-disorderly charge, was also a motorcyclist who well understood the temptations of speeding. A long-accepted boundary between respectable citizens and the distinct 'criminal classes' was in the process of being eroded. As we shall see later in this chapter, Waugh's comic novel takes that contemporary fact and exaggerates it farcically, coolly taking for granted a generalised criminality at all levels of British society, its plot culminating in a home secretary conspiring to 'spring' a convict from Egdon Heath and to fake his death, with the connivance of corrupt physicians and prison governors. Compared with that all-engulfing tide of institutional decadence suggested by the novel's title, the description we have quoted of the guilt-stricken sightseers at Egdon Heath stands as an unusual passage of modest social realism. Its most significant word is 'agreeably': these people know that they too have broken the law in some way, but they have the pleasure of reflecting that, unlike the convicts, they have got away with it.

This chapter is concerned with impunity in 1920s literature. It is about people getting away with murder and lesser offences, and about people being let off lightly for non-criminal but socially disreputable activities such as adultery. The 'people' involved here are of course all fictional characters in plays and novels, most of them comical, but our working assumption is that the treatment of crime and non-punishment in works of fiction nonetheless indicates something, at least obliquely, about shifting perceptions of morality in this decade. Literary works can of course never simply 'reflect' their moral environments directly, but what they can do is adjust their own internal conventions according to their audiences' changing standards of acceptable representation. Our focus here will be upon those long-standing conventions that reward or punish characters with exemplary fates according to their moral deserts, and upon how such codes of 'poetic justice' significantly break down in this decade. The old code maintained by the Victorian circulating libraries and in the theatre by the Lord Chamberlain's censors, requiring that a criminal or merely sinful character be shown to meet a Bad End had begun to fray a little in the 1890s, but it was in the 1920s that it came to be broken in an almost generalised fashion.

Before we engage with the fiction, a glance at the non-fictional annals of public scandal in the early 1920s may provide some relevant background. The summer of 1922 was particularly memorable for the exposure of corruption in high places. An Old Etonian stockbroker, Gerard Bevan, chairman of the City Equitable Fire Insurance Company, suddenly fled the country in an aeroplane bound for the Continent, carrying with him suitcases stuffed with cash; arrested in Vienna, he was sentenced to seven years imprisonment for defrauding the company. Meanwhile the sometime founder of the *Financial Times*, Horatio Bottomley MP, was arrested after the collapse of one of his many popular investment schemes, and also sentenced to seven years imprisonment for fraud. Bottomley, as proprietor of the aggressively patriotic and anti-German magazine *John Bull*, had been a major shaper of public opinion during the War, and (as we saw in the previous chapter) an object of D. H. Lawrence's special loathing. In Parliament, a huge political scandal erupted over the sale of peerages and other political honours by the prime minister himself, David Lloyd George, the 'man who won the war'. Such corrupt practices had long been carried on discreetly by both Liberal and Conservative administrations to replenish their party funds, but Lloyd George had been lining his own pocket too, on the basis of a tariff widely known to involve bribes of £10,000 for a knighthood or £30,000 for a peerage. The prime minister had unwisely failed to cut his Conservative coalition partners in on these deals, and so they soon turned on him, ejecting Lloyd George from Downing Street along with his private secretary Frances Stevenson, who was known in political circles to be his live-in mistress. The Liberal Party which had swept all before it at the 1906 general election (at which Horatio Bottomley had first been returned as member for Hackney South) was now finished as a governing party. To an innocent young student such as Evelyn Waugh, aged 19 at the time, it could well appear that the whole country was corrupt from top to bottom.

Similar conclusions had already been reached by a slightly older generation of men who had served in the Great War itself. As we noted in the Introduction, the *Manchester Guardian* journalist C. E. Montague had earlier in 1922 published a book of essays on the moral impact of the war, and given it the simple but telling title *Disenchantment*. It begins by describing the confident idealism of the 1914 volunteers, who had been brought up to believe in the honour and integrity of British institutions, and goes on to describe how the soldiers' trust in those institutions, beginning with the army itself but soon incriminating Parliament, press and Church too, collapsed into a kind of stoical cynicism. Even before the most destructive battles of 1916–17, the ardent recruits of 1914 had begun to notice confusion and incompetence among their superiors, along with all kinds of petty corruption whereby promotions and 'cushy' postings might be awarded on the basis of bribery or favouritism. On this basis, they had soon concluded that almost anyone in a safe position behind the front lines had secured it corruptly. The public pronouncements of newspaper editors, politicians and bishops had contradicted their own experience so flatly that these had soon come to be dismissed as lies. Montague summarises the resulting post-War attitude among ex-servicemen:

> Great masses of men have become more freely critical of the claims of institutions and political creeds and parties which they used to accept without much scrutiny [. . .] For men who have seen cities pounded to rubble, men who with little aid or guidance from their own rulers have chased emperors from their thrones, are pretty fully disengaged, at last, from the Englishman's old sense of immutable fixity in institutions which he may find irksome or worthless. (Montague 1928: 91–2)

There are many ways of assessing the impact of the War, beginning most often with statistics of death, injury, blindness and psychological trauma; but Montague's focus upon the less visible sapping of national morale is more directly relevant to our consideration here of a certain cynical flavour found so often in 1920s literature. Before we come to the lighter comedies and satires in which that spirit is most evident, we shall examine some darker tales.

Maugham: *The Casuarina Tree*

Some of the most memorable short stories of the decade are to be found in W. Somerset Maugham's collection *The Casuarina Tree* (1926). These tales have all the appearance of being about life in Malaya and Borneo, which is indeed the setting for all but one of them. Really they are about the English middle class and the fearsome code of respectability it maintains regardless either of geographical location or of moral reality. Two of the volume's six stories are about secret unpunished murders concealed behind the masks of English propriety, while another concerns a murder that is in effect condoned by an English official.

Significantly the first of the stories in *The Casuarina Tree* is set in the English Home Counties, in the family home of a respected solicitor. 'Before the Party' concerns the solicitor's 36-year-old elder daughter Millicent, who has lately returned from Borneo as a widow, her husband Harold, a colonial official, having apparently died from fever. The drama begins as Millicent's parents and sister prepare to attend a local clergyman's garden party with her, discussing which clothes it would be 'good form' to wear. The sister, Kathleen, who is honorary secretary to the local golf club, reveals that she has heard and denied a rumour that Millicent's husband really cut his own throat in a fit of *delirium tremens*. Millicent concedes the truth of the story, and we notice that the drink habit clearly strikes the family as more horrifying than the suicide. Millicent's father urges her to come out with the whole story so that they will all have the same version to give to any questioning neighbours. Her eight-year marriage had been, she now tells them, a recurrent struggle against Harold's drinking, apparently resolved after a two-year abstention, until she had returned from a trip away to find him unconscious from drink again – at which point Millicent had momentarily lost control and cut his throat with a decorative Malay sword he kept over the bed, successfully passing the death off as suicide. Millicent's pitiful story wins sympathy from the reader, but not from her family. Her father's response is to complain of the awkward position this confession of murder puts him in as a respectable lawyer, while her sister unleashes the worst condemnation of which she is capable: 'Oh, I think the whole thing is such frightfully bad form' (Maugham 1993: 31). In the interests of good form, though, the family agrees that they must all now attend the garden party, because it would look odd if they did not appear; so off they go, chauffeured by their gardener.

The ironies of 'Before the Party' dissect Millicent's family with merciless precision, Millicent herself being the bearer of the ironic perspective. Before she begins her full account, she notices her father's discomfort: 'Millicent looked at him and in her eyes, unmistakably, was a look of irony which was quite cynical' (Maugham 1993: 13). Her mother too has already noticed an odd remoteness about Millicent's manner, and has 'an uneasy impression that she looked at them as though they were mannequins at a dressmaker's. She seemed to live in a different world from theirs and to have no connection with them' (Maugham 1993: 14). One of the story's minor ironies is that the father inadvertently indicates why this should be so, when he misquotes Rudyard Kipling's line from 'The English Flag' as 'What can they know of England who only England know?' (Maugham 1993: 4). Maugham invites us to see – and see through – the England of garden parties and golf clubs as an alien, unreal world from the perspective of one who has lived through horrors in a very different place. Maugham's readers in 1926 would have recognised Millicent's disconnection and apparent cynicism, seeming as these do to match the attitudes of many returned war veterans of the time. Maugham himself was a veteran not of combat but of espionage duties in Switzerland (the basis of his next collection of stories, *Ashenden* (1928)) but he was sufficiently well-travelled in Borneo and elsewhere to see English customs from the outside.

The final story in *The Casuarina Tree* is the most famous, later adapted successfully for stage (1927) and screen. 'The Letter', set in Singapore, is a tale of discreet legal corruption in which a Western lawyer, Mr Joyce, saves his client from being hanged on a murder charge. His client is Leslie Crosbie, an elegant but shy Englishwoman in her thirties, married to the rubber planter Robert Crosbie, a personal friend of Mr Joyce himself. She has shot dead a neighbouring planter, Geoff Hammond, a handsome war veteran, consistently claiming that he had turned up unexpectedly at her house while her husband was in town and tried to rape her. Her story is universally accepted among the white community, in which Hammond's reputation is now worthless because it has just been revealed that he had a Chinese mistress. Leslie's impending acquittal seems to be a matter of course until Mr Joyce's impeccably polite Chinese clerk Ong Chi Seng discloses the existence of an incriminating letter sent by Leslie to

Hammond on the day of the killing, inviting him urgently to meet her in her husband's absence. The letter is held by Hammond's bereaved Chinese mistress, who expects to be paid a large sum if she is not to send it to the public prosecutor and thus explode Leslie's defence. Confronted with these facts by Mr Joyce, Leslie understands the real danger of her being hanged, and her composure cracks: 'She stared at Mr Joyce with eyes that started from their sockets. He was looking now at a gibbering death's head' (Maugham 1993: 191). Reluctantly, Mr Joyce decides to set aside his professional integrity and pervert the course of justice out of sympathy for Leslie's husband, who is given an apparently innocent explanation for the letter but is strongly advised to pay the blackmail, equivalent to his entire savings. Guided with perfect discretion by Ong Chi Seng – who will get his own cut from the transaction – Joyce and Crosbie pay off Hammond's mistress, and Leslie is duly acquitted, the prosecution offering only a token pretence of a case. A celebration party is held, from which Crosbie departs early, having now grasped the truth, eventually confessed by his wife to Mr Joyce, that she and Hammond had been secret lovers for years, and that she murdered him in a frenzy of jealousy over his stronger attachment to the Chinese woman.

The expertly managed plot of 'The Letter' has some resemblances to that of 'Before the Party', in that an Englishwoman gives two false accounts of a homicide before revealing her guilt in the third version. The chief difference is that Leslie Crosbie is too culpable to earn the reader's sympathy, so the discrepancy between appearance and truth is met not with irony but with moral horror: at the close of her final confession, Mr Joyce recoils aghast as his quietly refined client's expression reveals her fiendish cruelty. There are ironies to the story (both Leslie's husband and her friend Mrs Joyce are certain at the start that she is incapable of hurting a fly) but its dramatic focus is upon the gulf between Leslie's reserved composure and the murderous passions it conceals. The violence at the heart of the tale is cunningly offset by the polished courtesy with which Ong Chi Seng, who clearly holds all the cards in this game, leads his employer down the path of corruption while both men pretend there is nothing amiss. Whatever views the Chinese characters may have about the quality of British colonial justice, they keep a discreet silence on the matter, as does the narrator, who hardly needs to state the obvious.

In between those two tales of unpunished murderesses we find in *The Casuarina Tree* an insidiously sardonic story that invites the reader to condone both a murder and what amounts to its official toleration. Maugham manages to provide in 'The Outstation' not only a sudden 'twist' at the ending but a more gradual revolution in the reader's attitudes through the course of the narrative. In a remote part of Borneo the long-standing official resident, Mr Warburton, is an old-fashioned snob who reveres the British aristocracy and the tradition of his regiment, and always dresses for his solitary dinner in the correct boiled shirt and collar despite the humidity. He is sent a new assistant, a younger man called Cooper, whose manner is more informal and whose attitude to the British class system is more sceptically modern. They take an immediate dislike to each other, and it seems we are all set here for another of those clashes, so common in the 1920s, between the stiff representative of outmoded values and the coming man. But Maugham has artfully misled us: it emerges that the rigid traditionalist Warburton has one redeeming virtue, which is that he genuinely loves and respects the local people in his care, while Cooper turns out to be a racist bully who mistreats his servants, despite repeated warnings from the more experienced Warburton. One of the houseboys, Abas, driven to exasperation by Cooper's insults, stabs him to death with a *kriss* and then flees to another village. Warburton now has an official decision to make. Over his regular breakfast of eggs, toast, marmalade, tea and *The Times*, he calls his own head servant and tells him that justice must be done. The form this justice will take is that Abas will give himself up on the understanding that he will not be hanged but serve only a token term of imprisonment, after which he will be employed in Warburton's own house: a promotion equivalent to a reward for ridding the resident of his detested enemy.

Maugham's attitude to the unpunished murders in his tales is cool, unshocked and essentially sardonic: Millicent's husband and Mr Cooper, we are to understand, had it coming to them, and even the guiltless Hammond goes unlamented. The cover-ups by means of which the murderers are let off may appal the reader, but Maugham presents them unsensationally as predictable consequences of colonial power. It is in this worldly-wise unshockable attitude to murder that Maugham partly resembles the contemporary writers of detective murder-mysteries, although in other ways these stories are very different: there is no detective figure, no puzzle for the reader to solve and no reassurance that the truth will out.

Murder Most Frivolous: Detective Fiction of the Early Golden Age

The literature of crime in the 1920s is dominated by the decade's huge boom in detective fiction, within which the full-length murder-mystery or whodunit increasingly replaced the old kind of short story in which non-homicidal mysteries could be found as often as murders. This was a decade of transition in which the earlier masters of the mystery tale were still practising their art – Arthur Conan Doyle in his final Holmesian collection *The Case-Book of Sherlock Holmes* (1927), G. K. Chesterton in *The Incredulity of Father Brown* (1926) and *The Secret of Father Brown* (1927) – even while the leaders of the new school were building their careers: Agatha Christie from 1920 (*The Mysterious Affair at Styles*), Freeman Wills Crofts from the same year (*The Cask*), Dorothy L. Sayers from 1923 (*Whose Body?*), Anthony Berkeley from 1925 (*The Layton Court Mystery*), Margery Allingham from 1929 (*The Crime at Black Dudley*) and Gladys Mitchell from the same year (*Speedy Death*). The generic shift from short mystery to longer murder-puzzle was by no means a clean break: full-length murder novels had often appeared before, while the murderless short story was also part of the new arrivals' repertoires too, in Christie's collection *Poirot Investigates* (1924) and Sayers's *Lord Peter Views the Body* (1928: a dozen cases, only four of them murderous). Ernest Bramah's short stories about the blind detective Max Carrados (*The Eyes of Max Carrados*, 1923) were still admired too. The absence of crime, though, let alone murder in some of Doyle's *Case-Book* stories (enigmas in 'The Creeping Man', 'The Blanched Soldier' and 'The Lion's Mane' are all explained as freaks of nature) indicates the last gasp of the 'old' school, as the enormous success of Christie's murder-puzzle formula showed what the reading public in the 1920s now preferred. What they wanted was not just a spot of jewel-theft or forgery, but proper murder with several suspects entangled in a complex plot unravelled over some 200 pages.

As the so-called Golden Age of English detective writing dawned, it brought with it other notable indicators of changing taste. The most important transformation here was the widespread tone of frivolity and facetious high spirits in the handling both of murder and of detection. In this decade, detective fiction in effect tilted away from melodrama and towards comedy, as the sheer fun of unpicking the puzzles displaced older solemnities about crime and the battle against it. The clearest symptom of the shift lies in the new semi-comical type of detective figure. Although there were still serious professional investigators to be found, including Crofts's Inspector French (from 1924), the most remarkable new sleuths were the clownish amateurs: Christie's Hercule Poirot is both a master-sleuth and a figure of ridicule noted for his undignified personal vanity. Sayers's detective Lord Peter Wimsey is in a similar way intellectually heroic yet at the same time idiotic in his languid style of upper-class slang joviality – a trait seemingly derived from P. G. Wodehouse's Bertie Wooster (the likeness is indeed explicitly noted in Sayers's novel *Unnatural Death* (1927) (Sayers 1968a: 59)). This kind of 'silly-ass' detective reappeared in the figure of Margery Allingham's aristocratic hero Albert Campion. The absurd mannerisms of the new kind of detective may be regarded as cunning feints that mask a resolute heroism, but they also add a good deal to the larger comic effect of the decade's detective writing.

The unfolding of the detective plot in 1920s crime fiction presents itself more as an entertaining game than as an earnest mission to root out criminality. Moral indignation at crime, along with sympathy for its victims, is downplayed in the interests of the puzzle itself. Figuring out puzzles had become a widely popular pastime with the advent of the crossword in British newspapers from the early 1920s, and the parallel with crime fiction was seized upon both by detractors of the genre who thought it all a pointless waste of time and by Dorothy L. Sayers, who set out to defend her craft by analogy with crossword puzzles. Her 1928 short story 'Uncle Meleager's Will' involves an elaborate treasure hunt conducted by means of a crossword puzzle set (with the clues composed in rhyming couplets) by a wealthy eccentric as a posthumous challenge to his serious-minded niece to find the document through which she will inherit his fortune. Luckily the niece has Wimsey and his formidably educated sister to help her, but significantly it is a farcical pratfall on Wimsey's part – he trips into an ornamental pond – that provides them with the breakthrough they need. The story's key term is Frivolity: a value that the niece must learn to appreciate in order to earn her inheritance, and that Sayers herself is keen to promote so as to vindicate the sheer pointless fun of modern fictional detection.

While Christie's Poirot and most of his counterparts manage to keep a straight face about the horror of murder itself, they render the investigation of it lightly amusing. Dorothy L. Sayers, though, shows a more resolutely aesthetic attitude to homicide, voiced through her detective Wimsey, whose connoisseurship of old books and wines extends to his appreciation of distinguished crimes. In *Unnatural Death*, for instance, Wimsey enthuses about the death of a wealthy old lady, which he believes offers him the perfect case of a murder without apparent motive, means, or clues:

> 'Miss Dawson fascinates me, Charles. Such a beautiful subject. So old and ill. So likely to die soon. Bound to die before long. No near relations to make inquiries. No connections or old friends in the neighbourhood. And so rich. Upon my soul, Charles, I lie in bed licking my lips over ways and means of murdering Miss Dawson.' (Sayers 1968a: 92)

Wimsey's adoption of a murderer's standpoint here could of course be defended as a necessary step towards solving the criminal mystery, but that would overlook the gleeful relish with which he approaches the case. His aesthetic indifference to the morality of murder involves an identification not only with the killer but with the *reader*. And indeed Wimsey, like most 1920s detectives, is also a reader of crime fiction himself, as he reminds us in the short story 'The Man with No Face' (1928): 'I like a nice, quiet, domestic murder myself, with the millionaire found dead in the library' (Sayers 1989: 227). The reader of detective fiction in the 1920s was increasingly encouraged to suspend moral considerations for the sake of the sheer entertainment. A more startling example of the same trend appears in Gladys Mitchell's debut novel *Speedy Death*, in which very little to do with murder or justice is taken in the least seriously. Among the novel's several mischievous amusements are a male murder victim who turns out to have been a cross-dressing woman, and a merrily cackling psychoanalyst detective, Mrs Lestrange Bradley, who decides to commit a murder herself and gets away with it at the subsequent trial.

It is usually thought that the whole point of a detective fiction plot is to conclude satisfyingly with the solution of the criminal enigma and thus with the criminal apprehended and brought to justice. In fact the detective tradition from its earliest days had featured criminals who escape justice in various ways, so it should not surprise us to find plenty of unpunished malefactors in the decade's writing. Some of these suffer fatal accidents while attempting further crimes (as in Christie's *The Murder on the Links* (1923)) or while fleeing, or are killed by treacherous accomplices or by relatives of their victims. Others take their own lives rather than face the gallows (as happens in Christie's *The Murder of Roger Ackroyd* (1926)), or are discreetly allowed to take that way out by the detective, as with the ending of Sayers's *The Unpleasantness at the Bellona Club* (1928). There are indeed plenty of cases, mostly non-homicidal, in which the detective pre-empts the judicial process by deciding to let the malefactor off with a warning: in the *Case-Book* of 1927, Sherlock Holmes chivalrously covers up the crimes of two women, one of whom has commissioned a burglary ('The Three Gables'), the other being clearly guilty of conspiracy to murder ('The Veiled Lodger'). A more unusual kind of impunity is found in Anthony Berkeley's self-conscious spoof novel *The Poisoned Chocolates Case* (1929), in which there is simply not enough hard evidence available to convict the culprit.

Mrs Bradley's decision to commit murder in *Speedy Death* is justified primarily by our entertainment, although it does have the supplementary excuse that the victim is a poisoner who has killed already and may well do again unless stopped. This is an extreme case of the conventional indulgence whereby amateur detectives in fiction are permitted to take the law into their own hands, either by allowing a decent offender to get off lightly or by breaking the law themselves in pursuit of clues. Housebreaking is regularly condoned as permissible to Lord Peter Wimsey and his manservant Bunter, and even Sherlock Holmes himself is plainly guilty of burglary in 'The Illustrious Client' (1925), this being a case in which Holmes steals the incriminating 'little black book' of a womanising bounder, who is suspected of having murdered his first wife, simply in order to dissuade another woman from marrying him. Dr Watson's closing words to the tale are significant: 'Sherlock Holmes was threatened with a prosecution for burglary, but when an object is good and a client is sufficiently illustrious, even the rigid British law becomes human and elastic. My friend has not yet stood in the dock' (Doyle 1993: 132). The general tendency of detective fiction in this period is to encourage in these ways a flexible or 'human and elastic' interpretation of the law of the land.

Open sympathy with burglars and jewel-thieves was not, aside from the generic indulgences already mentioned, a permissible attitude in detective fiction. In the related genre of the comedy-thriller, however, there were modern precedents for exactly that kind of permissiveness in fiction. E. W. Hornung had introduced his character A. J. Raffles the stylish gentleman-burglar in *The Amateur Cracksman* (1899), and brought him back for further 'sporting' adventures in robbery in *The Black Mask* (1901) and two further sequels, despite the objections of Arthur Conan Doyle, who happened to be Hornung's brother-in-law. Doyle regarded it as wrong for an author to glamorise theft, but the popularity of the Raffles tales (narrated, like the Holmes stories, by a reverent sidekick) seemed to show that readers had no serious objection. In the 1920s, a similar fictional hero, likewise derived from romantic traditions of Robin Hood and of good-hearted highwaymen, was launched by Leslie Charteris in *Meet the Tiger* (1928): Simon Templar, nicknamed 'The Saint', is a modern Robin Hood type, a righter of wrongs who often resorts to criminality in the interests of a higher good. Some of the lesser heroes of P. G. Wodehouse's comic stories and novels are in the Raffles mould, too: Psmith in *Leave it to Psmith* (1923) helps to pull off a jewel-robbery, while the charmingly unprincipled Ukridge of the story-collection *Ukridge* (1924) engages in various kinds of thieving, blackmail and petty fraud. Otherwise the sympathetic portrayal of thieves is found in the Twenties most significantly upon the comic stage.

The Comedy of Crime I: On Stage

In Act II of Bernard Shaw's *Heartbreak House* (published 1919, British première 1921), a group of upper- and middle-class characters is assembled in a country house when noises of crashing furniture and gunfire are heard, and an elderly burglar is dragged in. He is a comic burglar, whose function is to highlight Shavian paradoxes, so the first thing he does after complaining about the dangerous pistol fired at him is to insist that the police be called, as his capture has been 'a fair cop' (Shaw 1964: 116). He makes sure to mention that his likely sentence will be ten years in prison, which at his age he is unlikely to survive, but still demands that justice be done. The ladies of the house are reluctant to follow that course, though, because they do not want their family affairs mentioned in the newspapers, and the menfolk are likewise unwilling to go through the inconvenience of involving the police in the matter. When the burglar says he will turn himself in, they stop him, protesting that he has no right to inconvenience them for the sake of his moral salvation. One of them even suggests that he rob a bank and use the proceeds to go straight by starting a locksmith's business. Eventually they pay him off with a modest bribe, at which point he admits that this kind of pay-off is how he really makes his living, not being a real burglar after all but a kind of beggar who exploits the propertied classes' preference for privacy, in a mild version of blackmail. This is only a passing episode in *Heartbreak House*, soon forgotten amid other business, but the curious situation it presents has dramatic possibilities that were to be developed by others.

Lonsdale: The Last of Mrs Cheyney

Among the most successful comic playwrights of the decade, now almost forgotten, was Frederick Lonsdale, a semi-educated Channel Islander of humble origins (his father was a tobacconist) who had found success as a librettist for musical comedies before switching to 'straight' theatre. Among his minor plays, it may be worth mentioning in passing, was a serious melodrama called *The Fake* (1924), in which the heroine is married off by her father to an abusive drunkard, until rescued by a gallant friend of the family who murders the husband, much to the relief and approval of the audience. Lonsdale's greatest success was his comedy of manners *The Last of Mrs Cheyney* (1925; filmed 1929), in which the title character, an attractive young woman claiming to be an Australian widow, infiltrates a circle of aristocrats with the secret purpose of carrying out thefts of jewels. In this play, robbery and blackmail are central to the entire action.

By the end of the first Act, set in Mrs Cheyney's house, we are aware that the hostess's unflappable butler Charles is in fact the leader of a criminal gang and that Mrs Cheyney, otherwise Fay, is his star protégée, although she has some momentary doubts about stealing from people she has found to be surprisingly likeable. We have also been introduced to two rich young aristocrats who have become attracted to Mrs Cheyney: Lord Elton, a dull and rather pompously respectable man, and the hard-drinking Lord Arthur Dilling, who has a 'fast' reputation as an unscrupulous seducer. The fascinating complications unfold in the second Act, set in a weekend party at the home of the wealthy Mrs Ebley, who is understood to be a retired courtesan turned respectable. The assembled guests expect Lord Elton to propose marriage to Mrs Cheyney, as does Dilling, who gets his own proposal in earlier, only to be rejected. Dilling then recalls that he has seen the butler Charles somewhere before, and his suspicions are raised further when he intercepts a conspiratorial message from Charles to Mrs Cheyney. Dilling finds a pretext to exchange bedrooms with his hostess Mrs Ebley without divulging his true reason for this. In the small hours, Mrs Cheyney sneaks into the room in search of Mrs Ebley's valuable pearls, only to be locked in by Dilling, who immediately blackmails her by threatening to expose her unless she succumbs to his advances. At this point the two 'lead' characters are both seen at their worst, but each then surprises us – and one another — by making spur-of-the-moment decisions of an unexpectedly honourable kind. Mrs Cheyney rings a bell to alert the household, fully prepared to confess her attempted crime rather than submit to Dilling's unprincipled offer. Dilling then covers up for her by telling the awakened company that he is the guilty party in the disturbance, having lured Mrs Cheyney into the room to take sexual advantage of her; but his confession is trumped by her insistence that, on the contrary, she was in the room to steal her hostess's pearls.

Lonsdale's most impressive feat is the third and final Act, in which everyone but Mrs Cheyney and her butler gathers for a breakfast conference, overshadowed less by the attempted nocturnal crime than by the revelation that Lord Elton has sent (prior to her exposure, of course) a proposal of marriage to Mrs Cheyney by letter, in which he has advised her that his hostess and fellow-guests are not the sort of people his future wife should associate with (Mrs Ebley we already know to be a 'woman with a past', while another of the ladies is an adulteress, another swears like a trooper and so forth). Elton's own copy of the letter is circulated to general horror, as it dawns on the company that the jewel-thieves have the advantage of them, possessing as they do a document that could disgrace them all, including Elton himself, who cannot let it be known that he has proposed marriage to a criminal. Mrs Cheyney's arrest would lead to this letter being produced in a court of law and therefore in the newspapers, so the only way out is for them to buy her off. She and Charles are called in, and at first refuse to be bought off, insisting on going to jail rather like Shaw's burglar; but then the serious blackmail negotiations begin, which appear to settle on a price of £10,000 to be paid by Elton, until Mrs Cheyney pulls another surprise, announcing that she has already destroyed his letter. Relieved, the aristocratic group, again like Shaw's, plans to reward her generosity by setting her up as a shopkeeper, but in the final dialogue Dilling proposes marriage to her again and is accepted. Fay, the pretended Mrs Cheyney, whose real name is never revealed, has already admitted that she is not an Australian widow but a former shop-girl from Clapham. She will now become Lady Dilling.

The Last of Mrs Cheyney is by no means a corrosive satire. Indeed it can be seen as a sentimental presentation of honour among thieves and scoundrels, in which the low-born criminal and the high-born rake are redeemed by discovering an inner decency in each other. Nonetheless, in the course of its cleverly designed plot it casts some interesting light upon the shifting moral ground of its time. The part of Charles the bogus butler is particularly intriguing, being a combination of Wodehouse's Jeeves and Hornung's gentleman-burglar Raffles. Charles reveals towards the end of the play that he is an Oxford-educated Old Etonian who has taken to crime out of sheer boredom with his safely privileged existence, and that he will now go on to further criminal adventures in high society as a cardsharp. In the first Act Charles overcomes Fay's scruples about robbing nice people by reminding her that Mrs Ebley's pearls have been in their own way ill-gotten, taken, as he puts it, from the wives of her admirers; and in the last Act he presents his straightforward sort of thieving as less harmful than the corruptions of the assembled patricians: 'I'm just an ordinary sort of feller, who only takes material things that can be replaced. How many of you can say that?' (Lonsdale 2000: 176). Mrs Cheyney herself adopts a superior tone when addressing Lady Maria Frinton 'as one fallen woman to another', and refers to her own criminal vocation as 'a profession in some form or other we are all members of', her 'we' embracing the titled company and possibly the play's audience too (Lonsdale 2000: 173, 171). She and Charles manage to suggest that crooks and aristocrats are mirror-images of each other, and so should settle their apparent differences amicably; the impending marriage of Lord Dilling and the light-fingered heroine seems to seal just such an arrangement.

Travers: Plunder

Stage plays about crime took many forms, of which the comedy of manners was only one. In the late 1920s there was a brief boom in crime drama, beginning with Maugham's stage version of his story, *The Letter* (1927), and including thrillers and detective puzzlers by the prolific Edgar Wallace (*The Ringer*, 1927; *The Flying Squad*, 1928), by A. A. Milne (*The Fourth Wall*, 1928), by Patrick Hamilton (*Rope*, 1929) and by Agatha Christie (*Alibi*, 1928, adapted from her novel *The Murder of Roger Ackroyd*). An unusual hybrid in this context is Ben Travers's *Plunder* (1928), which manages to build an entertainment comprising blackmail, jewel-theft, bigamy and police investigation upon the generic basis of the bedroom farce. Travers had pioneered this form of farce, known at the time as the 'Aldwych farce' after the theatre of its origin, with *A Cuckoo in the Nest* (1925) and *Rookery Nook* (1926). The latter play exemplifies the form in its essentials, which involve a crescendo of panic on the part of the male protagonist as a pretty young woman, expelled from her nearby home by a disciplinarian stepfather and dressed only in pink pyjamas, turns up unexpectedly seeking refuge at his holiday home shortly before his wife is due to arrive. Exposure of this seemingly scandalous but actually innocent situation threatens constantly: the nubile visitor could emerge from a door (there are as many as eight on the set) at the wrong time, or the man's relatives could – and do – show up unannounced, or one of the friends with whom he is obliged to share the secret could give the game away by contradicting the various lies he has told. After many alarms and confusions, and much dialogue laden with naughty double entendre, all ends happily enough with the wife acknowledging her husband's innocence while his bachelor friend gets the scantily-clad girl.

With *Plunder*, Travers takes that formula and grafts onto it a wholly different story of robbery and indeed suspected murder, while retaining the central principle of farce, which is the constantly impending risk of the protagonist's secret being exposed. In this comedy, the hero for whom we are rooting is another Rafflesesque gentleman burglar, Freddy Malone, who has identified a vulgar and obese but wealthy Mrs Hewlett as his next victim. Mrs Hewlett, formerly Mrs Veal, is the ex-housekeeper of a rich elderly man, and now his widow, having married him during his final illness while failing to tell his granddaughter of this alliance. As Freddy worms his way into Mrs Hewlett's family by using his attractive 'sister' Prudence as bait for her witless son, the disinherited granddaughter arrives from Australia to show her fiancé the mansion she thinks is now theirs. The fiancé, D'Arcy Tuck, happens to be an old school chum of Freddy's, which is where Freddy's plan to steal Mrs Hewlett's jewels starts to come unstuck: he is obliged to bring D'Arcy in on the plot, despite knowing that his new accomplice is an unreliable buffoon who never thinks before opening his mouth. Meanwhile

Mrs Hewlett's brother-in-law Simon Veal threatens her with mysterious references to a secret of hers.

The second Act of *Plunder* is set in Freddy's country residence, to which he has invited the Hewlett family (including Simon Veal and the resentful granddaughter), and where he plans to stage a robbery that will be blamed on a non-existent nocturnal intruder. As Freddy and D'Arcy are taking the sleeping Mrs Hewlett's jewels, though, they are unexpectedly disturbed by Simon Veal, who has noticed a suspicious ladder outside that bedroom and climbed up to investigate; following a struggle with Freddy, he loses his balance, falls off the ladder and is found dead after D'Arcy has run off to conceal the loot. Although the audience has witnessed the accidental nature of Veal's fall, his death means, as Freddy tells D'Arcy, that both of the thieves could be facing the gallows on a murder charge.

The third and final Act follows the course of the police investigation, as Freddy and D'Arcy are summoned for questioning. D'Arcy flounders absurdly under this pressure, and the police interrogators are convinced they have their culprits. As they call the next day to make their arrests, though, Freddy makes a crucial discovery: that Mrs Hewlett has come into her fortune illegally through bigamy, her first husband being alive and undivorced, this being the secret about which Simon Veal was blackmailing her. Freddy now takes over as her blackmailer, obliging her under threat of exposure to tell the police that Veal was the real thief. This allows her to get away with the bigamy offence while forfeiting the property to Hewlett's granddaughter and the jewels to Freddy and D'Arcy, who of course now get away with the theft. All's well that ends well, except for the deceased Simon Veal, who as a blackmailing villain goes unmourned. Once again the suspension of normal moral scruples that is permitted by comedy – but now permitted more indulgently than ever before – allows the audience to cheer the unpunished success of a criminal intrigue. Just as we hope at the edge of our seats that the innocent hero of the bedroom farce will not be caught alone with the underdressed beauty, so in the criminal farce of *Plunder* we find ourselves praying that the charmingly clever Freddy will get away with his jewel heist. The crime of blackmail that allows us to make light of Simon Veal's death as somehow merited is of course the same offence, with the same victim, that Freddy commits in order to elude punishment; but we happily condone it in his case.

The Comedy of Crime II: Narrative Comedy

We have noticed in passing that in a period in which crime fiction adopts a more comical tone, the new kind of 'silly-ass' detective resembles P. G. Wodehouse's famous comic creation Bertie Wooster. This kind of connection can be followed both ways, though, because at the same time comical fiction, of which Wodehouse was the emerging master, makes increasing use of the fun to be had with criminal capers. Wodehouse's novel *Money for Nothing* (1928), for instance, as its title partly indicates, revolves around an attempted insurance fraud based upon a faked burglary, while the absurdities of his *Summer Lightning* (1929) include the criminal abduction of a prize-winning pig. In addition to the Raffles tradition of gentlemanly crime, to which Wodehouse's characters Ukridge and Psmith partly belong, the famous pairing of Jeeves and Wooster from *My Man Jeeves* (1919) onwards seems to draw significantly upon Wodehouse's known admiration for Conan Doyle's Sherlock Holmes stories. The apocryphal catchphrase 'Elementary, my dear Watson', never actually uttered by Doyle's Holmes, appears most probably to have been coined by Wodehouse in *Psmith Journalist* (1909, in serial form; as a book, 1915). As Richard Usborne has noticed, there are recurrent resemblances between Doyle's and Wodehouse's twin series, not only in the central relationship between the more slow-witted narrator (Watson/Wooster) and the omnicompetent hero (Holmes/Jeeves) but in certain stock situations such as the breakfast discussion of the story's problem and the final rewarding of the genius for his secretive machinations (Usborne 2003: 58–9). Several of the Jeeves stories involve either some minor crime or a dubiously 'flexible' morality, as when Jeeves in 'Jeeves and the Hard-Boiled Egg' (1919) suavely employs blackmail against the Duke of Chiswick, threatening to inform the newspapers of his supposed mercenary exploitation of his title unless he restores the financial allowance he has withdrawn from Wooster's chum.

Of particular interest here is a story called 'Without the Option' (in *Carry On, Jeeves*, 1925), which starts dramatically with Wooster in the dock of a magistrate's court being fined £5 for the offence of stealing a policeman's hat while on his annual drunken rampage after the Varsity Boat Race. His less fortunate friend Sippy, who gets thirty days in prison for going so far as to punch the policeman, is desperate to conceal his disgrace from his fearsome aunt Vera, and Jeeves is, as usual, called upon to devise some means of getting the chum out of his fix. The first scheme, in which Wooster has to impersonate Sippy during a social visit to the aunt's friends, collapses as a 'loony-doctor' recognises Wooster from an earlier encounter; then Jeeves, acting on mysterious private information, recommends a direct penitent appeal to Aunt Vera herself. When Wooster nervously confesses to the offence and explains that Sippy is in prison, the aunt surprises him by bursting out into laughter and declaring herself proud of her nephew. In fact her unorthodox view of the matter is that England would be a far better place if every young man went about assaulting policemen. From a respectable gentlewoman this is unexpected, until Jeeves discloses that the local constable has recently summonsed her for a variety of minor offences including speeding in her car, and thus inflamed Aunt Vera into a vengeful attitude towards the Force as a whole. Nor has the constable's zealous persecution of the aunt been accidental: he happens to be Jeeves's cousin, and has recently had a visit from that manservant.

> 'Good Lord, Jeeves! You didn't bribe him?'
> 'Oh no, sir. But it was his birthday last week, and I gave him a little present. I have always been fond of Egbert, sir.' (Wodehouse 1957: 170)

This story begins, then, with a typical outbreak of upper-class hooliganism, and it ends with a respectable lady encouraging generalised assaults on the police because she resents being found out exceeding the speed limit, these being the consequences of the local constable being bribed with the 'present' of a five-pound note. We are in legal and moral territory that Bertie Wooster might describe as 'rum'.

Waugh: Decline and Fall

It is time to return to Evelyn Waugh's first novel, *Decline and Fall*, which shows many of the characteristics of farce, although without the sense of panic about vulnerable secrets that Travers exploited at the Aldwych. Apart from the *naif* protagonist Paul Pennyfeather and his friend the clergyman Prendergast, most of the people in Waugh's story are ludicrously caricatured scoundrels, the action being a sequence of fiascos and far-fetched coincidences in which Paul is endlessly manipulated by the depraved and corrupt characters around him. In Waugh's later novels, from *Vile Bodies* (1930) onwards, the moral turpitude and criminality exhibited here would form part of a satirical design in which the emptiness of modern society would be held up for condemnation from a broadly Catholic standpoint. *Decline and Fall*, though, is as innocent of satirical purposes as its anti-hero is of worldly knowledge. In fact the narrative adopts a version of Paul's own naïvety by coolly pretending not to notice that anything is wrong with the characters' incorrigibly criminal behaviour. The story is really a farcical escapade in which serious moral considerations do not apply, so that the most attractive characters are precisely those with no principles or scruples. The one-legged pederast Captain Grimes is assumed to be a war hero, but in fact his leg was lost in a traffic accident, and he has evaded a wartime court martial and likely execution thanks to his public-school connections; despite his homosexuality he commits the crime of bigamy but escapes by faking his death. Philbrick, the butler at a school in which Paul and Grimes teach, is a fraudster who poses as 'Sir Solomon' in order to run up unpaid hotel bills, meanwhile telling tall stories of his career as a safebreaker. The irresistibly attractive young aristocratic widow Margot Beste-Chetwynde runs a business trafficking prostitutes, but sends Paul, whom she has seduced and is all set to marry, to the Marseille red-light district to arrange their passage to the brothels of South America, whereupon Paul, still unaware of the nature of Margot's trade, is arrested and imprisoned while Margot slips away to Corfu with a stainless reputation and breaks off their engagement. She later makes it up to her former fiancé by marrying the home secretary and arranging for him to get Paul sprung from prison.

These characters are only the most prominent among several, including his guardian, his Oxford tutors and his academic employer Dr Fagan, who fleece Paul and ensure that he suffers for the crimes of others. The unshockable deadpan narrative voice, though, invites no condemnation against them, and indeed solicits hardly any sympathy for Paul either. Grimes, Philbrick and Margot all appeal to us not only as colourful rogues who get away with anything on account of their sheer panache, but as somehow untouchable or even indestructible like forces of nature. In a mock-heroic passage about another of Grimes's escapes from justice, the peg-legged reprobate is hailed as one 'of the immortals' (Waugh 2001: 185). It is the breathtaking impunity of these characters that places them on a different level from born losers like Paul: while he almost contentedly acquiesces in his role as the fall-guy, they are (and rightly so, as Paul concludes) above the law, and so in the strict sense of the term privileged. If *Decline and Fall* has any social 'meaning', it is not as a satirical exposé of British institutions but as a perverse tribute to Privilege.

Types of Promiscuity

The glamorously unprincipled Margot Beste-Chetwynde belongs to a recognisable Twenties 'type' of modern *femme fatale* or vamp, a figure whose flagrantly promiscuous conduct tends to go unpunished in significant ways. As a representative period type, she is of course a conscious inversion of the Victorian domestic angel, and her regular appearance in the decade's fiction signals a revolution in the literary presentation of women's sexuality, albeit distorted under pressures of censorship. Margot herself belongs to a special category of 1920s temptress, a version of the 'merry widow' archetype but with a kind of jaded boredom replacing the merriment. Her literary sisters in widowhood include Lucy Tantamount in Aldous Huxley's *Point Counter Point* (1928) and Iris Storm in Michael Arlen's *The Green Hat* (1924). These women may entertain themselves with one lover after another, but the special moral opprobrium still attaching to adultery does not directly concern them. Rather, they have other burdens to carry, in particular a deeply corrosive *ennui* that seems to afflict them all. As Samuel Hynes has pointed out, the siren of the 1920s is no longer the victim of social ostracism for her sexual laxity; rather, she is self-punished, and thus condemned to nihilistic self-loathing and infinite boredom (Hynes 1990: 365, 378). This may be taken in one sense as a residue of older 'Victorian' codes of disapproval and remorse, but at the same time the punishment is internalised as the siren's own business. The Twenties vamp, then, gets away with her promiscuity in the social sense but still finds no full impunity in the privacy of her conscience. So much at least may be observed of the general pattern; but individual cases are more complicated.

Arlen: The Green Hat

Among the most celebrated siren figures of the decade was the heroine of Michael Arlen's fashionably 'advanced' novel *The Green Hat*. Iris Storm's convoluted history is designed to illustrate a dramatic – indeed, melodramatic – discrepancy between her reputation as a 'shameless, shameful lady' who conducts numerous affairs (Arlen 1983: 64) and her privately unblemished integrity: the misunderstood siren turns out to be a kind of modern saint. By the time the novel's narrator, a friend of her brother, meets her, Iris is aged about 30 and twice-widowed, her second husband, a war hero, having been assassinated by Irish Republicans. The more important figure in her background is her first husband, Boy Fenwick, who was found dead below a hotel window on the morning after their wedding night in 1913. Resisting all attempts to cover this death up as a drunken accident, Iris had confirmed that it was suicide, its motive being, as she had enigmatically put it, 'for purity' – which leads everyone to assume that the idealistic Fenwick had discovered his bride to be unvirginal. Iris's action is clearly honourable, in that it puts the preservation of Fenwick's legend (he is a much-adored figure of pre-War youthful promise, on the Rupert Brooke model) above her own now permanently stained reputation. The same almost impossible sense of honour comes through in the main plot, in which Iris renews her romance with her true childhood sweetheart, Napier, taking him to bed just before his marriage to a young woman called Venice, and conceiving a child whose stillbirth almost kills her. In spite of their continuing rivalry (Napier and Iris are planning to run away together), Iris manages to save Venice from drowning during a swimming party. In the final crisis, Napier reveals the stunning secret that Iris has nobly kept for all these years: that Boy Fenwick's suicide 'for purity' was prompted by guilt at his own contraction of syphilis, and that she had covered that up at the expense of her own name in order to preserve the reputation of his family, which has since shunned her. She finally saves the marriage of Napier and Venice by making her last gesture of self-sacrifice, speeding off in her stylish yellow Hispano-Suiza and driving over a cliff to her death.

The point Arlen is trying to make with all this lavish melodrama is clear enough: that a sexually promiscuous woman can be inwardly pure, noble, selfless and honourable. Indeed Iris's character and situation place her above petty considerations of her own reputation, indifferent as she is to her status as a moral outlaw. *The Green Hat* implies that a woman's moral character has little to do with sexual 'virtue', and that chastity is not to be confused with integrity. A linked subplot indicates the same thing negatively: Iris's alcoholic brother Gerald, who had hero-worshipped Fenwick and despises his sister for causing his death, is arrested for accosting a woman sexually in a park, whereupon he blows his brains out from shame. Iris herself seems more heroic for carrying the stigma that her brother could not face, and wiser for seeing sexual conduct as of minor significance in moral terms. Iris is a case of a doomed nobility of spirit misunderstood by those who can see only her disrepute. The larger implication here is that the 'bohemian' sexual pariah may indeed be the true representative of an old-fashioned code of honour no longer recognised in the ethical confusion of post-War life. It is significant that in the first chapter the narrator makes mention of 'the England of Horatio Bottomley, the England of lies, vulgarity, and unclean savagery' (Arlen 1983: 11). Amid all that public mendacity, an apparently wicked woman could be discovered to be the bearer of a lost integrity – an implication also found in *The Last of Mrs Cheyney* by Arlen's close friend Frederick Lonsdale, in which the female jewel-thief turns out to be more principled than her apparently respectable accusers. A curious feature of *The Green Hat*, though, is that its liberalism in the sexual sphere can be embodied in a heroic figure only by reversion to a model of self-sacrificial inner purity that clearly derives from Victorian traditions of tear-jerking melodrama. In this sense its attempt to redeem a modern sexual outlaw by presenting her as a curiously 'Victorian' kind of self-abnegating heroine resembles that of Radclyffe Hall in her sapphic tear-jerker *The Well of Loneliness*.

Arlen's novel is more sophisticated than Hall's in its narrative technique, employing as it does the kind of puzzled fallible narrator-witness found in Ford Madox Ford's *The Good Soldier* (1915; mentioned among Iris's favourite books), Arlen's narrator finding himself similarly perplexed by upper-class English sexual mores and the hidden torments they inflict. This unnamed narrator is particularly knowing in his awareness of the contemporary literary conventions within which the discussion of women's sexuality is hedged around with evasive pretences. He mentions a fictional novelist, Trehawke Tush, who has found and profitably exploited a loophole in his readers' guarded attitude to adultery:

> He had hit on the discovery that English library subscribers will wholeheartedly bear with any racy and illegal relation between the sexes if the same is caused by Pique. He had observed that the whole purpose of a 'best-seller' is to justify a certain amount of adultery in the eyes of suburban matrons. He had observed that in no current English novel was there ever a mention of any woman having a lover because she wanted a lover: she always took a lover because something had upset her, as in real life she might take an aspirin. Mr Trehawke Tush had then created Pique, and was spoken of as a 'brilliant feminine psychologist'. (Arlen 1983: 83)

It is worth remembering these remarks as we move on to examine the figure of the adulteress in 1920s drama and fiction. The wife who takes a lover is in this period and for some time after a character whose presentation is always a matter of delicate negotiation, complicated by pressures of direct censorship (especially on the stage), by pre-emptive self-censorship and by disingenuous Tush-like conventions of mitigation. Writers of the 1920s found many curious ways to 'justify a certain amount of adultery' to their still shockable readers. By the end of the decade, though, Tush's claim that no fictional woman took a lover because she wanted one was already out of date, some writers having come to abandon the old pretences of justification as increasingly irrelevant.

Straying and Misbehaving

Of the three notorious 'banned books' of the Twenties – Hall's *The Well of Loneliness*, Joyce's *Ulysses* and Lawrence's *Lady Chatterley's Lover* – two are about marriages in which the wife engages guiltlessly and joyously in adultery with a lover because she wants one. It is true that Joyce's and Lawrence's books were in any case unpublishable in Britain on account of their explicit sexual vocabularies, but the centrally scandalous fact about each is that the woman's adulterous pleasure goes unaccompanied by racking guilt and unrebuked by the authorial voice. As late as 1960 it was clear that the 'problem' with *Lady Chatterley* was not obscenity as such but, in the eyes of the judge in the test-case obscenity trial of that year, that it seemed to encourage women readers to seek extra-marital pleasures. It is also the case that Connie Chatterley's erotic liberation is covered by multiple mitigations in that her war-damaged husband is impotent and in need of an heir, so he encourages her to conceive a child by a lover. Nonetheless, her adultery and planned elopement with the 'wrong' kind of lover – her husband's gamekeeper – is presented as wholly affirmative and in no need of special excuses. Similarly Molly Bloom's affair with her manager Blazes Boylan in *Ulysses*, and her cuckolded husband's reluctant acceptance of the matter, appear to us simply as established facts of her situation that never call for either justification or condemnation.

That the essential dividing line between the acceptable and the unacceptable lay here is confirmed by a less celebrated case of censorship, that of Noël Coward's play *This Was a Man*, which was produced in New York in 1926 but banned in Britain. It concerns the serially adulterous wife of an artist, Edward Churt, who is aware of her misbehaviour but unconcerned about keeping up respectable appearances. When his best friend Major Bathurst attempts to remonstrate with the errant Carol Churt about her sins, he too is seduced by her and feels obliged to confess his shameful lapse to her husband, at which point Churt bursts into cynical laughter. The age-old topic of a wife's adultery itself could not be excluded from the stage, but the censors of the Lord Chamberlain's office drew the line at representing a husband who clearly accepted such behaviour not with pained stoicism but with open amusement. The new element exposed here in 1920s sexual morality was a *blasé* indifference to marital respectability; an attitude officially judged too improper to be openly voiced on the stage, but increasingly found in prose fiction and sometimes suggested in the theatre.

The classic case of the apparently carefree but secretly anguished adulteress in this period is that of Florence Lancaster in Noël Coward's *The Vortex* (1924), a scandalous melodrama of contemporary decadence that enjoyed huge success on both sides of the Atlantic. Mrs Lancaster is a former society beauty, much photographed in her youth, and now unable to accept that she is ageing and has adult responsibilities. Her latest young lover is the athletic 24-year-old Tom, the same age as her son Nicky, a pianist just returned from studying in Paris and newly engaged to the tough-minded young aristocrat Bunty. Florence is plainly bored with her kindly old husband David, only superficially interested in her own son, and in love only with her own photographic image. At a weekend house party, Bunty rediscovers her former passion for Tom, so Florence and her son are both left jilted. The final Act, presumptuously echoing a scene from *Hamlet*, shows mother and son embattled in hysterical recriminations until Nicky confesses to his drug habit – a shock that seems at last to persuade Florence that she must give up her youthful lovers, become a true mother to Nicky and perhaps even grow up.

When first staged, with Coward himself taking the part of Nicky Lancaster, *The Vortex* encountered initial objections from the censors, until Coward managed to persuade the Lord Chamberlain's officials that its true purpose was to expose the evils of drug-taking: a most unlikely excuse, but he got away with it. The play's commercial success seems more credibly attributable to the opportunity it gave audiences to take a prurient peek at fashionable high-society debauchery, complete with cocktails, hectic dancing to gramophone records, bitchy dialogue, superlative-heavy slang ('how too divine' and so forth) and of course the adultery, which is casually connived in by most of Florence's friends. As Nicky puts it in his agonised protest against his mother's degrading promiscuity, 'We swirl about in a vortex of beastliness' (Coward 1989: 169). Coward's disingenuous implication here is that this idle life of drinking, dope-taking, dancing and casual sex is not an enviable one in the least, as its participants really find it all a hellish torment. With the censors appeased, Coward's audiences could come away both tickled by their brush with modern decadence and satisfied that the bohemian pleasure-seekers were, at least inwardly, suffering for their sins.

Florence Lancaster justifies her adulterous affairs on the grounds that she has a youthful 'temperament' and a husband too old to match it, but apart from that euphemism for sexual appetite she has no mitigating excuse, least of all – to revert to the terms of Arlen's fictional novelist Trehawke Tush – the excuse of Pique. Some other straying wives of the Twenties theatre, though, were amply provided with Pique and more. In W. Somerset Maugham's best comedy, *The Circle* (1921), for instance, the young heroine Elizabeth is married to an emotionally stunted politician, Arnold Champion-Cheney, who has refused to communicate with his own mother because of her elopement with a lover long ago, and seems more interested in his hobby of collecting old furniture than he does in his wife. In spite of his family's various plans to dissuade Elizabeth from 'bolting' with a more appealing admirer, she too elopes rather than live as an item of Arnold's domestic furniture. She knows she will face a life of exile and social ostracism, but takes that risk all the same.

A few years later, the most talked-about British play of 1928 was John van Druten's *Young Woodley*, a melodrama about a boy at an English public school falling in love with his housemaster's young wife, Laura Simmons. Mrs Simmons is clearly dissatisfied with her irritable older husband, whose behaviour throughout is pompous and vindictive. This version of Pique drives her to take a sentimental interest in young Woodley, and to discuss the poetry of Shelley and Swinburne with him, even going so far as to invite him for a walk in the nearby woods. By this point we are aware that walking in those woods is, among Woodley's less innocent schoolfellows, a customary prelude to having sex with the local shop-girls; but Laura's interest in Woodley is not consummated by anything more than afternoon tea and one passionate kiss, interrupted by the unexpected reappearance of Laura's enraged husband. Woodley is discreetly removed from the school by his father, and Laura apologises to the boy for the emotional confusion caused by her lapse, imploring him not to become embittered but rather to treasure the memory of their brief encounter. The audience is invited to regard Laura as an essentially decent character, understandably tempted by a youthful admirer but determined not to mislead him into ruinous scandal.

Semi-tragic in a sentimental way, *Young Woodley* represents only a minor current in 1920s theatre. More typical in its light-hearted approach to adulterous wives is Coward's comedy of manners *Fallen Angels* (1925). The simple situation of this play is that two young women friends have formerly both had the same lover, the Frenchman Maurice, but are now both married to dull English golf-playing types. The plot concludes with Maurice's reappearance and the clear final suggestion that both women will resume their liaisons with him. The critics found that unpleasantly cynical, but theatre-goers flocked to see it, largely because it starred the notorious American actress Tallulah Bankhead, whose own promiscuity was something of a legend among gossip-writers. When *Fallen Angels* reached the end of its run, Bankhead immediately took on the role of Iris Storm in a stage adaptation of *The Green Hat*.

There was no such thing in 1920s literature as a shared or consistent attitude to the figure of the adulterous wife, for the obvious reason that each such fictional character is given unique circumstances, varying kinds of temptation and differing balances of appetite and self-restraint, while authors themselves differ in the degrees to which they apply any code of sexual morality to them. At one end of the spectrum lies Sylvia Tietjens in Ford Madox Ford's *Parade's End* sequence of novels (1924–8), a selfishly vindictive woman whose adulterous affair appears as perhaps the least of her offences, although she is far more complex than any melodramatic she-devil. Somewhere in the middle we might place Kitty Fane of Maugham's *The Painted Veil* (1925), initially an unsympathetic character, but one whose adulterous affair sets her unexpectedly on a path to fuller self-understanding. Significantly, when Kitty comes to regret the affair, she regards it not morally as wicked but aesthetically as a blunder that was 'stupid and ugly' (Maugham 1952: 176). At the far end of this spectrum lies the similarly-named but blameless Silvia Tebrick of David Garnett's novella *Lady into Fox* (1922), who has an excuse for straying from her husband that is far stronger than mere Pique: she has inexplicably been transformed into a vixen, and forgotten her human upbringing so far as to take a dog-fox as her new mate, breeding cubs with him. Her human husband, a rather comically prim and virtuous Victorian, finds it in himself to forgive her: after some wrestling with his religious principles, he concludes that Silvia 'does right to be happy according to the laws of her being' (Garnett 1985: 70). Garnett's tale seems designed to show the futility of censuring the inevitable course of nature.

For all that inevitable variety in characters and in assessments of them, there is nonetheless a discernible tendency among the younger writers of the 1920s (notably Coward and Huxley) to accept wifely infidelity as a fact of life, more or less amusing or intriguing, but neither as an occasion for scandalised excitement nor as a symptom of general corruption. It was certainly no longer the duty of the writer to provide exemplary punishments for their fictional sinners. The new nonchalant approach is exemplified by Huxley's *Antic Hay* (1923), in which the two adulterously promiscuous women, Myra Viveash and Rosie Shearwater, are spared any requirement to justify themselves. Myra's husband is absent on a never-ending big-game hunting expedition in Africa, which is understood to be sufficient reason for her to relieve her boredom with the attentions of lovers; while Rosie feels neglected by her husband's infatuation with Myra, and eventually insists that the marriage be continued on an 'open' basis. The narrative voice passes no comment, let alone censure, on behaviour that is assumed simply to be the way of the world.

The literature of this decade, then, is reluctant to cast the first stone at the straying wife; and in the same manner it indulges other human weaknesses it assumes to be trivial or excusable, provided there is no malice in their expression. An important index of this lies in juvenile literature, formerly the realm in which morally improving examples and punishments for wrongdoing had been obligatory. The most significant new child hero of the period is the anarchically unruly 11-year-old William Brown of Richmal Crompton's series of stories for the *Ladies' Home Magazine* and *Happy Mag* first collected as *Just – William* (1922) and continuing in nine further volumes in the 1920s alone, including *William the Outlaw* and *William in Trouble* (both 1927). William always gets into trouble with his parents, elder siblings and neighbours, but always from an essentially innocent failure to understand the temptations to which he is subject, or to foresee their likely consequences: he will happily burn the paintwork off his bedroom door just to see what happens, or 'borrow' his brother's bicycle before inevitably damaging it, or even kidnap a neighbour's baby, but we know all along that there is no harm in the boy. In fact we are invited to share his contempt for 'goody-goody' children, and to see William's regularly disastrous scrapes as part of a necessary process of experiment, discovery and rebellion. Disobedience simply comes naturally to him, and can be smiled away indulgently on the basis that boys will be boys.

To some kinds of ostensibly adult character, usually in comic fiction and drama, similar kinds of indulgence apply: Wodehouse's Bertie Wooster is perhaps the most obvious case, essentially an overgrown child who is helpless without his valet Jeeves, unable to resist the temptations of immediate gratification (knocking off a policeman's hat, as Bertie does, is just the kind of prank that puts him in William Brown's company) and terrified of his Aunt Agatha. Another such type is the spoilt egotistical bohemian found so often in Coward's early plays. Florence Lancaster and her son Nicky in *The Vortex* are the melodramatic versions of the type, although their counterparts in Coward's finest comedy of the decade, *Hay Fever* (1925), turn out to be remarkably similar. The Bliss family in *Hay Fever*, written shortly after *The Vortex*, recapitulate the action of the earlier play's second Act, inviting guests of the opposite sex to a weekend house party and ending up rejected by them. This time there are four family members and four guests, and the mood is certainly lighter, but the problem is the same: this constantly bickering household is dominated by a faded beauty, Judith Bliss, who tries to deny her age and to relive her heyday as an actress, while her late-adolescent children, Simon and Sorel, blame their own ill-mannered selfishness on their upbringing; meanwhile Judith's husband David is trying to write a sensational novel, *The Sinful Woman*, which appears to resemble Arlen's *The Green Hat* (its heroine drives a scarlet Hispano, matching Iris Storm's yellow one).

The comic effects of *Hay Fever* feed off melodrama in other ways too: Judith's most famous role has been as the heroine of a lavishly clichéd melodramatic play, the dialogues of which her children know by heart, and her current infatuations are really just excuses for her to resume that role. The second Act culminates in a moment of uproarious parody with the family's re-enactment of Judith's most extravagant scene, to the bemusement of the four guests, who have felt rudely ignored by the self-obsessed Blisses since their arrival. The play itself is as inward-looking as the family it presents, being a theatrical performance of incorrigibly theatrical people performing their theatricality; but therein lies its strength, or at least its attraction. Irresponsible characters who are incapable of sincerity or of consideration for others are more dramatically compelling than responsible citizens, as Coward always understood. As a minor figure in *The Vortex* says of Nicky, 'He's divinely selfish; all amusing people are' (Coward 1989: 99). The often noted 'cynicism' of 1920s literature is perhaps only a rediscovery of that long-established comic principle.

Outlaws, miscreants and flamboyantly selfish narcissists are attractive fictional figures on the old principle that the Devil has the best tunes. The Devil, indeed, makes a personal appearance at the end of one of this decade's most intriguing 'spinster' novels, Sylvia Townsend Warner's *Lolly Willowes* (1926), as a rather kindly old rogue who listens sympathetically to the heroine's account of her boredom and frustration. *Lolly Willowes* is a fantastical romance that follows the transformation of Laura or 'Lolly' from the dutiful Victorian role of respectable maiden aunt to liberation amid a rural coven of witches. By the end of the tale, Laura has dedicated herself freely and comfortably to the service of the Devil, in what amounts to an allegory of feminine emancipation in the post-Victorian era.

Aren't We All? Amorality and the Rise of Camp

In many respects, then, writing of the 1920s turns its back upon what had not so long since been the symbolically punitive moral functions of literature. Except in the crudest popular thrillers (although there were plenty of those, by Edgar Wallace, Sax Rohmer and others), scowling villains fade away along with pure-hearted redemptive heroes and heroines, giving way to a largely comical array of harmless grotesques and eccentrics. Even in crime fiction, where we might expect to find clear lines drawn between good and evil, we often find instead a cheerfully cynical assumption of universal depravity, or at least of temptation and murky motives. The entertainment provided by Agatha Christie's novels in particular has much to do with the sheer range of potentially culpable characters whose dubious secrets are exposed by Poirot at the story's close. In *The Murder of Roger Ackroyd*, indeed, Poirot announces as a general principle that in cases of murder, 'Everyone concerned in them has something to hide' (Christie 1957: 71). Gladys Mitchell's psychoanalytic detective Mrs Bradley in *Speedy Death* puts it more strongly:

> 'We are all murderers, my friend,' said Mrs Bradley lugubriously. 'Some in deed and some in thought. That's the only difference, though.'
> 'Rather a considerable difference,' said Carstairs, putting into his tone a lightness which he was very far from feeling.
> 'Morally, there is no difference at all,' said Mrs Bradley more briskly. 'Some have the courage of their convictions. Others have not. That's all . . .'
> (Mitchell 1943: 67)

Detective fiction carried the general implication that everyone is just one strong temptation away from murder. The widely-known Freudian extension of that principle, understood by Mitchell and her readers, is that every individual conceals a violent and lustful Id only precariously constrained by his or her responsible Ego, so that the distinction between the normal citizen and the monster of criminality is almost a matter of accident. Much of the decade's literature takes it for granted, in such ways, that we are all potentially guilty, and thus all in a sense blameless.

The perfect motto for the indulgent and sometimes openly amoral attitude of the times went up in bright lights over the Globe Theatre, London in April 1923 at the opening of Frederick Lonsdale's comedy *Aren't We All?* In that play, the rhetorical question of the title (and of the final line) refers to fools rather than to sinners or criminals, but the light plot is about the temptations of adultery, and the need for a young husband and wife to forgive one another by acknowledging their common weakness in the face of temptation. The moral basis of the play is in fact eminently Christian, behind its veneer of modern naughtiness. The colloquially inclusive title, though, echoed the tones in which modern spirits of the time shrugged off the hard-and-fast moral distinctions they associated with the most forbiddingly puritanical aspects of Victorian culture.

The new 'elastic' morality and indulgent levity of 1920s literature should not be mistaken for an outright rejection of moral distinctions, let alone a generalised indifference. Where we hear the voices of unabashed amorality, we are just as often invited to suspect them of being merely self-serving. Thus when the heartless pleasure-seeker Lucy Tantamount in Huxley's *Point Counter Point* is called a 'bad angel' by one of her many former lovers, Maurice Spandrell, she replies 'For an intelligent man, Maurice, you talk a lot of drivel. Do you genuinely believe that some things are right and some wrong?' (Huxley 1994e: 153). Lucy tends to regard morality merely as an outmoded delusion of the older generations, and believes herself to be too sophisticated for that, but in the context of her characterisation the reader is most likely to treat her dismissive speech as a symptom of a generation that has lost its way. Similarly, Florence Lancaster in Coward's *The Vortex* responds to her son Nicky's anguished denunciations with a commonplace of the new liberal ethic: 'If you're preaching morality you've no right to – that's my affair – I've never done any harm to anyone' (Coward 1989: 170). In context, though, that self-exculpation appears flimsy, the point being that she has indeed harmed her own family by running after young boyfriends while ignoring Nicky's problems. Authors such as Huxley and Coward who were associated at the time with moral laxity and even degeneracy were in fact more inclined to cast suspicion upon their fictional amoralists than to endorse them.

All the same, amid the post-War dissolution of 'Victorian' moral certainties a certain flippancy encapsulated in the phrase 'aren't we all?' makes itself heard in the Twenties, often in the tones that we would now call *Camp*. To use this term does involve a certain element of anachronism, because it was not at the time in general currency outside the codes of underground slang (*OED2* records an example of the adjective from 1909, denoting an effeminately mincing manner, but no examples of the verb – as in 'camping it up' – before 1931). I use it here in the extended sense analysed in Susan Sontag's fragmentary but famous essay of 1964, 'Notes on "Camp"', in which she speaks of Camp taste as an indulgently 'sweet cynicism', of the kind that 'neutralizes moral indignation' (Sontag 1994: 119, 118). In Sontag's enlarged sense, Camp is not so much a mannerism of gesture or voice; it is a cultural stance or attitude, a playful modern version of nineteenth-century dandyism, refashioned by its pioneer, Oscar Wilde (much quoted in the essay), as a generalised triumph of aesthetic considerations over moral ones. 'The whole point of Camp', Sontag writes, 'is to dethrone the serious [. . .] One can be serious about the frivolous, frivolous about the serious' (Sontag 1994: 116). This kind of inversion, in which murder may be treated as a matter for giggling while questions of dress or interior décor are addressed with inflexible severity, is found more generally in the 1920s than in Wilde's own time.

That style of humour in which solemnity and frivolity are knowingly inverted is not of course a new discovery of the 1920s. Thomas De Quincey's essay 'On Murder Considered as One of the Fine Arts' (1827) is an early landmark in its emergence, and in some respects a prior tradition of mock-heroic poetry could be said to prefigure it too. It is the provocative Aestheticism of Oscar Wilde in the 1880s and 1890s, though, that provides the dominant example for 1920s Camp. Noël Coward's musical comedy *Bitter-Sweet* (1929), set partly in the 1890s, provides in its third Act a chorus of late-Victorian 'Pretty boys' singing about their green carnations, as a kind of tribute to a founding father. A distinctive line of elegantly languid and cruel humour indeed leads from Wilde through the short stories of 'Saki' (H. H. Munro, 1870–1916) and the novellas of Ronald Firbank into the more generalised Camp sensibility of the post-War period. Saki's tales had commonly treated murderous outrages with undisguised glee, and often in clearly Wildean style. The fictional world of Firbank was still in the 1920s a fantastical fairyland of aristocratic hauteur, as in his *The Flower Beneath the Foot* (1923), in which choicely Camp dialogue teeters constantly on the edge of disclosing some sexual depravity without ever being so vulgar as to name it. Firbank's work, with its sidelong but unmistakable implications of same-sex desire, was 'cult' reading-matter among a necessarily secretive subculture of educated homosexual men. For those circles, Wilde was a presiding spirit of the times in another sense, his personal fate in the trials and criminal conviction of 1895 having cast a long shadow of reticence (and thus also of teasing semi-disclosure) over the literary culture of homosexuality, one that helped to give Camp humour of the time a sometimes defiant edge. Direct and indirect censorship of literature was more severe on this topic than on others, giving rise to a huge discrepancy between public cultural representation and private informal knowledge, within which Camp humour could serve as a badge of 'knowing' sophistication.

A typical moment of 1920s Camp writing comes in Lytton Strachey's brief essay on T. B. Macaulay, the early-Victorian author of the popular *History of England* (1849–55), and a figure whose complacency and philistinism made him an irresistible target for the Stracheyan rapier. In 'Macaulay' (1928), Strachey concentrates not upon the obvious problem of the historian's Whig optimism but upon his prose style, bemoaning its torrent of clichés:

> When he wished to state that Schomberg was buried in Westminster Abbey, he *had* to say that 'the illustrious warrior' was laid in 'that venerable abbey, hallowed by the dust of many generations of princes, heroes and poets'. There is no escaping it; and the incidental drawback that Schomberg was not buried at Westminster at all, but in Dublin, is, in comparison with the platitude of the style, of very small importance. (Strachey 1980: 96)

A glaring factual error in a historical work is, in the Camp perspective, a trivially 'incidental' matter, whereas any failure in style must be counted as unforgivable.

Camp humour and Camp taste more generally have always been associated primarily with male homosexuals or bisexuals (there were no 'gay men' in the Twenties: colloquially, they were queers or nancies; in sexological jargon they were inverts). That link should not be understood as a necessary identification, though. On the one hand, there were homosexual writers of the time (E. M. Forster, Siegfried Sassoon, W. Somerset Maugham, among others) who showed little inclination to cultivate the Camp style in their writings. On the other hand, one of the most notable features of Twenties Camp is that it comes to be adopted by heterosexual authors and readers too (including such cases as the 'reformed' ex-homosexual Waugh), in a new shared spirit of refined frivolity. Many of the Camp characters in fiction and drama of the time are to be understood implicitly as homosexual: Pawnie, for instance, in Coward's *The Vortex*, who is quoted above saying that all amusing people are divinely selfish; or the giggling figure of the Hon. Miles Malpractice in *Decline and Fall*, who finds the images of kings on playing-cards adorably naughty-looking. Again in E. F. Benson's series of comically-mock-heroic 'Lucia' novels beginning with *Queen Lucia* (1920), the sustained camping over small-town feminine rivalries and battles of snobbery is enhanced by the attendance of the anti-heroine's sidekick, the bachelor Georgie Pilling, whose perfectionism about dress and grooming indicates that he is not as other men. On the other hand a Camp manner of emphasis on triviality is to be found among clearly heterosexual women such as Waugh's Margot Beste-Chetwynde, as when she decides against marrying Sir Humphrey Maltravers on the grounds that the married name Margot Maltravers sounds too alliterative to her taste.

More indicative of the diffusion of Camp humour well beyond the private circles of homosexual subculture is the popularity of certain comic types in light fiction of the Twenties. P. G. Wodehouse's stories of Bertie Wooster and his manservant Jeeves do not fall under any definition of 'gay fiction', and yet Jeeves is in his own way an unmistakably Camp creation, imposing a fanatically exacting supervision over Bertie's choices of neckties, spats, bathrobes and other items of dress. In the realm of detective fiction, Hercule Poirot again is a Camp figure in his perfectionism about such matters. Still more Camp at times is Dorothy L. Sayers's presentation of her undoubtedly heterosexual hero Lord Peter Wimsey, as in this description of him in the short story 'The Article in Question' (1928):

> On the morning of the wedding-day, Lord Peter emerged from Bunter's hands a marvel of sleek brilliance. His primrose-coloured hair was so exquisite a work of art that to eclipse it with his glossy hat was like shutting up the sun

in a shrine of polished jet; his spats, light trousers, and exquisitely polished shoes formed a tone-symphony in monochrome. It was only by the most impassioned pleading that he persuaded his tyrant to allow him to place two small photographs and a thin, foreign letter in his breast-pocket. (Sayers 1989: 34)

This description is given to us immediately after we have heard Lord Peter confess that 'I have rather an unwholesome weakness for policemen' (Sayers 1989: 34). He intends the remark in a non-sexual sense, but phrases it with Camp suggestiveness all the same, all the better to signal his aristocratic nonchalance, and his cultured disregard for any imputation of effeminacy. In such ways did comic writing of the time shrug off bourgeois seriousness and redefine a new style of modern frivolity.

Chapter Five

But It Still Goes On: The Passing of the Twenties

> It is for the historian of literature to decide; for him to say if we are now beginning or ending or standing in the middle of a great period of prose fiction, for down in the plain little is visible.
> Virginia Woolf, 'Modern Fiction' (1925)

It might be tempting to pretend that the literary 1920s signed themselves off with some neatly conclusive flourish before standing back to allow the Thirties to introduce themselves on the next fresh page. The appearance of Robert Graves's *Good-bye to All That* in November 1929 offers itself as a promising candidate for the decade's final bow, and not only on account of its boldly valedictory title. In Graves's case, though, any impression of timely closure was soon to be spoiled by the publication a few months later of his curious medley of dramatic and autobiographical pieces, *But It Still Goes On* (1930), whose title of course contradicts the finality of its predecessor's. The year 1929 was for Graves a personal and financial turning-point, the start of a new life in Majorca, but the war-books 'boom' to which he had contributed with *Good-bye* was the literary development that linked the late Twenties most strongly to the Thirties: it rumbled on continuously from 1928 through much of the next decade, with Sassoon's two 'Sherston' sequels (1930, 1936), H. M. Tomlinson's *All Our Yesterdays*, Henry Williamson's *The Patriot's Progress*, Frederic Manning's *Her Privates We* (all 1930), Vera Brittain's *Testament of Youth* (1933), T. E. Lawrence's *Seven Pillars of Wisdom* (1935), David Jones's *In Parenthesis* and Wyndham Lewis's *Blasting and Bombardiering* (both 1937).

An apparently more secure point at which to mark the end of the literary Twenties might seem to be provided by the death of D. H. Lawrence in March 1930; but here again we find that 'it still goes on', in that new works by Lawrence kept appearing posthumously: the verse collection *Nettles* two weeks after his death, *Assorted Articles* in April,

The Virgin and the Gipsy in May, *A Propos of Lady Chatterley's Lover* in June and *Love Among the Haystacks* in November. Lawrence carried on being resurrected in print over the next few years, too, both in his own works, *Apocalypse* (1931), *Etruscan Places*, *Last Poems* (both 1932) and *The Letters* (edited by Aldous Huxley, 1932), and in rival biographies of him, John Middleton Murry's *Son of Woman* (1931) and Catherine Carswell's *The Savage Pilgrimage* (1932). The deceased Lawrence indeed became one of the most visibly prolific authors of the early Thirties.

We are obliged, then, to regard the boundary offered by the calendar as permeable, and so to acknowledge considerable degrees of overspill and overlap between these decades, in which case the title of C. Day Lewis's *Transitional Poem* (1929) seems more fitting than Graves's misleadingly conclusive *Good-bye*. Elsewhere, I have offered an account of 1928 as a pivotal literary year in which 'the Thirties' may be said to have begun prematurely while certain developments of the 1920s reach a conclusion (McHale and Stevenson 2006: 73–81). In this brief chapter, I shall consider more broadly the permeability of the 1920s/1930s boundary, before going on to sketch some aspects of the Twenties' cultural legacy and then hazarding some general conclusions.

Previews of the Thirties

There was certainly no abrupt Changing of the Guard at the end of the decade, in that the distinctively new Twentyish authors – Huxley, Coward, MacDiarmid, Blunden, Muir, Sayers and Christie, for example – carried on publishing successfully through the Thirties, as did most of their established elders, including Yeats, Eliot, Woolf and even, as we have noticed, the late D. H. Lawrence. Even the discontinuities in literary careers were only partial: E. M. Forster retired from fiction after his short-story collection *The Eternal Moment* (1928), but not from the literary life of essay-writing; W. Somerset Maugham wrote only three more plays after *The Sacred Flame* (1929), but continued as a successful short-storyist and novelist; Edith Sitwell abandoned poetry for a decade after *Gold Coast Customs* (1929), but continued to write as a biographer. One exception was Lytton Strachey, whose career subsided into indolence and illness in the years before his death in 1932.

On the other hand, the last years of the 1920s are notable for the emergence of a number of new writers who came to define the new configuration of Thirties literature. In poetry, Louis MacNeice brought out his first collection, *Blind Fireworks* (1929), in the year of Day Lewis's

Transitional Poem. Day Lewis had been publishing verse since 1925 in the student anthology *Oxford Poetry*, which is also where Stephen Spender's poems first appeared in 1929, under the joint editorship of Spender and MacNeice. W. H. Auden was at this point visible only to readers of that anthology, which he co-edited in 1926–7, and to a small circle of friends who formed the readership of his privately-published *Poems* (1928). Among the novelists, Evelyn Waugh's début with *Decline and Fall* was the most striking of the late Twenties, but Christopher Isherwood's first novel, *All the Conspirators*, also appeared in 1928 (a critical failure, it was soon remaindered), while Graham Greene enjoyed his first – although scarcely merited – success with his second novel, *The Man Within* (1929). Eric Blair was living an impoverished 'down-and-out' life in Paris in 1928–9, later to be written up when he became 'George Orwell' in 1933. Ivy Compton-Burnett had already published two novels by this date (one of them disowned), but it was with her *Brothers and Sisters* (1929) that she at last found her true subject in the realm of domestic tyrannies and acidic breakfast-table dialogue: the topic is Twentyish, its development mostly delayed until the Thirties and after. Readers of detective fiction, mourning the retirement (and subsequent death, 1930) of Arthur Conan Doyle, were compensated by the arrival of new talents in the late 1920s, notably Margery Allingham and Gladys Mitchell.

The first late-Twenties steps of some authors later to be known as 'Thirties' writers exhibit two especially interesting features of the 1920s/1930s transition. One of these is a shift in their European literary orientations, from the French-speaking to the German-speaking zones. The Paris of Proust, Joyce and Gertrude Stein had been without question the world's literary-artistic capital in the 1920s, drawing in more Anglophone literary migrants during that decade: Ezra Pound, Ernest Hemingway, Ford Madox Ford, Edith Sitwell, Jean Rhys, Samuel Beckett and others, while W. Somerset Maugham, a Parisian by birth, settled in the south of France from 1928. Among the rising generation of the late Twenties, though, the Weimar Republic began to exert a magnetism both cultural and erotic: Auden's decision after graduating in 1928 to spend a year cruising the homosexual underworld of Berlin proved to be a crucial switch of directions. He urged his friend Christopher Isherwood to join him there in 1929, thereby handing the young novelist the terrain upon which his reputation was later established. Meanwhile, Stephen Spender spent some of the summer of 1929 in a personally liberating exploration of Hamburg, and at the same time Edwin and Willa Muir were at work on the first English translation of Kafka, *The Castle* (1930). The transition from the 'aesthetic' 1920s to the 'political' 1930s was in part a change of European location and language.

The second peculiarity of this transition is that the new 'Thirties' generation was ushered onto the literary scene in great part by two Twenties institutions, namely the Hogarth Press established in 1917 by Leonard and Virginia Woolf, and the publishing house of Faber and Faber (founded 1925, as Faber & Gwyer), directed by T. S. Eliot. The Woolfs' small press had become notable as publishers of the English versions of Sigmund Freud's works (from 1924) and of course of Woolf's own novels and essays. It was Eliot at Faber who came to publish Auden's *Poems* (1930) and subsequent works, along with Spender's *Poems, 1933* and eventually MacNeice's *Poems* (1935), but the Hogarth Press, fortified in the late 1920s by the healthy American sales of *Orlando*, engaged more fully with the rising generation. It launched Day Lewis by publishing *Transitional Poem* in 1929 and went on to publish an early example of Thirties working-class fiction with John Hampson's *A Night at the Greyhound* (1931), before bringing out both Isherwood's second novel, *The Memorial* (1932), and the two showcase verse anthologies of that generation, *New Signatures* (1932) and *New Country* (1933). The significance of this is that the new generation, as it followed sociopolitical concerns beyond the aesthetic purism of Bloomsbury and of high Modernism, was in fact consistently sponsored by the publishing arms of just those 1920s groupings. Virginia Woolf's own trajectory at the time may be seen to follow in part a parallel course, her famous lecture-series *A Room of One's Own* (1929) addressing the challenges facing women writers in a male-dominated culture in socio-political terms that would later be followed up in her *Three Guineas* (1938).

In this context, an especially interesting Hogarth Press publication of the late Twenties is Henry Green's second novel, *Living* (1929), a book that manages to combine the 'poetic' aspirations of Modernist fiction with a fresh interest in working-class life that recurs strongly in the literature of the Thirties. Set in and around a Birmingham engineering works, it presents the daily lives of both factory-managers and working-class households in a Modernist prose style evidently influenced by Joyce and Stein, and marked by an avoidance of articles, as in this opening of the eighth chapter:

> She lay, above town, with Jones. Autumn. Light from sky grew dark over town.
> She half opened eyelids from her eyes, showing whites. She saw in feeling. She saw in every house was woman with her child. In all streets, in clumps, were children.
>
> (Green 2000: 81)

The story, almost plotless, follows Twentyish generational conflicts in two connected spheres: the determination of the 26-year-old Richard Dupret (based upon Green himself), who has inherited the business from his father, to promote his younger employees by getting rid of the old hands; and the household of Craigan (one of those made redundant), maintained by the young Lily Gates, who dreams of escape from industrial Birmingham but has to return after a failed attempt to elope to Canada with her boyfriend. The novel is a surprisingly successful extension of experimental Twenties methods, notably in the recurrent poetical motif of the homing pigeon, into realms explored more often in the next decade – although rarely with Green's resolutely unsentimental sensitivity.

The Twenties Revisited: Waugh and Isherwood

The literature of the early 1930s is in part occupied with unfinished business of the late 1920s, especially so in certain books of the year 1930. Wyndham Lewis's enormous and unwieldy satirical novel *The Apes of God* (June 1930) is an essentially Twentyish book set at the time of the 1926 General Strike. Auden's *Poems* (September 1930) includes 'It was Easter as I walked in the public gardens', later helpfully retitled '1929', a spring poem deliberately echoing in miniature some of the motifs of 'The Waste Land'. A more substantial case is Evelyn Waugh's second novel, *Vile Bodies*, which very nearly became the swan song of the 1920s but in the event appeared two weeks after the decade's close, on 14 January 1930. Like Graves's *Good-bye*, *Vile Bodies* was written at a frantic pace through the summer of 1929 in the shadow of personal upheavals. It is set in what looks very much like the year of its composition, referring to such public events of the time as the rapid alternations of government, and obliquely incorporating private events that interrupted the writing of the novel: the sudden break-up of Waugh's marriage in July, and a trip to a major motor-race in Belfast in August. The central basis of the novel's success – and despite its obvious structural flaws it sold far better than *Decline and Fall* – was its caricatured portrayal of the fashionable set already known since 1924 as the Bright Young People, and the celebrity culture of parties and gossip columns that had in the late 1920s kept this ostentatiously decadent group in the public eye. This book was the first of a number of 1930s productions that look back upon aspects of Twenties life. Another is F. Tennyson Jesse's *A Pin to See the Peepshow* (1934), a fictional reinterpretation of the Thompson–Bywaters murder case of 1922.

The Thirties writer most given to revisiting the 1920s was Christopher Isherwood, who followed up his Twenties-set novel *The Memorial* with the remarkable autobiographical volume *Lions and Shadows: An Education in the Twenties* (Hogarth Press, 1938). These books offer fascinating insights into the peculiar mentality of young literati in the 1920s, although it should be borne in mind that Isherwood between the ages of 16 and 26 had not been a normal specimen of that class but, as he insists in *Lions and Shadows*, an even more disturbed case than most within 'the vast freak museum of our neurotic generation' (Isherwood 1985: 134). *The Memorial*, appropriately dedicated to Isherwood's father, who had been killed in action in 1915, is an ambitious study of family tensions in the wake of the War. Among its most striking episodes is a family reunion brought about by that most Twentyish occasion, the ceremonial dedication of a local war memorial. The book's title is justified not only by that occasion but also by the recurrent importance of memory to the characters' inner lives: one of the principal characters, Lily Vernon, is a war-widow who prefers to live on her idealised memories of early Edwardian life, resenting the post-War world as a whole and especially the post-War youth, whom she regards as 'enemies' (Isherwood 1978: 45). Another is a homosexual war veteran who travels to Berlin seeking psychoanalytic treatment. Despite its largely familial and private focus, the novel is in many respects a commemoration of the 1920s, the chronology of its action running from the summer of 1920 to December 1929. A further Twentyish feature of this chronology is that the narrative follows a discontinuous anachronic design in four parts, the first set in 1928, the second – including the war-memorial episode – in 1920, the third in 1925 and the final part in 1929.

The self-tormenting and sometimes suicidal gloom that colours *The Memorial* is decisively dispelled in the semi-fictionalised memoir *Lions and Shadows*, which is enlivened by sardonic hindsight in Isherwood's treatment of his own youthful delusions and virginal neuroses, and by colourful anecdotes of his friends Edward Upward (renamed 'Chalmers'), W. H. Auden ('Weston') and Stephen Spender ('Savage'). The book is often read primarily as a kind of preamble to the Thirties, but to students of the 1920s too, *Lions and Shadows* affords remarkable glimpses of post-War youth – of the expensively educated male variety – struggling with its extraordinary historical burdens and responding to literary developments of the time. On the general predicament of Twenties youth, Isherwood offers a psycho-historical diagnosis according to which young men of his generation felt secretly shamed at having missed the chance to prove themselves in the War, and so pursued a pseudo-war against their parents and teachers, who became the Enemy in their Us/

Them mythology. The literary aspect of this cultural conflict involved idolising certain literary heroes who, being safely dead before they had reached maturity, could never go over to the Enemy camp: Wilfred Owen and Katherine Mansfield were especially honoured by Isherwood and Chalmers/Upward in their early-Twenties schooldays. Perhaps more interesting are the new kinds of literary awareness that these two adjust to when studying at Cambridge, and that Weston/Auden encounters while at Oxford. Isherwood and Upward had been privileged in 1924 to attend the lectures on modern poetry given by the dynamic young critic I. A. Richards, who exhilarated them as a new 'evangelist' but at the same time shattered their Baudelaire-influenced Romanticism so that 'everything we had valued would have to be scrapped' (Isherwood 1985: 74–5). It is at this point that Isherwood first comes to see the importance both of T. S. Eliot and of modern psychology, including Freud's work. Later, we hear of Weston/Auden's conversion in 1926 from being a poetic disciple of Thomas Hardy to acknowledgement of Eliot as the new master. Meanwhile Isherwood trains himself for a future as a novelist by studying André Gide's *Les Faux-Monnayeurs* (1925) and E. M. Forster's *Aspects of the Novel* (1927).

The greatest of all retrospective evocations of the 1920s came a few years later, in Evelyn Waugh's *Brideshead Revisited* (1945), a novel divided into three parts, of which the first two are set in 1923–4 and 1924–6 respectively. The third part opens with the narrator, a successful artist now serving as an officer on home-front duties during the Second World War, declaring 'My theme is memory' (Waugh 2000: 211). Memory is indeed the basis of the novel, as the fictional Charles Ryder recalls events from twenty years before he begins his tale. *Brideshead Revisited* is a Twentyish work not only in its principal time-setting but in its ambitions too: it sets out clearly to compete with and to provide the English counterpart to Marcel Proust's work, and specifically the Proust of *Sodome et Gomorrhe* (1922), lovingly reconstructing a vanished age of stylishly languid upper-class homosexuality, but with the Oxford of 1923–5 now standing in for Proust's Parisian *Belle Époque*. Waugh's portrayal of the stammering super-aesthete Anthony Blanche in particular bids to rival Proust's creation of the eccentric homosexual Baron de Charlus. Waugh sets up for his narrator two matching dinner scenes, one with Blanche, exhibiting the perfect distillation of Twenties decadence, the other with the vulgarly ambitious politician Rex Mottram, which is the perfect distillation of Twenties snobbery. In the course of the story, Waugh recreates this niche of early 1920s life with the aid of references to Ryder's and his friends' reading-matter, which includes Strachey's *Eminent Victorians* (1918), Roger Fry's *Vision and Design*

(1920), David Garnett's *Lady into Fox* (1922) and Huxley's *Antic Hay* (1923). The high point of these period literary allusions, though, is the scene in which Blanche recites passages of 'The Waste Land' through a megaphone to a crowd of passing student athletes. (Behind the open reference to Eliot's famous poem here lies a further allusion to Edith Sitwell's use of the same instrument in her recital of her own *Façade* sequence in 1923.)

It is not only through literary references, though, that Waugh evokes the period of the early 1920s. He makes sure to include the shadow of the Great War, so for example Lady Marchmain, the mother of Ryder's debauched companion Sebastian Flyte, is occupied in producing a book commemorating her three brothers, all of them killed in the War. Ryder himself invokes the War when suggesting an explanation (intriguingly different from Isherwood's equivalent) for the childish antics of his Oxford generation, telling us that he caught up as a student with the carefree childhood he had been denied by the anxieties of the War years. The observation is offered only as an account of Ryder's own irresponsibility, but the constant presence of Sebastian's teddy-bear Aloysius indicates a broader generational infantilism. As if to complete the period picture, Waugh has Ryder go through a momentary but telling brush with 'disillusionment'. Having fallen in love not only with Sebastian but with his whole aristocratic-Catholic family, but then having offended Lady Marchmain, the young Ryder departs from their country estate, Brideshead, for what he mistakenly believes to be the last time, saying to himself 'I have left behind illusion,' in the expectation that he will now set out to confront the real 'world of three dimensions'. The older Ryder of the 1940s, though, immediately adds: 'I have since learned that there is no such world' (Waugh 2000: 158). Ryder's farewell to the illusory turns out to be another case of what Eliot had called the illusion of being disillusioned.

Conclusions

The reader will have noticed, and perhaps by now become irritated by, the degree to which the text of this book is sprinkled with numerical dates. My defence of that eyesore relies first on an appeal to the responsibilities of literary history, a discipline which, unlike literary criticism or theory, is obliged to keep its eye carefully upon the chronologies of composition, publication and performance. Not all of the numbers displayed in my text, though, are publication dates: some are dates of fictional settings, while others indicate the ages of various writers active in the decade. Here a further consideration, broached already in the opening sections of the Introduction, justifies the insistent registration of dates: the preoccupation of so many 1920s writers with the differences between their own times and pre-War era, and the resultant 'literature of hindsight', as I have termed it, requires careful specification, which I have attempted in various parts of this book when examining fictions set in the late-Victorian or Edwardian periods, and again in analysing the chronological designs of war-novels and war-memoirs in Chapter 3. So too do the age differences among authors of the time, given the significance of generational suspicion and resentment in the decade's writings.

These observations lead us to the principal claim upon which my account of 1920s literature has been founded in the previous chapters: that the chief clue to the distinctiveness of the decade, not only in openly expressed attitudes but in its unusual new configuration of literary genres, is to be found in its 'time-sense', which is always in turn a version of its sense of a special historical predicament. Writers in the 1920s thought of themselves and their contemporaries as people who had lived through an epochal transformation that disconnected them from the world of their own childhoods and of their parents' upbringings too. The Great War was of course the watershed to which most of them referred, but there were additional reminders in daily post-War experience too that everything seemed to have changed. 'Every day,' wrote Virginia Woolf, 'we find ourselves doing, saying, or thinking things that would have been impossible to our fathers' (Woolf 1994: 238). And indeed things seemed to be changing fast, in the pace of life (increased use of motor transport and of civil aviation), in public behaviour (young women in shorter skirts smoking and swearing), in popular culture (successive dance crazes, the rise of cinema), in the scientific and intellectual spheres (Relativity, psychoanalysis) and in world politics (the maps of Ireland, Europe and the Middle East all redrawn). All eyes were on the striking discontinuities between 1920s life and everything that came before it, especially the pre-War world, rather than on the – mostly unremarked – continuities; and abrupt Revolution seemed at the time to have replaced former expectations of steady Evolution.

For these reasons I have taken the decade's preoccupation with the discontinuity of recent public and private histories, documented it at some length under various headings in this study, pursued it as a key to 1920s literature (especially in Chapters 2 and 3) and found it more reliable than approaching that literature through such a nebulous *Zeitgeist* notion as 'disillusionment' – which I have argued is a much more uncertain concept than it seems. Nor do I take post-War 'despair' as a safe guide to the decade's literature: in Chapter 4 especially I have attempted to present instead the predominance of comedy in this decade as a clue to certain period tones of cynicism and flippancy. At the same time I have tried to bear in mind the strong element of exaggeration in the 1920s sense of being (to quote Woolf again) 'sharply cut off' from the past, and so I have traced important continuities in Chapter 1 between the Edwardian scene and the 'ideational' current of 1920s writing. Elsewhere I have tried to resist the common temptation to concentrate on Modernist classics or upon the war generation, by bringing into my account several writers who persisted in the use of pre-1920 literary modes and conventions, and have highlighted the often-forgotten contributions of elder writers (Bridges, Hardy, Shaw and others) to the decade's literary culture. I hope to have offered, then, a more carefully discriminating and more fully rounded account of the literary 1920s than could be provided on the basis of received wisdoms or restrictive academic canons.

Of the legacy left by 1920s literature it is safer to comment only very selectively, as the subject is of the kind that ramifies in several directions. Particular lines of influence from individual writers of the decade through to later British literature can be identified, some of these being well established. One such line, for example, runs from the D. H. Lawrence of *Birds, Beasts and Flowers* (1923) to the poetry of Ted Hughes; another may traced from the vernacular dialogue of Noël Coward's plays to that of Harold Pinter's. The influences exerted by Joyce and Yeats were felt not only by their compatriots, from Samuel Beckett to Seamus Heaney and beyond, but by later British authors: notable post-Joyceans included Malcolm Lowry and Anthony Burgess, while both W. H. Auden and Philip Larkin found themselves trying to resist the spell of Yeats by drawing upon the contrary example of Thomas Hardy. Few post-1930 British poets could safely claim to have escaped the long shadow of T. S. Eliot, either. Auden's 1947 poem 'The Fall of Rome', written in the wake of another World War, shows a convincing revival of anachronistic techniques found in the 1920s 'prophetic' poetry of Yeats and Eliot. Among the outstanding novelists of our own time, Alan Hollinghurst is a champion of Ronald Firbank, although his own work draws upon a wider range of examples including that of E. M. Forster.

Rather than list too many such individual cases, though, it may be better to address a few consequences of that tension in 1920s literature between the 'classicist' faction of Eliot and the 'Romantic' camp of D. H. Lawrence. One of the miracles of Auden's poetic career was that he managed to hold those incompatible authorities in productive balance: as an Eliotic anti-Romantic, Auden ought in principle to have rejected

Lawrence, but in fact he continued to revere him, although more as a lay-psychological prophet than as a poet. On the other hand, the most influential and charismatic British literary critic of the mid-century period, F. R. Leavis (a student at Cambridge during the 1920s) found his work profoundly shaped, and eventually torn, by divided loyalties to those rival masters: his early writings develop suggestions drawn from Eliot, but an increasingly idolatrous commitment to Lawrence's memory eventually led him to dismiss Eliot as a writer essentially hostile to 'life'. The internal antagonisms of 1920s literature were still being felt as late as the 1960s.

There is a good case, although it is not now an original case, for understanding much of the literary and cultural Sixties as a resumption of battles fought in the 1920s. The resemblances are often seen primarily in terms of the persistence of values (sexual tolerance, anti-militarism) associated with the Bloomsbury Group; but there are broader cultural similarities too in the revived cult of Youth and in a renewed appetite for pseudo-religious charlatanisms. The legendary dawn of the Sixties in Britain involved the reappearance of a 1920s novel – Lawrence's *Lady Chatterley's Lover* – in paperback and the acquittal of its publisher, Penguin Books, in a landmark obscenity trial in which such veterans of the Twenties as E. M. Forster and Rebecca West appeared as defence witnesses. Thereafter, Lawrence became a presiding spirit of Sixties libertarianism, usually being misread as a benign prophet of Love – the very principle he had in fact spent most of the 1920s railing against. In some respects, the Sixties were the Twenties repeated as farce, and quite literally as farce in the case of Joe Orton, whose camp-farcical play *Loot* (1965) plunders many of its elements from Ben Travers's *Plunder* (1928). A particularly important revival of 1920s preoccupations can be found in certain 1960s versions of the War Myth. The title of my third chapter is taken from Philip Larkin's elegiac poem about the outbreak of the Great War, 'MCMXIV' (1914). Other works of the time, notably the Theatre Workshop's musical satire *Oh What a Lovely War* (1963), resuscitated the War Myth in more propagandist terms that even Siegfried Sassoon might have found too simplified.

At the end of her 1924 essay 'Character in Fiction', Virginia Woolf hazards 'one final and surpassingly rash prediction – we are trembling on the verge of one of the great ages of English literature' (Woolf 1988). We may now be surprised less by the boldness of her prediction than by her trepidation, and indeed her tardiness, in advancing it. At the time, it seemed to Woolf a reckless gamble, and one that she did not risk either in the first (1923) or the second (1925) version of her essay 'How It

Strikes a Contemporary', where she weighs the prospects far more cautiously, even doubting whether a single book of her own times would come to be regarded a century later as fit to stand alongside the classics of the nineteenth century. Woolf could not foresee the transformations of literary culture, including the paperback revolution in publishing and the growth of academic literary study, that would propel her own novels to the status of 'modern classics', then simply 'classics' and of course 'set texts'. The same processes – by no means automatic, but shaped by continuing critical reassessment – have in the event preserved the 1920s poems of Eliot and Yeats, and the contemporary fiction of Joyce (especially), Forster, Lawrence and a few others. Outside the academy, revivals of Coward's and Shaw's work of the 1920s still attract audiences, while unflagging popular interest in the Great War keeps the war-books of Sassoon and Graves in print, along with R. C. Sherriff's play *Journey's End* (1928). Feminist projects of rediscovery since the 1970s have also brought such writers as Dorothy Richardson, Sylvia Townsend Warner, Radclyffe Hall and Rose Macaulay to the attention of new generations. More surprisingly, popular taste has clung tenaciously to some light literary entertainers of the 1920s, most notably Agatha Christie and P. G. Wodehouse, and made classics of them too.

I have quoted as epigraph to this chapter another of Woolf's hesitant guesses about the future reputation of 1920s literature. Her uncertainty, issuing from the 'plain' in which no vantage-point was yet available, is quite understandable; but where she is wrong is in saying that the literary historian of the future will decide upon the greatness or otherwise of the period. In fact we literary historians decide very little, as we always arrive after the party is over, and simply tidy up the mess left by critics. These days we speak rather less about great ages of English literature, and more about momentous phases, years (1922, for instance), movements (Modernism, mostly) and indeed decades of – in this series of books, at least – British literary production. In those terms, there is now no longer any excuse for the hesitancy Woolf showed at the time. While not immune to shifts of emphasis and revaluation, the reputation of the 1920s in Britain as an outstandingly creative literary phase is already secure, even though its clarification as a period, which this book has attempted, is not yet widely confirmed. Some German cultural historians are in the habit of referring to the period of recovery in their country that followed the hyperinflation of 1923 as *die goldenen zwanziger Jahre* (the Golden Twenties). 'Golden' is perhaps too immodest an epithet for British ears, but if there were any justice in such things, we should be able to agree that the literature of the Twenties is at the very least Glittering.

Works Cited

Aldington, Richard [1929] (1984), *Death of a Hero*, London: Hogarth Press.
Arlen, Michael [1924] (1983), *The Green Hat: A Romance for a Few People*, Woodbridge: Boydell Press.
Ayers, David (1999), *English Literature of the 1920s*, Edinburgh: Edinburgh University Press.
Baldick, Chris (2004), *The Oxford English Literary History, Volume 10. 1910–1940: The Modern Movement*, Oxford: Oxford University Press.
Bennett, Arnold (1974), *The Evening Standard Years: 'Books and Persons' 1926–1931*, ed. Andrew Mylett, London: Chatto and Windus.
Blunden, Edmund [1928] (1937), *Undertones of War*, Harmondsworth: Penguin.
— (1982), *Selected Poems*, ed. Robyn Marsack, Manchester: Carcanet.
Bolt, Sydney, ed. (1967), *Poetry of the 1920s*, London: Longmans.
Boulton, James T., ed. (1979), *The Letters of D. H. Lawrence, Volume 1: 1901–1913*, Cambridge: Cambridge University Press.
Branson, Noreen (1975), *Britain in the Nineteen Twenties*, London: Weidenfeld and Nicolson.
Bridges, Robert (1929), *The Testament of Beauty*, London: Oxford University Press.
Christie, Agatha [1926] (1957), *The Murder of Roger Ackroyd*, Glasgow: Fontana Collins.
Coward, Noël (1989), *Plays: One: Hay Fever, The Vortex, Fallen Angels, Easy Virtue*, London: Methuen.
Doyle, Arthur Conan [1927] (1993), *The Case-Book of Sherlock Holmes*, ed. W. W. Robson, Oxford: Oxford University Press.
Eliot, T. S. (1928), *For Lancelot Andrewes: Essays on Style and Order*, London: Faber and Gwyer.
— [1920] (1950), *The Sacred Wood: Essays on Poetry and Criticism*, 7th edn, London: Methuen.
— (1951), *Selected Essays*, 3rd edn, London: Faber and Faber.
— (1974), *Collected Poems 1909–1962*, London: Faber and Faber.
— (1975), *Selected Prose*, ed. Frank Kermode, London: Faber and Faber.
— (2001), *The Waste Land: Authoritative Text, Contexts, Criticism*, ed. Michael North, New York: W. W. Norton.

Ford, Ford Madox [1924] (2010), *Parade's End, Volume I: Some Do Not . . . , A Novel*, ed. Max Saunders, Manchester: Carcanet.
— [1926] (2011), *Parade's End, Volume III: A Man Could Stand Up—, A Novel*, ed. Sara Haslam, Manchester: Carcanet.
Forster, E. M. [1927] (1962), *Aspects of the Novel*, Harmondsworth: Penguin.
— [1924] (1989), *A Passage to India*, ed. Oliver Stallybrass, London: Penguin.
Foster, R. F. (2003), *W. B. Yeats: A Life, II: The Arch-Poet 1915–1939*, Oxford: Oxford University Press.
Fussell, Paul [1975] (1977), *The Great War and Modern Memory*, New York: Oxford University Press.
Garnett, David [1922, 1924] (1985), *Lady into Fox* and *A Man in the Zoo*, London: Hogarth Press.
Graves, Robert (1929), *Good-bye to All That: An Autobiography*, London: Jonathan Cape.
— (1995), *Good-bye to All That: An Autobiography*, ed. Richard Perceval Graves, Providence, RI: Berghahn.
Graves, Robert and Alan Hodge [1940] (1971), *The Long Week-end: A Social History of Great Britain, 1918–1939*, Harmondsworth: Penguin.
Green, Henry [1929] (2000), *Living*, London: Vintage.
Harding, Jason (2002), *The Criterion: Cultural Politics and Periodical Networks in Inter-War Britain*, Oxford: Oxford University Press.
Hardy, Thomas (1994), *The Oxford Poetry Library: Thomas Hardy*, ed. Samuel Hynes, Oxford: Oxford University Press.
Heywood, Christopher, ed. (1987), *D. H. Lawrence: New Studies*, Basingstoke: Macmillan.
Housman, A. E. (1989), *Collected Poems and Selected Prose*, ed. Christopher Ricks, London: Penguin.
Hulme, T. E. (1924), *Speculations: Essays on Humanism and the Philosophy of Art*, ed. Herbert Read, London: Routledge and Kegan Paul.
Huxley, Aldous [1925] (1994a), *Along the Road: Notes and Essays of a Tourist*, London: Flamingo.
— [1923] (1994b), *Antic Hay*, London: Flamingo.
— [1921] (1994c), *Crome Yellow*, London: Flamingo.
— [1926] (1994d), *Jesting Pilate: The Diary of a Journey*, London: Flamingo.
— [1928] (1994e), *Point Counter Point*, London: Flamingo.
— [1925] (1994f), *Those Barren Leaves*, London: Flamingo.
Hynes, Samuel (1990), *A War Imagined: The First World War and English Culture*, London: Bodley Head.
Isherwood, Christopher [1928] (1967), *All the Conspirators*, London: Sphere.
— [1932] (1978), *The Memorial: Portrait of a Family*, London: Triad Panther.
— [1938] (1985), *Lions and Shadows: An Education in the Twenties*, London: Methuen.
Joannou, Maroula (1995), *'Ladies, Please Don't Smash These Windows': Women's Writing, Feminist Consciousness and Social Change 1918–38*, Oxford: Berg.
Kipling, Rudyard (1999), *The Oxford Authors: Rudyard Kipling*, ed. Daniel Karlin, Oxford: Oxford University Press.
Lawrence, D. H. (1971a), *The Complete Poems*, ed. Vivian de Sola Pinto and Warren Roberts, New York: Viking Penguin.

—[1923] (1971b), *Fantasia of the Unconscious* and *Psychoanalysis and the Unconscious*, Harmondsworth: Penguin.
—[1924] (1971c), *Studies in Classic American Literature*, Harmondsworth: Penguin.
—[1926] (1983), *The Plumed Serpent*, ed. Ronald G. Walker, Harmondsworth: Penguin.
—[1928] (1990), *Lady Chatterley's Lover*, ed. John Lyon, London: Penguin.
—[1923] (1997), *Kangaroo*, ed. Bruce Steele, London: Penguin.
—[1921] (1998), *Women in Love*, ed. David Bradshaw, Oxford: Oxford University Press.
Lewis, Wyndham [1927] (1993), *Time and Western Man*, ed. Paul Edwards, Santa Rosa, CA: Black Sparrow Press.
Lonsdale, Frederick (2000), *Plays One*, ed. Clifford Williams, London: Oberon.
Lucas, John (1997), *The Radical Twenties: Aspects of Writing, Politics and Culture*, Nottingham: Five Leaves.
Macaulay, Rose [1923] (1983), *Told by an Idiot*, London: Virago.
—[1926] (1985), *Crewe Train*, London: Methuen.
MacDiarmid, Hugh [1926] (1987), *A Drunk Man Looks at the Thistle*, ed. Kenneth Buthlay, Edinburgh: Scottish Academic Press.
McHale, Brian and Randall Stevenson, eds (2006), *The Edinburgh Companion to Twentieth-century Literatures in English*, Edinburgh: Edinburgh University Press.
Mansfield, Katherine (2002), *Selected Stories*, ed. Angela Smith, Oxford: Oxford University Press.
Maugham, W. Somerset [1925] (1952), *The Painted Veil*, Harmondsworth: Penguin.
—[1926] (1993), *The Casuarina Tree*, London: Mandarin.
Melman, Billie (1988), *Women and the Popular Imagination in the Twenties: Flappers and Nymphs*, Basingstoke: Macmillan.
Mitchell, Gladys [1929] (1943), *Speedy Death*, Harmondsworth: Penguin.
Montague, C. E. [1922] (1928), *Disenchantment*, London: Chatto and Windus.
Montgomery, John (1957), *The Twenties: An Informal Social History*, London: Allen and Unwin.
Mottram, R. H. [1928] (1930), *Ten Years Ago*, London: Chatto and Windus.
—(1979), *The Spanish Farm Trilogy, 1914–1918*, Harmondsworth: Penguin.
Owen, Wilfred (1985), *The Poems of Wilfred Owen*, ed. Jon Stallworthy, London: Chatto and Windus.
Pound, Ezra (2003), *Poems and Translations*, ed. Richard Sieburth, New York: Library of America.
Powys, T. F. [1927] (1937), *Mr Weston's Good Wine*, Harmondsworth: Penguin.
Rickword, Edgell (1974), *Essays & Opinions, 1921–1931*, ed. Alan Young, Cheadle: Carcanet New Press.
Sackville-West, V. [1926] (1933), *The Land*, London: Heinemann.
Sassoon, Siegfried [1928] (1960), *Memoirs of a Fox-Hunting Man*, London: Faber and Faber.
—(1984) *Collected Poems, 1908–1956*, London: Faber and Faber.
Sayers, Dorothy L. [1927] (1968a), *Unnatural Death*, London: New English Library.

—[1928] (1968b), *The Unpleasantness at the Bellona Club*, London: New English Library.
—[1923] (1968c), *Whose Body?*, London: New English Library.
—[1928] (1989), *Lord Peter Views the Body*, London: Coronet.
Shaw, Bernard [1921] (1939), *Back to Methuselah: A Metabiological Pentateuch*, Harmondsworth: Penguin.
—[1924] (1946), *Saint Joan: A Chronicle Play in Six Scenes and an Epilogue*, Harmondsworth: Penguin.
—[1919] (1964), *Heartbreak House: A Fantasia in the Russian Manner on English Themes*, Harmondsworth: Penguin.
Sinclair, May (1922), *Life and Death of Harriett Frean*, London: Collins.
Sitwell, Osbert [1926] (1985), *Before the Bombardment*, Oxford: Oxford University Press.
Sontag, Susan [1966] (1994), *Against Interpretation*, London: Vintage.
Stevenson, John (1984), *British Society 1914–45*, Harmondsworth: Penguin.
Strachey, Lytton [1928] (1950), *Elizabeth and Essex: A Tragic History*, Harmondsworth: Penguin.
—(1980), *The Shorter Strachey*, ed. Michael Holroyd and Paul Levy, Oxford: Oxford University Press.
Travers, Ben (1979), *Five Plays*, Harmondsworth: Penguin.
Trewin, J. C. (1958), *The Gay Twenties: A Decade of the Theatre*, London: Macdonald.
Usborne, Richard (2003), *Plum Sauce: A P. G. Wodehouse Companion*, London: Ebury.
Warner, Sylvia Townsend [1927] (1978), *Mr Fortune's Maggot*, London: Virago.
Waugh, Evelyn (1983), *The Essays, Articles and Reviews of Evelyn Waugh*, ed. Donat Gallagher, London: Methuen.
—[1945] (2000), *Brideshead Revisited: The Sacred and Profane Memories of Captain Charles Ryder*, London: Penguin.
—(2001), *Decline and Fall*, ed. David Bradshaw, London: Penguin.
Webb, Mary [1924] (1978), *Precious Bane*, London: Virago.
Williams, T. G., ed. (1929), *Tradition and Experiment in Present-day Literature*, London: Oxford University Press.
Wodehouse, P. G. [1925] (1957), *Carry On, Jeeves*, Harmondsworth: Penguin.
Woolf, Virginia (1988), *The Essays of Virginia Woolf, Volume III: 1919–1924*, ed. Andrew McNeillie, London: Hogarth Press.
—[1922] (1992a), *Jacob's Room*, ed. Kate Flint, Oxford: Oxford University Press.
—[1925] (1992b), *Mrs Dalloway*, ed. Stella McNichol, London: Penguin.
—(1994), *The Essays of Virginia Woolf, Volume IV: 1925–1928*, ed. Andrew McNeillie, London: Hogarth Press.
Wordsworth, William (1984), *The Oxford Authors: William Wordsworth*, ed. Stephen Gill, Oxford: Oxford University Press.
Yeats, W. B. [1926] (1937), *A Vision*, London: Macmillan.
—(1990), *The Poems*, ed. Daniel Albright, London: Dent.

Index

Adelphi, 13
adultery, 79, 125–6, 142, 158–62
Aldington, Richard, 2, 5, 6, 8, 10, 27, 28, 29–30, 58–9, 103, 130
   Death of a Hero, 5, 10, 28, 34, 58–9, 101, 104, 107, 110, 116, 129, 130
Allingham, Margery, 144, 145, 172
Arlen, Michael, 21
   The Green Hat, 12–13, 22, 156, 156–8, 161, 163
Arnold, Matthew, 39
Asquith, Herbert H., 49, 105, 121
Auden, W. H., 1, 2, 62, 172, 173, 174, 175, 176, 179, 179–80
Austen, Jane, 3–4, 6, 26, 56
Ayers, David, 35n

Bagnold, Enid, 108
Bankhead, Tallulah, 161
Barrie, J. M., 19, 20, 29
Baudelaire, Charles, 84, 176
Beckett, Samuel, 21, 172, 179
Belloc, Hilaire, 46
Bennett, Arnold, 11, 18, 26, 28, 29, 48, 56, 76, 130
   Lord Raingo, 16, 108
   Riceyman Steps, 16, 56
Benson, E. F., 168
Beresford, J. D., 53, 60
Bergson, Henri, 46, 73, 92, 93
Berkeley, Anthony, 144, 146
Berlin, 172, 175
Bevan, Gerard, 138
Bildungsroman, 11–12, 53, 112, 114, 116, 125
Birmingham, 17, 48, 173–4
Blake, William, 40
Bloomsbury Group, 57, 180

Blunden, Edmund, 14, 15, 17, 24–5, 30, 101, 107, 136n, 171
   Undertones of War, 108, 111–12
Bottomley, Horatio, 121, 138, 139, 157
Bowen, Elizabeth, 15, 30
Bramah, Ernest, 144
Breton, André, 52
Bridges, Robert, 27, 29, 61–3, 179
   The Testament of Beauty, 27, 61–4
Brittain, Vera, 170
Buchan, John, 9, 16, 19, 29, 30
Burgess, Anthony, 179
Burns, Robert, 25, 64, 65
Butler, Samuel, 50
Butts, Mary, 17, 23, 108

Calendar of Modern Letters, 34, 134–5
Cambridge, 112, 176, 180
Camp writing, 166–9
Carswell, Catherine, 12, 20, 171
Chaplin, Charlie, 93
Charteris, Leslie, 147
Chekhov, Anton, 25
Chesterton, G. K., 17, 29, 46, 47, 61, 144
Christie, Agatha, 3, 9, 23, 24, 27, 30, 108, 144, 145, 146, 151, 164–5, 171, 181
   The Murder of Roger Ackroyd, 27, 146, 151, 165
comedy of manners, 8, 12, 37
Compton-Burnett, Ivy, 172
Comte, Auguste, 46
Condition-of-England novel, 60
Conrad, Joseph, 21, 29, 35n
Coward, Noël, 3, 8, 9, 10, 27, 30, 37–8, 159–60, 162, 163–4, 166, 171, 179, 181
   Bitter-Sweet, 10, 167
   Fallen Angels, 161
   Hay Fever, 17, 37, 163–4

The Vortex, 12, 101, 159–60, 163, 164, 166, 168
This Was a Man, 159
Criterion, 13, 32, 39, 47
Crofts, Freeman Wills, 144
Crompton, Richmal, 163
crossword puzzles, 21–2, 145

Dana, R. H., 44
Dane, Clemence, 8, 48
Dante, 25, 84, 86
Darwin, Charles, 45, 50
Davies, Rhys, 19
Davies, W. H., 14, 17, 19, 29
Day Lewis, C., 14, 29, 171, 171–2, 173
De la Mare, Walter, 8, 14, 17, 26, 29
De Quincey, Thomas, 166
Deeping, Warwick, 60
detective fiction, 8–9, 12, 143–7, 164–5, 172
Dorset, 17, 18, 93
Dostoevsky, Fyodor, 65
Doyle, Arthur Conan, 19, 29, 144, 147, 153, 172
  The Case-Book of Sherlock Holmes, 144, 146, 147
Drinkwater, John, 8, 12, 14
Dukes, Ashley, 25
Dunbar, William, 20, 25

Edinburgh, 20
Einstein, Albert, 67, 93
Eliot, George, 123
Eliot, T. S., 2, 3, 4, 13, 14, 21, 24–5, 26, 27, 29, 30, 33, 37, 38, 39, 42, 47, 66, 81–7, 87–8, 90–1, 91–2, 98, 101, 132, 134–5, 171, 173, 176, 177, 179, 180, 181
  The Sacred Wood, 13, 33, 36
  'The Waste Land', 4, 8, 16, 39, 64, 70, 81–7, 90, 134, 135, 177
  'Tradition and the Individual Talent', 42, 84, 91, 91–2
Ellis, Havelock, 100
Evans, Caradoc, 19

Faber and Faber, 173
Faulkner, William, 92
Firbank, Ronald, 15, 21, 29, 30, 167, 179
First World War *see* Great War
Flaubert, Gustave, 46, 123
Ford, Ford Madox, 7, 21, 29, 36, 37, 78–81, 90, 92, 98, 105–6, 158, 172
  A Man Could Stand Up—, 106, 109

Last Post, 11, 108
No More Parades, 108
Parade's End, 7, 22, 24, 78, 81, 110, 116, 161–2
Some Do Not . . ., 16, 78–81, 105, 108
Forster, E. M., 14, 26, 29, 30, 57, 59–60, 91, 92, 93, 98, 168, 171, 179, 180, 181
  A Passage to India, 14, 57, 59–60
  Aspects of the Novel, 13, 91, 176
Frazer, J. G., 19–20, 46, 85
Freud, Sigmund, 51–3, 67, 69, 93, 132, 165, 173
Fry, Roger, 176
Fussell, Paul, 102, 103, 103–4

Galsworthy, John, 28, 29, 46, 47, 48, 56, 116
  A Modern Comedy, 8, 22, 56, 60
  The Forsyte Saga, 11, 16, 24, 60, 109, 110, 116
Galton, Francis, 46
ganglia, 42–3, 58, 68
Garnett, David, 8
  Lady into Fox, 8, 162, 177
Gay writing *see* homosexual literature
General Strike, 60, 61, 66, 174
Georgian poetry, 17, 26
Gerhardi, William, 15
Gibbon, Lewis Grassic, 20–1
Gibbons, Stella, 18
Gide, André, 68–9, 176
gig-lamps, 32–3
Goldsmith, Oliver, 84
Grahame, Kenneth, 100
Graves, Robert, 13, 17, 26, 30, 34, 35n, 112, 170, 181
  Good-bye to All That, 34, 110, 111, 113–16, 136n, 170, 171, 174
Great War, 4–5, 7, 9, 11, 27–8, 28–9, 71, 84, 88, 92, 97, 102, 103–19, 121–2, 177, 178, 181
  Armistice, 4, 106, 108, 109
  memoirs of, 10, 16, 107, 108, 110–16, 181
  memorials, 10, 175
  outbreak of, 102, 105, 106, 127
  Somme, Battle of, 92, 106, 118
  veterans of, 4–5, 7, 10, 23–4, 27–8, 29, 30, 60, 77–8, 83, 101, 103, 108, 110, 111–16, 119, 121, 139, 141, 175
Green, Henry, 8, 17, 29, 173–4
Greene, Graham, 172
Grieve, C. M. *see* MacDiarmid, Hugh
Gunn, Neil M., 20, 21

Gurdjieff, G. I., 39–40
Gurney, Ivor, 34

Hall, Radclyffe, 16, 23, 30, 158, 181
   The Well of Loneliness, 13, 34, 60, 158
Hamilton, Patrick, 151
Hampson, John, 173
Hardy, Thomas, 17, 25, 26, 27, 29, 33, 130–1, 133–4, 176, 179
Heaney, Seamus, 179
Hemingway, Ernest, 172
Henryson, Robert, 20
historical fiction, 8–9
Hogarth Press, 53, 173
Holme, Constance, 18
Holtby, Winifred, 18, 23
Homer, 83–4, 87, 92
homosexual literature, 167–8
Hopkins, Gerard Manley, 63
Hornung, E. W., 147, 150
Housman, A. E., 17, 29, 33, 82, 131
Hughes, Richard, 15, 19, 29
Hughes, Ted, 179
Hulme, T. E., 132
Hutchinson, A. S. M., 60
Hutchinson, Ernest, 48
Huxley, Aldous, 3, 14, 21, 23, 30, 66–70, 127–8, 129, 135, 162, 166, 171
   Along the Road, 15, 128, 134
   Antic Hay, 16, 22, 66, 67–8, 69, 70, 129, 162, 177
   Crome Yellow, 17, 66–7
   Jesting Pilate, 15, 127–8
   Point Counter Point, 8, 16, 22, 28, 66, 67, 69–70, 156, 165–6
   Those Barren Leaves, 15, 23, 66, 67, 69, 70, 101, 129
Huxley, Julian, 66
Hynes, Samuel, 7, 102, 156

Ibsen, Henrik, 25, 46, 48, 123
Imagism, 26
Irish Free State, 18, 99
Isherwood, Christopher, 29, 129, 172, 175–6
   All the Conspirators, 129, 172
   Lions and Shadows, 175–6
   The Memorial, 173, 175

James, Henry, 13, 21, 36, 37, 55
Jesse, F. Tennyson, 174
Jones, David, 170
Joyce, James, 7, 12, 18–19, 21, 25, 28, 29, 30, 36, 37, 87, 90, 92, 93, 172, 173, 179, 181

Ulysses, 7, 16, 34, 75, 84, 87, 158–9

Kafka, Franz, 172
Kaye-Smith, Sheila, 18, 23
Keats, John, 90
Kennedy, Margaret, 13
Kipling, Rudyard, 29, 46, 109, 130, 141

Lamarck, Jean-Baptiste, 50
Larkin, Philip, 179, 180
Lawrence, D. H., 3, 4, 8, 11, 12, 14, 15, 18, 21, 25, 26, 27, 28, 29, 30, 35n, 42–5, 51, 57–8, 66, 67, 68, 101, 104, 108, 138, 170–1, 179, 180, 181
   Aaron's Rod, 15, 16, 108, 119
   Fantasia of the Unconscious, 40, 42–4
   Kangaroo, 15, 58, 59, 105, 109, 119–22
   Lady Chatterley's Lover, 4, 8, 11, 18, 23, 34, 56, 57, 60–1, 108, 134, 158–9, 180
   Pansies, 14, 61
   Studies in Classic American Literature, 13, 25–6, 44
   The Plumed Serpent, 15, 45, 59
   Women in Love, 8, 11, 33, 44–5, 57–8, 59, 119
Lawrence, T. E., 33, 170
Leavis, F. R., 180
Lehmann, Rosamond, 12, 22, 29
Lewis, Wyndham, 8, 17, 25, 27, 29, 30, 47, 93, 98, 170, 174
Lindsay, David, 20
Lloyd George, David, 19, 49, 105, 121, 138–9
London, 16–17, 19, 20, 77, 78, 83, 86–7, 121
Lonsdale, Frederick, 8, 148–50, 157, 165
   Aren't We All?, 165
   The Last of Mrs Cheyney, 148–50, 157
Lowry, Malcolm, 179
Lubbock, Percy, 13, 36, 37
Lucas, John, 35n
Lucretius, 61

Macaulay, Rose, 14, 29, 104–5, 181
   Crewe Train, 16, 21, 134
   Orphan Island, 8, 16
   Told by an Idiot, 11, 104–5, 109
Macaulay, T. B., 167
MacDiarmid, Hugh, 3, 14, 20–1, 25, 26–7, 30, 61, 63–6, 171

A Drunk Man Looks at the Thistle, 20, 26, 63–6
Machen, Arthur, 19
Mackenzie, Compton, 15
MacNeice, Louis, 14, 29, 171, 172, 173
Manning, Frederic, 170
Mansfield, Katherine, 8, 15, 21, 23, 25, 29, 33, 34, 39–40, 108, 123–4, 176
 'The Garden Party', 123–4
Marvell, Andrew, 84
Marx, Karl, 45
Masefield, John, 14, 29, 30
Maugham, W. Somerset, 8, 12, 15, 21, 26, 29, 37, 48, 52–3, 125–6, 127, 140–3, 151, 160–1, 162, 168, 171, 172
 'Rain', 15, 52–3
 The Casuarina Tree, 15, 140–3
 The Circle, 8, 17, 160–1
 The Painted Veil, 15, 34–5, 125–6, 162
Maurras, Charles, 132
Mayor, F. M., 23, 29
melodrama, 12, 158, 161
Melville, Herman, 25, 65
Mew, Charlotte, 13
Milton, John, 62, 85
Mitchell, Gladys, 144, 146, 165, 172
Mitchison, Naomi, 9, 20, 30
Monro, Harold, 14
Montague, C. E., 4–5, 29, 108, 139
Morrell, Ottoline, 67
Mottram, R. H., 10, 25, 30, 116–19, 128–9
 The Spanish Farm Trilogy, 109, 116–19, 128–9
Muir, Edwin, 13, 14, 20, 30, 171, 172
Muir, Willa, 172
Murry, John Middleton, 13, 27, 38, 40, 171

New Age, 39, 46
Nietzsche, Friedrich, 45, 46, 64, 69, 96, 123
Northcliffe, Lord, 23

O'Casey, Sean, 18–19
Orage, Alfred, 39–40, 46
Orton, Joe, 180
Orwell, George, 172
Ouspensky, P. D., 39
Owen, Wilfred, 19, 27, 33, 104, 176
 'Arms and the Boy', 131–2
 'The Parable of the Old Man and the Young', 34, 104, 107

Oxford, 20, 112, 114, 155, 176, 177
Oxford English Dictionary, 66, 95

Paris, 16, 21, 117, 172
Pater, Walter, 25
Pinter, Harold, 179
Poe, Edgar Allan, 44
Pound, Ezra, 2, 25, 37, 93, 134, 172
Powys, John Cowper, 18, 19, 29, 51
Powys, T. F., 18, 19, 93–4, 98
 Mr Weston's Good Wine, 93–4
Priestley, J. B., 8
Proust, Marcel, 7, 10, 20, 57, 73–4, 90, 93, 172, 176

Read, Herbert, 2, 14
Rhys, Jean, 15, 16, 19, 30, 172
Richards, I. A., 13, 135, 176
Richardson, Dorothy, 7, 12, 16, 29, 33, 181
Rickword, Edgell, 34, 134–5
Riding, Laura, 13
Rohmer, Sax, 164
Rothermere, Lady, 39

Sackville-West, Vita, 14, 15, 17
saga fiction, 11, 109, 110
Saki, 167
Santayana, George, 62
Sassoon, Siegfried, 8, 14, 17, 28, 29, 30, 61, 103, 104, 121, 136n, 168, 170, 181
 Memoirs of a Fox-Hunting Man, 108, 111, 112–13, 116
satire, 8, 12, 58, 61, 104, 114
Sayers, Dorothy L., 3, 16, 30, 144, 145–6, 168–9, 171
 The Unpleasantness at the Bellona Club, 22, 24, 108, 146
 Unnatural Death, 23, 144, 145–6
 Whose Body?, 23–4, 144
Schreiner, Olive, 21
Scott, F. G., 64
Scott, Walter, 3–4, 6
Scott Moncrieff, C. K., 10, 20
Scottish literature, 18, 19–21
Seldes, Gilbert, 134
Shakespeare, William, 10, 12, 37, 84, 86, 92
Shaw, Bernard, 12, 19, 21, 29, 46, 48–51, 66, 94–8, 99, 147–8, 179, 181
 Back to Methuselah, 48–50, 66
 Heartbreak House, 33, 147–8
 Saint Joan, 8, 12, 94–8

Shelley, Percy Bysshe, 90
Shepherd, Nan, 20
Sherriff, R. C., 181
Sinclair, May, 11, 29, 53–5
   Life and Death of Harriett Frean, 23, 53–5
Sitwell, Edith, 3, 14, 24–5, 26, 29, 52, 104, 171, 172, 177
Sitwell, Osbert, 2, 5, 6, 26, 28, 103
   Before the Bombardment, 5, 17, 108
Sontag, Susan, 166
Spencer, Herbert, 46
Spender, Stephen, 172, 173, 175
Spengler, Oswald, 93
spinster novel, 22–3
Stein, Gertrude, 93, 172, 173
Strachey, James, 52
Strachey, Lytton, 25, 27, 29, 30, 52, 135, 167, 171
   Elizabeth and Essex, 27, 52
   Eminent Victorians, 27, 52, 176
Swinburne, A. C., 113

Thackeray, W. M., 37
Thirties writing, 1–3, 9, 15, 21, 33–4, 36, 170–6
Thomas, Edward, 19
Thompson, Edith, 133, 174
Tolstoy, Leo, 25, 46, 56
Tomlinson, H. M., 15, 170
tragedy, 12–13, 96
Travers, Ben, 8, 27, 133, 151–2, 180
Turner, W. J., 21
Tylor, E. B., 46

Upward, Edward, 175, 176

Van Druten, John, 161
Virgil, 17

Wagner, Richard, 46, 48, 82, 86
Wallace, Edgar, 151, 164
war literature *see* Great War
Warner, Sylvia Townsend, 21, 30, 126–7, 164, 181
   Lolly Willowes, 23, 164
   Mr Fortune's Maggot, 16, 126–7
Waugh, Evelyn, 3, 29, 137, 154–5, 168, 174, 176–7

Brideshead Revisited, 176–7
Decline and Fall, 8, 34, 100, 116, 137–8, 154–5, 155–6, 168, 172, 174
Vile Bodies, 100, 154, 174
Webb, Mary, 9, 18
Webster, John, 85
Wells, H. G., 15, 28, 29, 46, 47, 60, 66, 76
Welsh literature, 18, 19, 21
West, Rebecca, 16, 20, 29–30, 180
Weston, Jessie L., 85
Whitman, Walt, 25
Wilde, Oscar, 166–7
Wilkinson, Ellen, 60
Williamson, Henry, 170
Wittgenstein, Ludwig, 67
Wodehouse, P. G., 9, 21, 29, 30, 144, 147, 153–4, 163, 168, 181
Woolf, Virginia, 3–4, 6–7, 7–8, 12, 13, 21, 25, 28, 29, 32–3, 53, 56–7, 72–8, 80, 90, 92, 93, 99, 103, 104, 129, 171, 173, 178, 179, 180–1
   A Room of One's Own, 173
   'Character in Fiction' *see* 'Mr Bennett and Mrs Brown'
   'How It Strikes a Contemporary', 3–4, 6, 180–1
   Jacob's Room, 8, 12, 16, 56, 108
   'Modern Fiction', 32–3, 75–6, 92
   'Mr Bennett and Mrs Brown', 28, 32, 47, 75–6, 103, 180–1
   Mrs Dalloway, 6–7, 8, 16, 23, 56, 72–5, 76–8, 81
   Orlando, 8, 56, 57, 76, 173
   The Common Reader, 13, 32–3, 36
   To the Lighthouse, 8, 11, 17, 56, 59, 76, 78, 109, 110
Wordsworth, William, 26, 89
Wren, P. C., 16

Yeats, W. B., 13, 14, 18, 21, 26, 27, 29, 37, 40–2, 61, 87–90, 93, 98, 171, 179, 181
   A Vision, 35, 40–2
   'Among School Children', 89
   'Leda and the Swan', 88–9
   'Sailing to Byzantium', 41, 89–90
   'The Second Coming', 41, 87, 88
Young, Edward, 111